Baltic
PHRASEBOOK

Acknowledgments
Associate Publisher Mina Patria
Managing Editor Angela Tinson
Editor Branislava Vladisavljevic
Series Designer Mark Adams
Managing Layout Designer Chris Girdler
Layout Designer Carol Jackson
Cover Image Researcher Naomi Parker

Thanks
Ruth Cosgrove

Published by Lonely Planet Publications Pty Ltd
ABN 36 005 607 983

3rd Edition – Sep 2013
ISBN 978 1 74104 014 2
Text © Lonely Planet 2013

Cover Image Līvu laukums, Rīga, Latvia, Brent Winebrenner/Getty
Images ©
Printed in China 10 9 8 7 6 5 4 3 2 1

MIX
Paper from
responsible sources
FSC™ C021741

About the Authors

This revised edition of the Estonian chapter with transliterations was prepared by Alan Trei, a marketing consultant and literary translator of Estonian origin living in Northampton, Massachusetts, working with Inna Feldbach. The Estonian section in the first edition was written by Lisa Trei, then a correspondent for the Wall Street Journal and a Fulbright Scholar at Tartu University in Estonia, assisted by Inna Feldbach, a governmental and literary translator.

Jana Teteris, author of the Latvian chapter, was born and brought up as a Latvian in the UK. She lived and worked in Latvia from the late 1980s to 1992 and then again from 1994 to 1998, when she returned to London. She now works at the Institute of Linguists and continues to do some translating and interpreting on a freelance basis.

Eva Aras updated the Lithuanian section based on the the first edition written by Paul Jokubaitis. Originally a teacher of French and German, then a university librarian, Eva now teaches Lithuanian at the Victorian School of Languages in Melbourne. She also translates between Lithuanian and English and does on-site and telephone interpreting for various agencies and government bodies. All these activities help to keep her well in touch with the language of her birth, despite spending most of her life in an English-speaking environment.

From the Authors

Jana Teteris would like to thank her mother and friends in Latvia for their assistance in re-writing the Latvian chapter. She is especially indebted to Judith Gill who managed to find the time in the run-up to her wedding to proofread the transliterations.

Eva Aras would like to thank her son Danielius for his technical assistance and also for some helpful language suggestions.

From the Publisher

This book was coordinated by Peter D'Onghia and Ingrid Seebus. Karin Vidstrup Monk and Karina Coates supervised. The book was edited with flair by Emma Koch and meticulously proofread by Lou Callan. The splendiferous illustrations were done by Patrick Marris, who also laid out the book, and Fabrice Rocher supervised layout. Natasha Velleley drew the map.

CONTENTS

LITHUANIAN 185

INTRODUCTION

The three Baltic countries, Latvia, Lithuania and Estonia, have been occupied by various powers throughout the centuries. During this time, and especially during Soviet occupation after World War II, when Russian was the official language of each of the three countries, language played a key role in maintaining national identity.

After their successful and remarkably peaceful individual bids for independence in 1991, Latvia, Lithuania and Estonia have become inextricably linked in many people's minds. However, you may be surprised to learn that the Latvian, Lithuanian and Estonian languages are not all related to one other. Estonian is a Finno-Ugric language, closely related to Finnish and more distantly to Hungarian. Estonian and Finnish are mutually intelligible and share a large proportion of their respective vocabularies. Latvian and Lithuanian belong to the Baltic branch of the Indo-European language tree and are the only surviving spoken Baltic languages. However, in spite of their close relationship, the two are not mutually intelligible.

This book will enable you to make the most of these exciting and dynamic countries. English is spoken in the cities, but if you learn at least a few phrases in the local language you'll find that you're more than rewarded for your efforts.

TRANSLITERATIONS

Simplified transliterations have been provided in pink throughout this book. Italic is used to indicate where to place stress in a word.

INTRODUCTION

POLITE FORMS

When a language has polite and informal forms of the singular pronoun 'you', the polite form has been used in most cases. However, you will come across the informal form of 'you' in some phrases, such as those for talking with children.

ARTHUR OR MARTHA?

When there are both feminine and masculine forms of a word, it's indicated in either of two ways, with the feminine form always appearing first:

- with a slash separating the feminine and masculine endings of a word:

  eg, hungry   ish-*ahl-k-*usi/-as   *išalkusi/ęs* (f/m)

- when the distinction between masculine and feminine is more complex, each word is given in full, separated with a slash:

  eg, married   ish-tak-*eh*-yu-si/vad-as   *ištekėjus/vedęs* (f/m)

ABBREVIATIONS USED IN THIS BOOK

f	feminine	n	noun
inf	informal	pl	plural
lit	literally	pol	polite
m	masculine	sg	singular

Map 9

INTRODUCTION

ESTONIAN, LATVIAN & LITHUANIAN

FINLAND

Gulf of Finland

TALLINN

Kohtla-Järve

Narva

Hiiumaa

ESTONIA

RUSSIAN FEDERATION

Lake Peipsi

Saaremaa

Pärnu

Tartu

Baltic Sea

Gulf of Riga

Sigulda

Ventspils

RIGA

LATVIA

Rēzekne

Daugava

Liepāja

Daugavpils

Palanga

Šiauliai

Panevėžys

Klaipėda

LITHUANIA

Nemunas

Kaunas

BELARUS

VILNIUS

Alytus

RUSSIAN FEDERATION

POLAND

| Estonian |
| Latvian |
| Lithuanian |

0   50   100 km
0   30   60 mi

INTRODUCTION

HOW TO USE THIS PHRASEBOOK
You *Can* Speak Another Language

Anyone can speak another language. Don't worry if you haven't studied languages before, or that you studied a language at school for years and can't remember any of it. It doesn't even matter if you failed English grammar. After all, that's never affected your ability to speak English! And this is the key to picking up a language in another country. You don't need to sit down and memorise endless grammatical details and you don't need to memorise long lists of vocabulary. You just need to start speaking.

Once you start, you'll be amazed how many prompts you'll get to help you build on those first words. You'll hear people speaking, pick up sounds from TV, catch a word or two that you think you know from the local radio, see something on a billboard – all these things help to build your understanding.

Plunge In

There's just one thing you need to start speaking another language – courage. Your biggest hurdle is overcoming the fear of saying aloud what may seem to you to be just a bunch of sounds. There are a number of ways to do this.

The best way to start overcoming your fear is to memorise a few key words. These are the words you know you'll be saying again and again, such as 'hello', 'thank you' and 'How much?'. Here's an important hint though: right from the beginning, learn at least one phrase that will be useful but not essential. Such as 'See you later' or even a conversational piece like 'It's nice today, isn't it?' (people everywhere love to talk about the weather). Having this extra phrase (just start with one, if you like, and learn to say it really well) will enable you to move away from the basics, and when you get a reply and a smile, it'll also boost your confidence. You'll find that people you speak to will like it too, as they'll understand that at least you've tried to learn more of the language than just the usual essential words.

Ways to Remember

There are several ways to learn a language. Most people find they learn from a variety of these, although people usually have a preferred way to remember. Some like to see the written word and remember the sound from what they see. Some like to just hear it spoken in context (if this is you, try talking to yourself in the foreign language, but do it at home or somewhere private, to give yourself confidence, and so others don't wonder about your sanity!). Others, especially the more mathematically inclined, like to analyse the grammar of a language, and piece together words according to the rules of grammar. The very visually inclined like to associate the written word and even sounds with some visual stimulus such as illustrations, TV and general things they see in the street. As you learn, you'll discover what works best for you – be aware of what made you really remember a particular word, and if it sticks in your mind, keep using that method.

Kicking Off

Chances are you'll want to learn some of the language before you go. The first thing to do is to memorise those essential phrases and words. Check out the basics and don't forget that extra phrase. Try the sections on making conversation or greeting people for a phrase you'd like to use. Write some of these words and phrases down on a piece of paper and stick them up around the place: on the fridge, by the bed, on your computer, as a bookmark – somewhere where you'll see them often. Try putting some words in context – the 'How much is it?' note, for instance, could go in your wallet.

Any Questions?

Try to learn the main question words. Each language chapter contains a box with the most common ones. As you read through different situations, you'll see these words used in the example sentences, and this will help you remember them. So if you want to take a bus, turn to the Bus section in each chapter (use the Index pages to find it quickly). You've already tried to memorise

INTRODUCTION

the word for 'which' and you'll see the word for 'bus'. When you come across the sentence 'Which bus goes to ...?', you'll recognise the key words and this will help you remember the whole phrase.

I Have a Flat Tyre

Doesn't seem like the phrase you're going to need? Well, in fact it could be very useful. As are all the phrases in this book, provided you have the courage to mix and match them. We have given specific examples within each section. But the key words remain the same even when the situation changes. So while you may not be planning on any driving during your trip, the first part of the phrase 'I have ...' could refer to anything else, and there are plenty of words in the other phrases that, we hope, will fit your needs. So whether it's 'a ticket' or 'a visa', you'll be able to put the words together to convey your meaning.

Finally

Don't be concerned if you feel you can't memorise words. You'll find the most essential words and phrases on the Quick Reference page at the start of each chapter. You could also try tagging a few pages for other key phrases, or use the notes pages at the back of the book to write your own reminders.

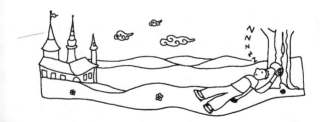

ESTONIAN

QUICK REFERENCE

Hello.	*te*-rre	*Tere.* (inf/pol)
Goodbye.	head *ae*-gah	*Head aega.* (inf/pol)
Yes./No.	yah/ay	*Jah./Ei.*
Excuse me/ Sorry.	*vah*-bahn-dah-ge	*Vabandage.*
Thank you.	*ta*-nahn	*Tänan.*
You're welcome.	*pah*-lun	*Palun.*

Please give me a ... ticket.	*pah*-lun ... *pi*-let	*Palun ... pilet.*
one-way	üks	üks
return	*e*-dah-si-*tah*-gah-si	*edasi-tagasi*

I don't understand.
  mah ay saah ah-rru   *Ma ei saa aru.*
Do you speak English?
  kahs te *rraa*-gi-te   *Kas te räägite*
  ing-li-se kehlt?   *inglise keelt?*
Where is ...?
  kus on ...?   *Kus on ...?*
Go straight ahead.
  ot-se   *Otse.*
Turn left/right.
  vah-sah-ku-le/   *Vasakule/*
  pah-rre-mah-le.   *Paremale.*
Where's the toilet?
  kus on tua-lett?   *Kus on tualett?*
Help!
  ahp-pi!   *Appi!*

1	üks	üks	6	koos	kuus
2	kahks	kaks	7	*sayt*-se	seitse
3	kolm	kolm	8	*kah*-hek-sah	kaheksa
4	*ne*-li	neli	9	*üh*-hek-sah	üheksa
5	vees	viis	10	*küm*-me	kümme

ESTONIAN

ESTONIAN

INTRODUCTION

Estonian, a Finno-Ugric tongue, is the official language of the Republic of Estonia and is spoken by about one million people. Closely related to Finnish, Estonian belongs to the Uralic language family and not to the Indo-European language family to which Latvian, Lithuanian, English and Russian belong.

Apart from a few names, words and phrases in earlier chronicles, the oldest surviving Estonian text dates from the 16th century. Estonian was regarded by the Germans, Danes, Swedes and Russians who ruled the land as a simple peasants' tongue and was not honoured as a language in its own right until the period of national awakening in the latter 19th century. An Estonian-German dictionary was published in 1869 and an Estonian grammar guide in 1875. In the early 20th century, language reformers de-Germanised the sentence structure, helped develop new vocabulary and made Estonian the language of instruction at Tartu University. During the first period of independence from 1920 to 1940, many people Estonianised their German surnames.

Through 800 years of occupation, Estonians kept their language alive as a means of maintaining their national identity. Although many foreign words and expressions crept into the language during the various occupations, Estonian has survived as a distinct and mellifluous tongue.

You'll find that Estonians are much more welcoming of visitors who make an effort to speak their language. So don't be shy!

BALKANS OR BALTICS?

Don't make the mistake of confusing the Balkans with the Baltics because the two are totally unrelated.

ESTONIAN

Help!

It's a good idea to take the time to learn a few basic words of Estonian to help you get by and to make your stay more enjoyable. 'Hello' is *Tere* (**te-rre**) and 'Goodbye' is *Head aega* (**head ae-gah**). *Palun* (**pah-lun**) is the word for 'Please' and is also used to mean 'You're welcome' and 'Here you are'. *Tänan* (**ta-nahn**) means 'Thank you'. The word for 'Yes' is *Jah* (**yah**) and 'No' is *Ei* (**ay**). If you find yourself stuck just say *Ma ei räägi eesti keelt.* (**mah ay rraa-gi ehs-ti kehlt**) which translates as 'I don't speak Estonian'. Pages 30–35 are crammed with handy phrases to help you make small talk with the locals.

PRONUNCIATION

You'll discover that Estonian words are not difficult to pronounce once you have learned the basics set out in this chapter. Unlike English, Estonian letters have only one pronunciation. The alphabet consists of 23 letters – *a, b, d, e, g, h, i, j, k, l, m, n, o, p, r, s, t, u, v, õ, ä, ö* and *ü*. The letters *c, č, f, q, š, z, ž, w, x* and *y* are used only in words of foreign origin.

Vowel combinations (diphthongs) don't form completely new sounds as they often do in English; each vowel is still pronounced individually. Estonian also uses many double vowels, which indicate that the vowel sound is extended.

FIRST IN, BEST STRESSED

In Estonian, stress is almost always on the first syllable with the exception of a few words such as *aitäh*, 'thanks', where it's on the second syllable, and some foreign words.

Vowels, Diphthongs & Double Vowels

Estonian	Translit	Sounds
a	ah	as the 'a' in 'father'
ä	a	as the 'a' in 'act'
e	e	as the 'e' in 'ten'
i	i	as the 'i' in 'in'
o	o	as the 'o' in British English 'hot'
ö	er	as the 'ir' in 'girl' (rounding the lips)
õ	y	roughly as the 'i' in 'girl' (without rounding the lips)
u	u	as the 'u' in 'put'
ü	ü	as the 'oo' in 'too' said with a small, round opening of the lips

ae	ae	as the 'ie' in 'diet' (two sounds)
ai	ai	as the 'ai' in 'aisle'
ää	aa	as the 'a' in 'Aaron'
äe	aeh	as the 'ae' in 'aesthetic'
ee	eh	as the 'e' in 'ten' but longer
ea	ea	as the 'ea' in 'bear'
ei	ay	as the 'ai' in 'paid'
ii	ee	as the 'ee' in 'see'
oo	aw	as the 'aw' in 'dawn'
oi	oy	as the 'oi' in 'loiter'
öö	err	as the 'yrr' in 'myrrh' (rounding the lips)
uu	oo	as the 'oo' in 'zoo'
ui	uy	as the 'oui' in 'Louie', but shorter and clipped
õi	yi	roughly as the word 'curly' leaving out the 'c', 'r' and 'l'

ESTONIAN

Consonants

Consonants are pronounced as in English, with the exception of the following:

Estonian	Translit	Sounds
p	**p**	halfway between English 'p' and 'b'
t	**t**	halfway between English 't' and 'd'
g	**g**	always as in 'good', never as in 'page'
k	**k**	softer than in English
j	**y**	as the 'y' in 'yes'
r	**rr**	always trilled, as the Italian 'r'
č	**ch**	as the 'ch' in 'change'
š	**sh**	as the 'sh' in 'shampoo'
ž	**zh**	as the 's' in 'treasure'

Stress

Stress is on the first syllable. There are very few exceptions to this rule but there's one that's very conspicuous – the word for 'thanks' *aitäh* (ai-*tahh*) stresses the second syllable.

Pronunciation Practice

Here are a few phrases. Practise these and you'll pick up Estonian pronunciation in no time. Stress is indicated by italics.

What are the Estonian flag's colours?
> **mis on *ehs*-ti *li*-pu *varr*-vid?**   *Mis on Eesti lipu värvid?*

They are blue, black and white.
> **nehd on *si*-ni-ne must yah *vahl*-ge**   *Need on sinine, must ja valge.*

Do you speak English?
> **kahs te *rraa*-gi-te *ing*-li-se kehlt?**   *Kas te räägite inglise keelt?*

I like this performance.
> **mul-le *mehl*-dib seh e-ten-dus**   *Mulle meeldib see etendus.*

Where do you come from?
kust te *pa*-rrit *o*-le-te?   *Kust te pärit olete?*

Happy birthday!
***pahl*-yu *yn*-ne**   *Palju õnne sünnipäevaks!*
***sün*-ni-paeh-vahks!**

GRAMMAR
Word Order
There are no articles or grammatical genders in Estonian. Sentences
don't have a strict word order. Parts of speech, such as the subject
and object, are identified by their different endings, called case
endings. Even if your sentence structure is slightly awkward, you'll
be understood if you use the endings correctly.

ESTONIAN

- What?/Who? (nominative case – no specific ending)

  plane   *lennuk*
  boy   *poiss*

- Of what?/Whose? (genitive or possessive case)

  plane's   *lennuk-i*
  The plane's size.   *Lennuki suurus.*

  boy's   *pois-i*
  The boy's size.   *Poisi suurus.*

- What?/Whom? (accusative or objective case)

  plane   *lennuk-it*
  I see the plane.   *Ma näen lennukit.*

  boy   *pois-si*
  I see the boy.   *Ma näen poissi.*

ESTONIAN

ON THE CASE

In English, we're able to recognise the 'role' of a noun in a sentence – who is performing an action, to whom, with what and so on – by its position in a sentence and/or by the use of prepositions.

However, like Latin, German and many other languages, Estonian uses what is known as 'case' to make these distinctions. Different suffixes known as case endings act like labels on nouns to indicate their relationship to other words in a sentence.

The case endings of other words in a sentence, such as adjectives and pronouns, must agree in number and gender with the case ending of the noun they refer to.

Estonian has fourteen cases, but you don't need to know them all. Here's a brief explanation of the three cases which are most important:

1. The nominative case refers to the subject of a verb in a sentence and is also the form you'll find in a dictionary. It indicates what or who is performing an action:

The audience threw flowers to the dancer, stomped the ground with their feet and yelled 'Encore!'.

2. The accusative is the direct object of a sentence. It indicates what or whom the verb refers to. Here it indicates what was given:

The audience threw *flowers* to the dancer, stomped the ground with their feet and yelled 'Encore!'.

3. The genitive case refers to possession, a bit like English 'of' or the possessive 's' ('s). It indicates whose or of what/of whom:

The audience threw flowers to the dancer, stomped the ground with *their feet* and yelled 'Encore!'.

Adjectives

Adjectives are placed before nouns and usually take the same case endings as the nouns they modify:

in a big city   *suures linnas*
               (lit: big city-in)

Both comparative and superlative adjectives add *-m* to the genitive case. Superlative adjectives also begin with the word *kõige* which translates as 'most'.

big	*suur*
bigger	*suurem*
biggest	*kõige suurem*
	(lit: most bigger)

beautiful	*ilus*
more beautiful	*ilusam*
	(lit: beautiful-er)
most beautiful	*kõige ilusam*
	(lit: most beautiful-er)

Adverbs

To form adverbs from adjectives, add the endings *-lt* or *-sti* to their genitive (second form given in the dictionary) forms:

slow	*aeglase*
slowly	*aeglaselt*

quick	*kiire*
quickly	*kiiresti*

ESTONIAN

Pronouns

Personal and possessive pronouns have two forms. Short forms are common in speech; long forms are used to stress a point.

Verbs

All Estonian verbs have either *-ma* or *-da* as an ending. The ending is dropped when the verb is conjugated. The following shows the present tense endings which are the same for most verbs:

to come	*tulema*
I come	*ma tulen*
you come (sg & inf)	*sa tuled*
she/he comes	*ta tuleb*
we come	*me tuleme*
you come (pl & pol)	*te tulete*
they come	*nad tulevad*

PRONOUNS		
PERSONAL		
I	mah/*mi*-nah	ma/mina
you (sg & inf)	sah/*si*-nah	sa/sina
she/he	tah/*te*-mah	ta/tema
we	me/*may*-e	me/meie
you (pl & pol)	te/*tay*-e	te/teie
they	nahd/*ne*-mahd	nad/nemad
POSSESSIVE		
my	mu/*mi*-nu	mu/minu
your (sg & inf)	su/*si*-nu	su/sinu
her/his	tah/*te*-mah	ta/tema
our	me/*may*-e	me/meie
your (pl & pol)	te/*tay*-e	te/teie
their	*nen*-de	nende

Present

In Estonian grammar, there's no distinction between a continuous activity and one that happens only once. Actions are expressed through context:

He comes here every day.	*Ta tuleb siia iga päev.* (lit: she/he comes to-here every day)
He is coming this way.	*Ta tuleb siiapoole.* (lit: she/he comes to-here-towards)

Future

The future tense is also expressed through context:

He will come tomorrow.	*Ta tuleb homme.* (lit: she/he comes tomorrow)

Past

Most verbs take a form of the suffix *-si* to create the simple past. To make the verb agree with the subject add, *-sin* for the subject 'I', *-sid* for 'you' (inf), *-s* for 'she/he', *-sime* for 'we', *-site* for 'you' (pl & pol) or *-sid* for 'they':

We asked for the menu.	*Me palusime menüüd.* (lit: we asked menu-for)
They went to the cinema.	*Nad läksid kinno.* (lit: they went cinema-to)

The verb 'to be' is an exception to this rule:

I was ill.	*Ma olin haige.* (lit: I was ill)

ESTONIAN

Imperatives

To make formal imperatives (commands), drop the *-ma* or *-da* ending of a verb and add *-ge*.

Infinitive	Imperative	
sööma	*Sööge!*	Eat!
kirjutama	*Kirjutage!*	Write!
vabandama	*Vabandage!*	Excuse me!
tulema	*Tulge siia!*	Come here!
	Ärge tulge!	Don't come!

TO BE

The bracketed form of the pronoun is used for emphasis.

I am	*(mina) ma olen*
you are (sg & inf)	*(sina) sa oled*
she/he is	*(tema) ta on*
we are	*(meie) me oleme*
you are (pl & pol)	*(teie) te olete*
they are	*(nemad) nad on*

TO HAVE

The verb 'to have' (*omama*) is rarely used in Estonian. Possession is expressed by using the third person of the verb 'to be'. Once again, the bracketed form is used for emphasis:

I have a car.	*(Minul) Mul on auto.*
	(lit: on-me is car)
We have two tickets.	*(Meil) Meil on kaks piletit.*
	(lit: on-us are two tickets)
She has a cat.	*(Temal) Tal on kass.*
	(lit: on-him/her is cat)

Questions

Who are you?	*Kes te olete?*
	(lit: who you are?)
Why are they shouting?	*Miks nad karjuvad?*
	(lit: why they shout?)
How do I get there?	*Kuidas ma sinna saan?*
	(lit: how I to-there get?)
What's your name?	*Mis te nimi on?*
	(lit: what your name is?)

Another way to turn a sentence into a question is to place the word *kas* (**kahs**) at the beginning of a sentence. This roughly translates as 'do':

You speak English.	*Te räägite inglise keelt.*
	(lit: you speak
	English language)
Do you speak English?	*Kas te räägite inglise keelt?*
	(lit: do you speak
	English language?)

ESTONIAN

QUESTION WORDS		
who?	kes?	kes?
what?	mis?	mis?
where?	kus?	kus?
when?	*mil*-lahl?	millal?
why?	miks?	miks?
how?	*kuy*-dahs?	kuidas?

ESTONIAN

Negatives

To make a sentence negative, place the word *ei* ('no') in front of the verb:

I am not.   *Ma ei ole.*
                                     (lit: I no am)

She/He doesn't drink.   *Ta ei joo.*
                                     (lit: she/he no drink)

Modals

A modal is a word or phrase placed in front of the verb that changes the mood of that verb by expressing ability, necessity, desire or need. Estonian modals denoting ability are more specific in meaning than their English counterparts. For example, the English modal verb 'can' translates into four different modals, with four different meanings, in Estonian:

I can dance.
(I can because I have learned)   *Ma oskan tantsida.*
(I may if I choose to)   *Ma võin tantsida.*
(I can because I will be invited)   *Ma saan tantsida.*
(I am able to, I am not too tired)   *Ma suudan tantsida.*

Prepositions

above	*ko*-hahl	kohal
at	*joo*-rres	juures
next to	*kyr*-vahl	kõrval
on	peal	peal
under	ahll	all
with	kaws	koos
without	*il*-mah	ilma

Conjunctions

and	yah	ja
because	sest	sest
but	*ah*-gah	aga
or	vyi	või

GREETINGS & CIVILITIES

Most Estonians, especially younger people, understand some English and Finnish. Many speak some Russian, although they are often sensitive about using it.

Estonians are a reserved and polite people and are generally rather shy with strangers. If you're lucky enough to be invited to someone's home, it's customary to bring flowers as a gift. When entering a household, it's considered unlucky to shake hands across the threshold. You should take off your shoes. Your host will usually give you slippers to wear instead.

ESTONIAN

Greetings & Goodbyes

Hello.	te-rre	*Tere.*
Welcome.	te-rre tu-le-mahst	*Tere tulemast.*
Good ...	te-rre ...	*Tere ...*
morning	*hom*-mi-kust	*hommikust*
afternoon	*paeh*-vahst	*päevast*
evening	*yh*-tust	*õhtust*
Good night.	head errd	*Head ööd.*
Goodbye.	head ae-gah	*Head aega.*
See you later.	na-ge-mi-se-ni	*Nägemiseni.*

Civilities

In Estonia, it's considered awkward to ask a stranger, 'How are you?'. Such a question is often taken literally and not as a courtesy question, but if you do ask, it will be understood.

How are you? (How's it going?)
   kuy-dahs *la*-heb?   *Kuidas läheb?*
Very nice (to meet you).
   va-gah *mehl*-div   *Väga meeldiv.*
Fine.
   has-ti   *Hästi.*
Okay (Nothing wrong).
   po-le *vi*-gah   *Pole viga.*
Please./You're welcome.
   pah-lun   *Palun.*
Thank you (very much).
   ta-nahn (*va*-gah)   *Tänan (väga).*
Thanks.
   ai-*tahh*   *Aitäh.*
Okay. (agreed)
   hea küll   *Hea küll.*
No, thank you.
   ta-nahn ay   *Tänan, ei.*

Forms of Address

Miss	*prray*-li	*preili*
Mrs	*prrou*-ah	*proua*
Mr	*har*-rah	*härra*

COME ON STRONG

When greeting someone who is working, it's customary to say *Jõudu!* (lit: strength-to-you!). The reply is *Tarvis!* (lit: it's-needed!).

ESTONIAN

Use the formal 'you', *te* (**te**) or *teie* (**tay-e**), when addressing strangers or people you just met. The informal *sa* (**sah**) or *sina* (**si-nah**) is reserved for children, family and friends. Except with children, don't use it until you are invited to.

Do you speak English?
kahs te *rraa*-gi-te   *Kas te räägite*
***ing*-li-se kehlt?**   *inglise keelt?*
You're a good child.
sah *o*-led *tub*-li lahps   *Sa oled tubli laps.*

ESTONIAN

Useful Words & Phrases

Yes.	yah	*Jah.*
No.	ay	*Ei.*
Pardon?	*kuy*-dahs?	*Kuidas?*
Certainly.	*kind*-lahs-ti	*Kindlasti.*
Of course.	*muy*-du-gi	*Muidugi.*
Just a moment.	üks hetk	*Üks hetk.*
Never mind.	*po*-le *vi*-gah	*Pole viga.*
Wait!	*aw*-dah-ke!	*Oodake!*
Excuse me/	*vah*-bahn-dah-ge	*Vabandage.*
I'm sorry.		
What a pity!	*kah*-yu!	*Kahju!*

Can I help you? (How can I be of service?)
***kuy*-das mah saahn**   *Kuidas ma saan*
***kah*-su-lik *ol*-lah?**   *kasulik olla?*

Where's the ...?	kus on ...?	*Kus on ...?*
hotel	ho-*tell*	*hotell*
telephone	*te*-le-fon	*telefon*
toilet	tuah-*lett*	*tualett*

SMALL TALK
Meeting People

What's your name?	mis te *ni*-mi on?	*Mis te nimi on?*
My name is ...	mu *ni*-mi on ...	*Minu nimi on ...*
I like Estonians.	*mul*-le *mehl*-di-vahd *ehst*-lah-sed	*Mulle meeldivad eestlased.*

This is my ...	seh on *mi*-nu ...	*See on minu ...*
friend	*sy*-berr	*sõber*
husband	mehs	*mees*
spouse	*ah*-bi-kaah-sah	*abikaasa*
wife	*nai*-ne	*naine*

Nationalities

When Estonians ask visitors about their nationality, it doesn't always mean their citizenship. An ethnic Russian, even though born in Estonia and holding an Estonian passport, will still be called a Russian.

I'm ...	mah *o*-len ...	*Ma olen ...*
American	ah-*meh*-rik-lah-ne	*ameeriklane*
Australian	aust-*rrahl*-lah-ne	*austraallane*
British	*ing*-lah-ne	*inglane*
Canadian	*kah*-nah-dah-lah-ne	*kanadalane*
Danish	*taahn*-lah-ne	*taanlane*
Estonian	*ehst*-lah-ne	*eestlane*
Finnish	*sawm*-lah-ne	*soomlane*
French	*prrahnts*-lah-ne	*prantslane*
German	*sahks*-lah-ne	*sakslane*
Latvian	*lat*-lah-ne	*lätlane*
Lithuanian	*leh*-du-lah-ne	*leedulane*
Norwegian	*nor*-rrah-lah-ne	*norralane*
Russian	ve-ne-lah-ne	*venelane*
Swedish	*rrawts*-lah-ne	*rootslane*

ESTONIAN

Age

How old are you?
    kuy *vah*-nah te *o*-le-te?   *Kui vana te olete?*

I'm ...
    mah *o*-len ...   *Ma olen ...*

WHEN IN ROME

Remember, in keeping with the polite and formal character of the Estonians, it's considered impolite to ask strangers their age.

ESTONIAN

Occupations

What's your line of work?
    mis terrd te *teh*-te?   *Mis tööd te teete?*

I'm (a) ...	mah *o*-len ...	*Ma olen ...*
business person	a-rri-nai-ne	*ärinaine* (f)
	a-rri-meehs	*ärimees* (m)
doctor	ahrrst	*arst*
farmer	*tah*-lu-nik	*talunik*
journalist	a-yah-kirr-yah-nik	*ajakirjanik*
labourer	terr-line	*tööline*
lawyer	*yu*-rrist	*jurist*
nurse	*y*-de	*õde*
retired	*pen*-sio-narr	*pensionär*
sailor/mariner	*me*-rre-mehs	*meremees*
state official	*rree*-gi-ah-met-nik	*riigiametnik*
student	*tu*-deng	*tudeng*
teacher	*y*-pe-ta-ya	*õpetaja*
tour guide	geed	*giid*
unemployed	terr-tu	*töötu*
waiter	*et*-te-kahnd-yah	*ettekandja* (f)
	kel-nerr	*kelner* (m)
writer	*kirr*-yah-nik	*kirjanik*

Religion

Most ethnic Estonians are Lutheran but only about 10% of them
actively practise it. Russian Orthodoxy is more common on the
islands and among the Russian population. On the island of
Saaremaa off the west coast (a popular holiday destination for
Estonians) you'll hear Orthodox services delivered entirely in
Estonian.

What's your religion?		
mis *us*-ku te *o*-le-te?		*Mis usku te olete?*

I'm ...	mah *o*-len ...	*Ma olen ...*
Buddhist	*bu*-dist	*budist*
Catholic	*kah*-to-leek-lah-ne	*katoliiklane*
Christian	*krrist*-lah-ne	*kristlane*
Hindu	*in*-du-ist	*induist*
Jewish	*yu*-dah-ist	*judaist*
Lutheran	*lu*-terr-lah-ne	*luterlane*
Muslim	*mu*-sul-mahn	*musulman*
Russian Orthodox	*ve*-ne *yi*-ge-usk-lik	*vene õigeusklik*

| I'm not religious. | mah ay *o*-le *usk*-lik | *Ma ei ole usklik.* |

Family

Are you married?		
kahs te *o*-le-te *ah*-bi-e-lus?		*Kas te olete abielus?*

I'm ...	mah *o*-len ...	*Ma olen ...*
divorced	*lah*-hu-tah-tud	*lahutatud*
gay	*les*-bi/gay	*lesbi/gei* (f/m)
married	*ah*-bi-e-lus	*abielus*
single	*vahl*-lah-li-ne	*vallaline*
widowed	lesk	*lesk*

ESTONIAN

Do you have any ...?	kahs tayl on ...?	*Kas teil on ...?*
children	*lahp*-si	*lapsi*
sisters/brothers	y-de-sid/ *ven*-di	*õdesid/vendi*

I have a daughter/son.		
mul on *tü*-tahrr/poeg		*Mul on tütar/poeg.*
I don't have any children.		
mul ei o-le *lahp*-si		*Mul ei ole lapsi.*

Is your ... here	kahs *tay*-e ... on	*Kas teie ... on*
as well?	kah seen?	*ka siin?*
boyfriend	*sy*-berr	*sõber*
girlfriend	*syb*-rrah-tarr	*sõbratar*
wife/husband	ah-bi-*kaah*-sah	*abikaasa*

aunt	*ta*-di	*tädi*
family	*pe*-rre	*pere*
father	*i*-sah	*isa*
mother	*e*-mah	*ema*
uncle	*o*-nu	*onu*

ESTONIAN

Kids' Talk

How old are you?
kuy *vah*-nah sah *o*-led? *Kui vana sa oled?*
When's your birthday?
***mil*-lahl su *sün*-ni-paehv on?** *Millal su sünnipäev on?*
What do you do after school?
***mi*-dah sah *parr*-ahst
kaw-li tehd?** *Mida sa pärast
kooli teed?*
Do you have a pet at home?
**kahss sul on *ko*-dus
lem-mik-law-mah?** *Kas sul on kodus
lemmiklooma?*

ESTONIAN

I have a ...	mul on ...	*Mul on ...*
bird	lind	*lind*
budgerigar	veerr-pah-pah-goy	*viirpapagoi*
canary	kah-nah-rri-lind	*kanaarilind*
cat	kahss	*kass*
dog	koerr	*koer*
duck	pahrrt	*part*
fish	kah-lah	*kala*
frog	konn	*konn*
guinea pig	me-rri-si-gah	*merisiga*
hamster	hahms-terr	*hamster*
horse	ho-bu-ne	*hobune*
tortoise	kilp-konn	*kilpkonn*

Expressing Feelings

I'm ...	mul on ...	*Mul on ...*
cold	külm	*külm*
hot	pah-lahv	*palav*
happy	hea tu-yu	*hea tuju*
in a hurry	kee-rre	*kiire*
scared	hirrm	*hirm*
sorry	kah-yu	*kahju*

I'm ...	mah o-len ...	*Ma olen ...*
angry	vi-hah-ne	*vihane*
grateful	ta-nu-lik	*tänulik*
sad	kurrb	*kurb*
sick	hai-ge	*haige*
tired	va-si-nud	*väsinud*

I feel ...	mul on ...	*Mul on ...*
bad	hahlb	*halb*
good	hea	*hea*

Expressing Opinions

What do you think?	mis te *ahr*-vah-te?	*Mis te arvate?*
I like this ...	*mul*-le *mehl*-dib seh ...	*Mulle meeldib see ...*
I don't like this ...	*mul*-le ay *mehl*-di seh ...	*Mulle ei meeldi see ...*
city	**linn**	*linn*
country	**maah**	*maa*
hotel	**ho-*tell***	*hotell*
performance	**e-ten-dus**	*etendus*
restaurant	**rres-to-rran**	*restoran*

I like her/him.
  ta *mehl*-dib *mul*-le   *Ta meeldib mulle.*
I don't like this/that.
  seh ay *mehl*-di *mul*-le   *See ei meeldi mulle.*

BODY LANGUAGE

Estonians tend to be reserved and formal with strangers. Friends shake hands rather than embrace when they greet each other. Shouting, arm gestures and standing too close are considered uncouth. The old-fashioned customs of men helping women on with their coats and holding doors open are commonplace.

ESTONIAN

ESTONIAN

BREAKING THE LANGUAGE BARRIER

I don't speak Estonian.
    mah ay rraa-gi ehs-ti kehlt   *Ma ei räägi eesti keelt.*
Estonian is difficult.
    ehs-ti kehl on rrahs-ke   *Eesti keel on raske.*
I don't understand.
    mah ay saah ah-rru   *Ma ei saa aru.*
Do you understand?
    kahs te saah-te ah-rru?   *Kas te saate aru?*

SIGNS

PARKIMINE KEELATUD	NO PARKING
SISSESÕIT KEELATUD	NO ENTRY
STOPP	STOP
TEE REMONT	ROADWORKS
ÜLEKÄIK	PEDESTRIAN CROSSING
VALUUTAVAHETUS	CURRENCY EXCHANGE
AVARII	ACCIDENT/DANGER
AVATUD/LAHTI	OPEN
KASSA	CASHIER/TICKETS
KURI KOER	VICIOUS DOG
LÕUNA	AT LUNCH
MEESTELE	MEN'S TOILET
MITTE SUITSETADA	NO SMOKING
NAISTELE	WOMEN'S TOILET
RESERVEERITUD	RESERVED
SISSEPÄÄS	ENTRANCE
SULETUD/KINNI	CLOSED
VÄLJAPÄÄS	EXIT
WC	PUBLIC TOILET

Please repeat it.

    pah-lun *kor*-rrah-ke   *Palun korrake.*

Please write it down here.

    pah-lun *kirr*-yu-tah-ge   *Palun kirjutage*
    seh *see*-ah   *see siia.*

Do you speak ...?	kahs te *rraa*-gi-te ... kehlt?	*Kas te räägite ... keelt?*
English	*ing*-li-se	*inglise*
Finnish	*saw*-me	*soome*
French	*prrahnt*-su-se	*prantsuse*
German	*sahk*-sah	*saksa*
Russian	ve-ne	*vene*

Sports & Interests

What do you do with your free time?

    mi-dah te *vah*-bahl   *Mida te vabal*
    ah-yahl *teh*-te?   *ajal teete?*

I like (to) ...	*mul*-le *mehl*-dib ...	*Mulle meeldib ...*
art	kunst	*kunst*
ballet	bahl-*lett*	*ballett*
the cinema	*fil*-mi-kunst	*filmikunst*
(classical) music	(*klahs*-si-kah-li-ne) *moo*-si-kah	*(klassikaline) muusika*
opera	*aw*-perr	*ooper*
reading	*lu*-ge-dah	*lugeda*
the theatre	*teah*-terr	*teater*
travelling	*rray*-si-dah	*reisida*
visit exhibitions	*kai*-ah *nai*-tus-tel	*käia näitustel*
visit museums	*kai*-ah *moo*-se-u-mi-des	*käia muuseumides*
visit national parks	*kai*-ah *rrah*-vus-pahrr-ki-des	*käia rahvusparkides*

ESTONIAN

ESTONIAN

I want to go ...	ma *tah*-han	*Ma tahan*
	min-nah ...	*minna ...*
bird watching	*lin*-de *vaaht*-le-mah	*linde vaatlema*
bobsledding	*saah*-ni-gah *syit*-mah	*saaniga sõitma*
camping	*tel*-gi-gah	*telgiga*
	maht-kah-mah	*matkama*
canoeing	*süs*-tah-*maht*-kah-le	*süstamatkale*
cycling	*yahlg*-rraht-tah-gah	*jalgrattaga*
	syit-mah	*sõitma*
(ice) fishing	(*yaa*-le)	(*jääle*)
	kah-lahs-tah-mah	*kalastama*
gliding	*pu*-rri-len-nu-ki-gah	*purilennukiga*
	syit-mah	*sõitma*
hiking	*maht*-kah-mah	*matkama*
horse riding	*rrat*-su-tah-mah	*ratsutama*
jogging	*yawks*-mah	*jooksma*
sailing	*purr*-ye-tah-mah	*purjetama*
skiing	*soo*-sah-tah-mah	*suusatama*
swimming	*u*-yu-mah	*ujuma*
tobogganing	*kel*-gu-tah-mah	*kelgutama*

I play ...	mah *man*-gin ...	*Ma mängin ...*
basketball	*korrv*-pahl-li	*korvpalli*
cards	*kaahrr*-te	*kaarte*
chess	*mah*-let	*malet*
guitar	ki-*tahr*-rri	*kitarri*
soccer	*yahlg*-pahl-li	*jalgpalli*
tennis	*ten*-nist	*tennist*
winter sports	*tah*-li-sporr-di-ah-lahd	*talispordialad*

Useful Words & Phrases

Well done!	*tub*-li!	*Tubli!*
Let's go.	*lah*-me	*Lähme.*
Let's start.	*hak*-kah-me *pih*-tah	*Hakkame pihta.*
Let's try.	*prraw*-vi-me	*Proovime.*
Just joking!	mah *te*-gin *nahl*-yah!	*Ma tegin nalja!*
Congratulations!	*pal*-yu *yn*-ne!	*Palju õnne!*

GETTING AROUND

You'll find many travel agencies in Tallinn that can help you with bookings and queries about travel within and out of Estonia. They also organise city tours, guided trips to other parts of the country and provincial accommodation.

Directions

Excuse me.	vah-bahn-dah-ge	Vabandage.

Where's the ...?	kus on ...?	Kus on ...?
airport	len-nu-yaahm	lennujaam
bus station	bus-si-yaahm	bussijaam
ferry terminal	sah-dahm	sadam
taxi rank	tahk-so-pea-tus	taksopeatus
train station	rron-gi-yaahm	rongijaam

Is it far?
  kahs seh on kau-gel? Kas see on kaugel?
Please show me on the map.
  pah-lun nai-dah-ke mul-le Palun näidake mulle
  se-dah kaahrr-dil seda kaardil.

Buying Tickets

I'd like a ticket to ... please.	pah-lun üks pi-let ...	Palun üks pilet ...
Tartu	tahrr-tus-se	Tartusse
Pärnu	par-nus-se	Pärnusse
Riga	rree-gah	Riiga
Vilnius	vil-nius-se	Vilniusse
Moscow	mosk-vahs-se	Moskvasse
St Petersburg	pe-terr-bu-rri	Peterburi
Helsinki	hel-sin-gis-se	Helsingisse
Stockholm	stock-hol-mi	Stockholmi

ESTONIAN

ESTONIAN

Air

Tallinn is served by several European airlines. The national airline is Estonian Air, but there are no domestic flights. Tallinn Airport is close to the city and easily reached by bus or taxi. It uses English as its international language so it's not difficult to ask for help there.

Is there a flight to ...?
   kahs tayl on *len*-nu-rray-si ...?   *Kas teil on lennureisi ...?*
Where's the ticket office?
   kus on *pi*-le-ti-kahs-sah?   *Kus on piletikassa?*
Where's the left luggage?
   kus-on *pah*-gah-si   *Kus on pagasi*
   ***hoy*-u-rroom?**   *hoiuruum?*

ON THE STREETS

TÄNAV	STREET
VÄLJAK/PLATS	SQUARE
PUIESTEE	AVENUE/BOULEVARD
TEE	ROAD
MAANTEE	HIGHWAY
SILD	BRIDGE

Bus & Train

Bus travel is comfortable and domestic routes are inexpensive. Links to Europe are good. Domestic trains go to many Estonian towns and there's only one class. Some trains continue to foreign destinations and they offer several classes of service.

It's advisable to buy tickets in advance, especially for holiday and weekend travel. Many trains have restaurant cars and facilities to carry bikes. Bus and train tickets are one-way. A return ticket is twice the one-way fare.

Please give me a ... ticket.	*pah*-lun ... *pi*-let	*Palun ... pilet.*
one-way	üks	*üks*
return	e-dah-si–*tah*-gah-si	*edasi-tagasi*

A student/child ticket, please.
pah-lun *y*-pi-lah-se/   *Palun õpilase/*
lahp-se *pi*-let   *lapse pilet.*

City Public Transport

Tickets for all city public transport are sold in kiosks and on board vehicles at a slightly higher cost. A ticket must be punched for every ride and failure to do this can result in a fine. You can buy tickets for unlimited rides for 10, 20 and 30 days. There are discounts if you can show an International Student ID Card.

Which ... do I take to get there?	mis ... mah *sin*-nah saahn?	*Mis ... ma sinna saan?*
bus	*bus*-si-gah	*bussiga*
tram	*trrahm*-mi-gah	*trammiga*
trolleybus	*trrol*-li-gah	*trolliga*

What time is the next ...?	mis kell on *yarrg*-mi-ne ...?	*Mis kell on järgmine ...?*
bus	buss	*buss*
train	rrong	*rong*

ESTONIAN

What time does the train depart?
    mis kell *la*-heb rrong?   *Mis kell läheb rong?*
Which platform?
    mis *plaht*-vorrm?   *Mis platvorm?*
What time does the bus arrive?
    mis kell *saah*-bub buss?   *Mis kell saabub buss?*
What bus stop?
    mis *peah*-tus?   *Mis peatus?*
This train is cancelled.
    seh rrong yaab *a*-rrah   *See rong jääb ära.*
How long will it be delayed?
    kui *pahl*-yu seh *hi*-li-neb?   *Kui palju see hilineb?*
I want to get off.
    mah *ta*-hahn *mah*-hah *min*-nah   *Ma tahan maha minna.*
Excuse me, you're sitting in my seat.
    vah-bahn-dah-ge te *is*-tu-te   *Vabandage, te istute*
    mi-nu *ko*-hah peal   *minu koha peal.*

Ferry

Many ferries and hydrofoils ply the Gulf of Finland between Tallinn and Helsinki, and there's also ferry services to Sweden and Germany. Baltic travellers continue to use ferries because they're inexpensive and convenient. There are also ferries between the mainland and the large Estonian islands.

boat	**paaht**	*paat*
ferry	**prraahm**	*praam*
harbour	*sah*-dahm	*sadam*
hydrofoil	*tee*-burr	*tiibur*

Where does the ferry leave from?
    kust *prraahm val-yub?*   *Kust praam väljub?*
What time does the ferry arrive?
    mis kell *prraahm saah-bub?*   *Mis kell praam saabub?*
Which ferry goes to ...?
    mil-li-ne *prraahm la*-heb ...?   *Milline praam läheb ...?*
Is this the ferry for ...?
    kahs seeh on ... *prraahm?*   *Kas see on ... praam?*

DID YOU KNOW ...   Estonia is only slightly bigger than Denmark or the Netherlands, and is the smallest of the three Baltic countries.

ESTONIAN

Taxi

I want to go to ...
    mah *tah*-han *min*-nah ...   *Ma tahan minna ...*
How much will it cost?
    mis seh mahk-sab?   *Mis see maksab?*
Please drive to ...
    pah-lun *syit*-ke ...   *Palun sõitke ...*
Go left.
    vah-sah-ku-le   *Vasakule.*
Go right.
    pah-rre-mah-le   *Paremale.*
Go straight ahead.
    ot-se   *Otse.*
Please stop here.
    pah-lun *pea*-tu-ge seen   *Palun peatuge siin.*
Please wait.
    pah-lun *aw*-dah-ke   *Palun oodake.*
How much does it cost?
    kuy *pahl*-yu seh *mahk*-sahb?   *Kui palju see maksab?*

Car

Where can I rent a car?
kus mah saahn
rren-ti-dah au-to?

*Kus ma saan
rentida auto?*

What is the daily/weekly rate?
mis on paeh-vah/
na-dah-lah rrent?

*Mis on päeva/
nädala rent?*

Does that include ...?	kahs seh on kaws ...?	*Kas see on koos ...?*
insurance	kind-lus-tu-se-gah	*kindlustusega*
mileage	ki-lo-met-rraah-zhi-gah	*kilomeetraažiga*

Where can I buy a parking card?
kus saahb os-tah
pahrr-ki-mis-kaahrr-te?

*Kus saab osta
parkimiskaarte?*

Where does this road go?
ku-hu seh teh veeb?

Kuhu see tee viib?

Where's a petrol station?
kus on ben-see-ni-yaahm?

Kus on bensiinijaam?

air (for tyres)	yhk	*õhk*
battery	ah-ku	*aku*
driving licence	yu-hi-lu-bah	*juhiluba*
engine	maw-torr	*mootor*
lights	tu-led	*tuled*
oil	y-li	*õli*
radiator	rrah-di-aah-torr	*radiaator*
road map	maahn-tee-de kaahrrt	*maanteede kaart*
windscreen	too-le-klaahs	*tuuleklaas*

My ... isn't/aren't
working.
mu au-to ... ay terr-tah

Mu auto ... ei tööta.

brakes	pi-du-rrid	*pidurid*
clutch	si-durr	*sidur*
gears	kai-gu-kahst	*käigukast*

ESTONIAN

My tyre is flat.
    mu *au*-to kumm on *tü*-hi   *Mu auto kumm on tühi.*
Where's a garage?
    kus on *au*-to-teh-nin-dus?   *Kus on autoteenindus?*
How much will repairs cost?
    kuy *kahl*-lis on *rre*-mont?   *Kui kallis on remont?*
When will the car be ready?
    mil-lahl *au*-to *vahl*-mis saahb?   *Millal auto valmis saab?*
My car has been stolen.
    mu *au*-to on *vah*-rrahs-tah-tud   *Mu auto on varastatud.*
Is your car insured?
    kahs *tay*-e *au*-to on *kind*-lus-   *Kas teie auto on*
    tah-tud?   *kindlustatud?*

ACCOMMODATION

There are hotels to suit all budgets in Estonia. Bed and breakfast accommodation is becoming increasingly common in the countryside. Camp sites can also be found.

Finding Accommodation

Where can I find a ...?	**kus** *ah*-sub ...?	*Kus asub ...?*
hotel	**ho-***tell*	*hotell*
pension	*vyy*-rrahs-te-mah-yah	*võõrastemaja*
camp site	*kam*-ping	*kämping*

Is it far?	**kahs** seh on *kau*-gel?	*Kas see on kaugel?*
Is it expensive?	**kahs** seh on *kahl*-lis?	*Kas see on kallis?*

At the Hotel

I'd like a ...	**mah** *tah*-hak-sin ...	*Ma tahaksin ...*
	tu-bah	*tuba.*
single room	*ü*-he *vaw*-di-gah	*ühe voodiga*
double room	*kah*-he *vaw*-di-gah	*kahe voodiga*
room with a bathroom	*vahn*-ni-toa-gah	*vannitoaga*

ESTONIAN

I'm staying ...	mah yaan ...	*Ma jään ...*
one day	ü-heks *paeh*-vahks	*üheks päevaks*
two days	kah-heks paeh-vahks	*kaheks päevaks*
one week	ü-heks *na*-dah-lahks	*üheks nädalaks*

Is there (a) ...?	kahs seal on ...?	*Kas seal on ...?*
hot water	soe *ve*-si	*soe vesi*
bathroom	*vahn*-ni-tu-bah	*vannituba*
sauna	saun	*saun*
shower	*du*-shi-rroom	*duširuum*
telephone	te-le-fon	*telefon*
television	te-le-vee-sorr	*televiisor*

How much is it per person/per night?
> kui *pahl*-yu *mahk*-sab
> vaw-di-koht/*err*-paehv?

Kui palju maksab
voodikoht/ööpäev?

Please write down the price.
> *pah*-lun *kirr*-yu-tah-ge
> *see*-ah hind

Palun kirjutage siia
hind.

Does it include breakfast?
> kahs *hom*-mi-ku-serrk on
> *hin*-nah sehs?

Kas hommikusöök on
hinna sees?

THEY MAY SAY ...

kahs tayl on pahss?
> Do you have a passport?

kah-yuks ay *o*-le mayl *vah*-bu *koh*-ti
> Sorry, we're full.

kuy *kau*-ahks te *yaa*-te?
> How long will you be staying?

vaw-di-koht/*err*-paehv *mahk*-sab ...
krraw-ni
> It's ... kroons per person/per day.

Can I see it?
    kahs mah vyin se-dah
    na-hah?

Kas ma võin seda
näha?

Can I see the bathroom?
    kahs mah vyin vaah-dah-tah
    vahn-ni-tu-bah?

Kas ma võin vaadata
vannituba?

Are there any cheaper rooms?
    kahs tayl on o-dah-vah-maid
    tu-be?

Kas teil on odavamaid
tube?

Fine, I'll take it.
    ke-nah mah vy-tahn sel-le

Kena, ma võtan selle.

I'd like to pay the bill.
    mah tah-hahks mahks-tah
    ahrr-ve

Ma tahaks maksta arve.

Requests & Complaints

Please order a taxi for me.
    pah-lun tel-li-ge
    mul-le tahk-so

Palun tellige
mulle takso.

Please wake me up at ...
    pah-lun a-rrah-tah-ge
    mind kell ...

Palun äratage
mind kell ...

My room needs to be cleaned.
    mu tu-bah vah-yahb
    ko-rris-tah-mist

Mu tuba vajab
koristamist.

Please change the sheets.
    pah-lun vah-he-tah-ge
    vaw-di-pe-su

Palun vahetage
voodipesu.

I can't open the window.
    mah ay saah
    ah-vah-dah ah-kent

Ma ei saa
avada akent.

I can't get into my room.
    mah ay paa-se o-mah tup-pah

Ma ei pääse oma tuppa.

The toilet won't flush.
    tuah-le-tis po-le vett

Tualetis pole vett.

ESTONIAN

My room is very cold.
    mu *tu*-bah on *va*-gah külm   *Mu tuba on väga külm.*
My telephone/television
isn't working.
    mu *te*-le-fon/*te*-le-vee-sorr   *Mu telefon/televiisor*
    ay *terr*-tah   *ei tööta.*
I don't like this room.
    mul-le ay *mehl*-di seh *tu*-bah   *Mulle ei meeldi see tuba.*

It's too ...	seh on *lee*-gah ...	*See on liiga ...*
expensive	*kahl*-lis	*kallis*
noisy	*ka*-rrah-rri-kahs	*kärarikas*
small	*vai*-ke	*väike*

Laundry

Can I have my clothes cleaned?
    kahs mah vyin *lahs*-tah *pe*-su   *Kas ma võin lasta pesu*
    pes-tah?   *pesta?*
How long will it take?
    kuy *kau*-ah seh *ae*-gah *vy*-tab?   *Kui kaua see aega võtab?*

Useful Words

bed	*vaw*-di	*voodi*
bill	*ahrr*-ve	*arve*
blanket	tekk	*tekk*
chair	tawl	*tool*
clean	*pu*-hahs	*puhas*
dark	*pi*-me	*pime*
dirty	must	*must*
double bed	*kah*-he-i-ni-me-se-*vaw*-di	*kaheinimesevoodi*
electricity	e-*lek*-terr	*elekter*
key	*vy*-ti	*võti*
lift (elevator)	lift	*lift*
light bulb	pirrn	*pirn*

lock (n)	**lukk**	*lukk*
mattress	**mahd-rrahts**	*madrats*
pillow	**pah-di**	*padi*
quiet	**vaik-ne**	*vaikne*
room (in hotel)	**ho-tel-li-tu-bah**	*hotellituba*
sheet	**li-nah**	*lina*
shower	**dush**	*duš*
soap	**sehp**	*seep*
suitcase	**koh-verr**	*kohver*
toilet	**tua-lett**	*tualett*
towel	**ka-te-rra-tik**	*käterätik*
hot/cold water	**soe/külm ve-si**	*soe/külm vesi*
window	**ah-ken**	*aken*

ESTONIAN

AROUND TOWN

Many Estonian towns have tourist information offices that offer visitors multilingual help. If you are planning a visit during the winter months, check in advance to ensure attractions and accommodations are open.

Where's (a/an/the) ...?	kus on ...?	*Kus on ...?*
art gallery	**kuns-ti-gah-le-rri**	*kunstigalerii*
bank	**pahnk**	*pank*
church	**ki-rrik**	*kirik*
city centre	**kesk-linn**	*kesklinn*
... embassy	**... saaht-kond**	*... saatkond*
my hotel	**mi-nu ho-tell**	*minu hotell*
market	**turrg**	*turg*
police	**po-lit-say**	*politsei*
post office	**post-kon-torr**	*postkontor*
toilet	**tua-lett**	*tualett*
tourist office	**tu-rris-mi-bü-rroo**	*turismibüroo*

ESTONIAN

ESTONIAN I AM

The power and imagery of 'Estonian I Am' are very difficult to convey in translation, but some of the emotion may be visible. The poet Jüri Leesment wrote the lyrics to Alo Mattiisen's music.

Eestlane olen

*Tuhat korda kas
või alata,
Tuhat aastat tõusu,
mitte luigelend.*

*Oma rahvust maha salata
sama ränk on nagu
orjaks müüa end.*

*Eestlane olen
ja eestlaseks jään,
kui mind eestlaseks loodi.*

*Eestlane olla on
uhke ja hää,
vabalt vaarisa moodi,
nende teiste meeste moodi.*

*Tuhat kõuehäälset küsijat,
vaba meri, põlistanud
püha muld.
Tuhat korda tuhat püsijat
kõige kiuste elus
hoiab püha tuld.*

Estonian I Am

We can have a thousand
beginnings
A thousand years rising,
not just a solitary
swan's flight.

To deny your own nation
is like selling yourself
into slavery.

Estonian I am and
Estonian I will stay
Since Estonian I was born.

To be an Estonian is a
proud and good thing.
As free as our forefathers,
Yes, like those other men.

A thousand thundering
questioners, our open sea,
our homeland's inviolate soil.
A thousand times a thousand
who prevail against all odds
to keep the sacred
flame burning.

At the Bank

The Estonian currency is the kroon, which is stable and tied to the German deutschmark. Credit cards are widely accepted. You'll find currency exchange offices everywhere, even in some supermarkets.

Where can I exchange money?
  kus mah saahn *vah*-he-tah-dah   *Kus ma saan vahetada*
  rrah-hah?   *raha?*
What's the ... rate today?
  mis on ... *paeh*-vah-kurrss?   *Mis on ... päevakurss?*
When is the bank open?
  mil-lahl on pahnk *ah*-vah-tud? *Millal on pank avatud?*

cash	*su*-lah-rra-hah	*sularaha*
cashier	kah-*seerr*	*kassiir*
coins	*mün*-did	*mündid*
credit card	krre-*deet*-kaahrrt	*krediitkaart*

At the Post Office

Post offices are open Monday through Saturday. In addition to handling mail, they offer telephone and telegraph services.

Where's the post office?
  kus *ah*-sub *post*-kon-torr?   *Kus asub postkontor?*

I'd like to	mah *ta*-hahks	*Ma tahaks*
buy some ...	*os*-tah ...	*osta ...*
envelopes	*ümb*-rrik-ke	*ümbrikke*
postcards	*post*-kaahrr-te	*postkaarte*
stamps	*mahrr*-ke	*marke*

I'd like to send a ...	mah *tah*-hahks	*Ma tahaks*
	saah-tah ...	*saata ...*
fax	*fahk*-si	*faksi*
parcel	*pahk*-ki	*pakki*
telegram	te-le-*grrahm*-mi	*telegrammi*

ESTONIAN

I'd like to send this to ...
    mah *tah*-hahks   *Ma tahaks*
    saah-tah *sel*-le ...   *saata selle ...*
How much does it cost?
    kui *pahl*-yu seh *mahk*-sahb?   *Kui palju see maksab?*
Is there a letter/parcel for me?
    kahs *mul*-le on   *Kas mulle on*
    kirr-yah/ *pahk*-ki?   *kirja/pakki?*

| airmail | *len*-nu-post | *lennupost* |
| letter box | *post*-kahst | *postkast* |

Telephone & Internet

It's possible to make direct international calls from most private telephones in Estonia. Pay phones need phone cards, sold in kiosks, filling stations and many shops. Mobile phones are very widely used. You can also book telephone calls at post offices through an operator.

I want to make a long-distance
call to ...
    mah *tah*-han *vyt*-tah   *Ma tahan võtta*
    kau-ge-ky-ne ...   *kaugekõne ...*
What does it cost per minute?
    kuy *pahl*-yu   *Kui palju*
    mahk-sahb *mi*-nut?   *maksab minut?*
I was cut off.
    ky-ne *kaht*-kes   *Kõne katkes.*
It's the wrong number.
    seh on *vah*-le *num*-berr   *See on vale number.*
It's engaged.
    seh on *kin*-ni   *See on kinni.*
I'd like to speak to ...
    mah *soo*-vin *rraa*-ki-dah ...   *Ma soovin rääkida ...*
I want to leave a message.
    mah *tah*-han *yat*-tah *sy*-na   *Ma tahan jätta sõna.*

ESTONIAN

| telephone | *te-le-fon* | *telefon* |
| telephone number | *te-le-fo-ni-num-berr* | *telefoninumber* |

I need to get on the Internet.
  mah *vah*-yahn
  in-terr-ne-ti-ü-hen-dust

*Ma vajan
internetiühendust.*

I need to check my email.
  mah pean *vaah*-tah-mah
  o-mah e-*lekt*-rron-pos-ti

*Ma pean vaatama oma
elektronposti.*

Sightseeing

Tallinn and many other towns in Estonia are picturesque and lend
themselves to walking. During summer there are organised walking
and bus tours. Guidebooks, maps and brochures are available in
tourist information offices and bookstores.

ESTONIAN

Do you have a ...?	kahs tayl on ...?	*Kas teil on ...?*
town guidebook	*lin*-nah-yuh-ti	*linnajuhti*
town map	*lin*-nah-plaah-ni	*linnaplaani*

What are the main attractions?
  mis on *pea*-mi-sed
  vaah-tah-mis-vaarr-su-sed?

*Mis on peamised
vaatamisväärsused?*

What's that?
  mis seh on?

Mis see on?

How old is it?
  kuy *vah*-nah seh on?

Kui vana see on?

Can I take photographs?
  kahs mah *to*-hin
  pil-dis-tah-dah?

*Kas ma tohin
pildistada?*

What time does it open/close?
  mis kell seh *ah*-vah-tahk-se/
  su-le-tahk-se?

*Mis kell see
avatakse/suletakse?*

What street is this?
  mis *ta*-nahv seh on?

Mis tänav see on?

I'd like to go to ...
    mah *tah*-haks *min*-nah ...   *Ma tahaks minna ...*
I'd like to go on a guided tour.
    mah *tah*-haks *min*-nah   *Ma tahaks minna*
    eks-kurr-*siaw*-ni-le   *ekskursioonile.*
I'd like to hire a guide.
    mah *tah*-hahks *tel*-li-da *gee*-di   *Ma tahaks tellida giidi.*

ESTONIAN

Useful Words

building	*haw*-ne	*hoone*
castle	loss	*loss*
cemetery	*kahl*-mis-tu	*kalmistu*
church	*ki*-rrik	*kirik*
exhibition	*nai*-tus	*näitus*
fortress	*kind*-lus	*kindlus*
historical	a-*yah-law*-li-ne	*ajalooline*
library	*rraah*-mah-tu-ko-gu	*raamatukogu*
monument	*mo*-nu-ment	*monument*
museum	*moo*-se-um	*muuseum*
national park	*rrah*-vus-pahrk	*rahvuspark*
nature trail	*low*-du-se	*looduse*
	yp-pe-rrah-dah	*õpperada*
park	pahrrk	*park*
ruins	*vah*-rre-med	*varemed*
statues	*ku*-yud	*kujud*
university	*ü*-li-kawl	*ülikool*

DID YOU KNOW ...   As well as the mainland, Estonia consists of 1521 islands, which make up nearly 10% of Estonian territory.

Going Out

Restaurants abound throughout Estonia, nearly all of them opened since independence. Prices are close to western levels and you'll also find fast food places and pizza parlours. Estonia's long musical heritage is reflected in the wide range of classical music performances, and events like the enormous song festivals. Theatre is vibrant and popular. Discos, cabaret shows, and casinos are booming. They often have a cover charge.

What's there to do here
in the evenings?
    mi-dah vyiks sehn   *Mida võiks siin*
    yh-tu-ti *te*-hah?   *õhtuti teha?*
Are there any discos?
    kahs sehn on *dis*-ko-sid?   *Kas siin on diskosid?*
Are there places where I can hear
Estonian folk music?
    kahs *ku*-sah-gil saahb   *Kas kusagil saab*
    koo-lah-tah *ehs*-ti   *kuulata Eesti*
    rrah-vah-moo-si-kaht?   *rahvamuusikat?*

Please recommend	*pah*-lun *saw*-vi-tah-ge	*Palun soovitage*
a good ...	*mu*-le head ...	*mulle head ...*
bar	*baah*-rri	*baari*
cafe	*koh*-vi-kut	*kohvikut*
nightclub	*err*-klu-bi	*ööklubi*

What's on tonight at the theatre?
    mis on *ta*-nah *teaht*-rris?   *Mis on täna teatris?*
What time does it begin?
    mis kell seh *al*-gab?   *Mis kell see algab?*
Where can I buy tickets?
    kust saahb *os*-tah *pi*-le-tayd? *Kust saab osta pileteid?*
One ticket/two tickets, please.
    üks *pi*-let/kahks   *Üks pilet/kaks*
    pi-le-tit *pah*-lun   *piletit, palun.*
Is this seat free?
    kahs seh koht on *vah*-bah?   *Kas see koht on vaba?*

ESTONIAN

cabaret	*kah-bah-rray*	*kabaree*
casino	*kah-seh-no*	*kasiino*
cinema	*ki-*no	*kino*
concert	*kont-*serrt	*kontsert*
disco	*dis-*ko	*disko*
theatre	*teah-*terr	*teater*

ESTONIAN

PAPERWORK

name	*ni-*mi	*nimi*
address	*aahd-*rress	*aadress*
age	*vah-*nus	*vanus*
birth certificate	*sün-ni-tun-nis-tus*	*sünnitunnistus*
border	*rree-gi-*peerr	*riigipiir*
car registration	*syi-*du-ki	*sõiduki*
document	*rre-gist-rreh-rri-mis-*	*registreerimis-*
	tun-nis-tus	*tunnistus*
citizenship	*ko-dah-*kond-sus	*kodakondsus*
customs	toll	*toll*
date of birth	*sün-*ni-aeg	*sünniaeg*
driver's licence	*yu-*hi-lu-bah	*juhiluba*
identification	*i-si-ku-tun-nis-tus*	*isikutunnistus*
immigration	*im-mig-rraht-siawn*	*immigratsioon*
marital status	*pe-rre-kon-nah-*says	*perekonnaseis*
passport	*pahss*	*pass*
passport number	*pahs-*si *num-*berr	*passi number*
place of birth	*sün-*ni-koht	*sünnikoht*
profession	*e-*lu-kut-*se*	*elukutse*
reason for travel	*rray-*si *pyh-*yus	*reisi põhjus*
religion	*kon-fes-siawn*	*konfessioon*
sex	*su-*gu	*sugu*
visa	*vee-*sah	*viisa*

IN THE COUNTRY
Weather

Today the weather is ...	*ta*-nah on ... ilm	*Täna on ... ilm.*
nice	*i*-lus	*ilus*
bad	hahlb	*halb*
cold	külm	*külm*
warm	soe	*soe*
windy	*too*-li-ne	*tuuline*
foggy	*u*-du-ne	*udune*

It will ... tomorrow.	*hom*-me *sah*-yahb ...	*Homme sajab ...*
rain	*vih*-mah	*vihma*
snow	lund	*lund*
sleet	*lert*-si	*lörtsi*

Directions

How far is it?

kuy *kau*-gel seh on?	*Kui kaugel see on?*

Can we walk there?

kahs *sin*-na sahb *yahlg*-si?	*Kas sinna saab jalgsi?*

north	*py*-hi	*põhi*
south	*lyu*-nah	*lõuna*
east	*i*-dah	*ida*
west	laas	*lääs*

ESTONIAN

RAINING SPRATS & DOGS

Kui müristab ja välku lööb, siis Vanapagan silku sööb.
'When it thunders and lightning strikes, then Old Pagan eats sprats.' – Estonian folk saying.

ESTONIAN

Animals

beaver	*kob*-rrahs	*kobras*
bird	lind	*lind*
boar	*mets*-sigah	*metssiga*
cat	kahss	*kass*
cow	lehm	*lehm*
deer	hirrv	*hirv*
dog	koerr	*koer*
fish	*kah*-lah	*kala*
fox	rre-bah-ne	*rebane*
horse	*ho*-bu-ne	*hobune*
lynx	*il*-ves	*ilves*
moose	*py*-derr	*põder*
otter	*saahrr*-mahs	*saarmas*
rabbit	*yah*-nes	*jänes*
sheep	*lahm*-mahs	*lammas*
wolf	hunt	*hunt*

Plants

birch	kahsk	*kask*
fir	koosk	*kuusk*
flower	lill	*lill*
oak	tahmm	*tamm*
pine	mand	*mänd*
tree	poo	*puu*

DID YOU KNOW ...   Estonia's national bird is the barn swallow, *suitsupääsuke*, and the national flower is the cornflower, *rukkilill*.

Camping

Where's a camp site?
    kus on *kam*-ping?   *Kus on kämping?*
Can we set up a tent here?
    kahs seen vyib *tel*-ki-dah?   *Kas siin võib telkida?*

ESTONIAN

air mattress	*yhk*-mahd-rrahts	*õhkmadrats*
axe	*kirr*-ves	*kirves*
backpack	*sel*-yah-kott	*seljakott*
can opener	*ah*-vah-yah	*avaja*
compass	*kom*-pahss	*kompass*
firewood	*lyk*-ke-pood	*lõkkepuud*
gas cylinder	*maht*-kah-gaahs	*matkagaas*
matches	*ti*-kud	*tikud*
penknife	*tahs*-ku-nu-gah	*taskunuga*
rope	kyis	*köis*
sleeping bag	*mah*-gah-mis-kott	*magamiskott*
stove	*ah*-hi	*ahi*
tent	telk	*telk*
tent pegs	*tel*-gi-vai-ahd	*telgivaiad*
torch (flashlight)	*tahs*-ku-lahmp	*taskulamp*

ESTONIAN

Useful Words

beach	rrahnd	*rand*
county/province	*maah*-kond	*maakond*
forest	mets	*mets*
island	saahrr	*saar*
lake	yarrv	*järv*
river	*yo*-gi	*jõgi*
sea	*me*-rri	*meri*
village	*kü*-lah	*küla*
weather forecast	*il*-mah-tea-de	*ilmateade*
windmill	*too*-le-ves-ki	*tuuleveski*

ISLAND HOPPING

Estonia's long coastline includes many islands. The two largest, Saaremaa and Hiiumaa, are among the most unspoiled and idyllic parts of Europe, thanks in large part to the 50-year Soviet occupation, during which they were off limits for all but the locals, and no significant industrialisation took place.

Saaremaa is the larger, about the size of Luxembourg, and it's a place for quiet wandering and looking at ancient churches, windmills, and manor houses. In the sleepy main town of Kuressaare is the only entirely preserved stone castle in the Baltics, dating back to the 14th century. With moat and towers, it fulfills any child's fantasy. Even more intriguing for many is the meteor crater at Kaali. The last giant meteorite to fall in an inhabited place, it may be the source of stories in Pytheas and northern mythology about the sun falling to earth.

Even wilder and more tranquil is the second island, Hiiumaa. Many writers, artists and musicians have summer houses here. In addition to churches and manor houses, worth seeing is the enormous lighthouse at *Kõpu*, first lit in 1531.

ESTONIAN

FOOD

Estonians prefer entertaining in their own homes, and while the food may not be exotic you'll be served tasty fish and pork, fresh vegetables and fruits. Even city dwellers take off weekends in the spring and autumn to tend allotments and visit family farms, and they bring back home-grown food to use during the rest of the year.

Estonians start any meal by saying *Head isu!* which is the equivalent of 'Bon appetit!'. When enjoying a drink, you'll often hear *Terviseks!,* 'To your health!'. In an informal situation, your host may say *Söö kõht täis,* 'Eat until your stomach is full'.

Restaurants can be found featuring every cuisine and they often provide multilingual menus. Tipping does not follow firmly established rules. In better restaurants, add 10%.

At the Restaurant

Please recommend	*pah*-lun *saw*-vi-tah-ge	*Palun soovitage*
a good ...	*mu*-le head ...	*mulle head ...*
restaurant	*rres*-to-*rrah*-ni	*restorani*
cafe	*koh*-vi-kut	*kohvikut*

I'd like to make a reservation
for ... people at ... pm.

mah *saw*-vin *tel*-li-dah	*Ma soovin tellida*
lau-dah ... *i*-ni-me-se-le	*lauda ... inimesele*
kel-lah ...	*kella ...*

I have a reserved table.

mul on *tel*-li-tud laud	*Mul on tellitud laud.*

Do you have a free table?

kas tayl on *vah*-bah *lau*-dah?	*Kas teil on vaba lauda?*

May I have a menu?

kas mah *saahk*-sin me-*nüü?*	*Kas ma saaksin menüü?*

I'd like ...

ma *saw*-vik-sin ...	*Ma sooviksin ...*

This isn't my order.
  **seh ay o-le mi-nu
  tel-li-mus**

I'd like the bill, please.
  pah-lun ahrr-ve

Can I pay by credit card?
  **kas tayl saab mahks-tah
  krre-deet-kaahrr-di-ga?**

I've had enough.
  sel-lest pee-sahb

*See ei ole minu
tellimus.*

Palun arve.

*Kas teil saab maksta
krediitkaardiga?*

Sellest piisab.

ESTONIAN

Useful Words

ashtray	**tu-hah-taws**	*tuhatoos*
bill	**ahrr-ve**	*arve*
cold	**külm**	*külm*
cup	**tahss**	*tass*
drink	**yawk**	*jook*
fork	**kah-vel**	*kahvel*
fresh	**varrs-ke**	*värske*
glass	**klaahs**	*klaas*
greasy	**rrahs-vah-ne**	*rasvane*
knife	**nu-gah**	*nuga*
plate	**tahld-rrik**	*taldrik*
spoon	**lu-si-kahs**	*lusikas*
stale	**vah-nah**	*vana*
sweet	**mah-gus**	*magus*

MENU DECODER

Special Dishes

These traditional foods are usually served during special holidays and festivals:

hani	**hah**-ni	goose (served at Christmas and Kadripäev)
heeringas	**heh**-rrin-gahs	herring
hernesupp	**herr**-ne-supp	pea soup
kilu	**ki**-lu	sprat
klimbisupp	**klim**-bi-supp	dumpling soup
mulgikapsas	**mul**-gi-kahp-sahs	sauerkraut with pork and barley
räim	**rraim**	Baltic herring

seajalad ubadega	**sea**-yah-lad **u**-bah-de-gah	pigs' legs with beans (served on Shrove Tuesday)
suitsuangerjas	**suyt**-su-ahn-gerr-yahs	smoked eel
suitsulest	**suyt**-su-lest	smoked flounder
sült	**sült**	'headcheese' (meat or fish in aspic)
verivorst	**ve**-rri-vorrst	blood sausage (served at Christmas)

Vegetarian Meals

It's not impossible to be a vegetarian in Estonia. Tallinn has at least one vegetarian restaurant, and most restaurants offer some vegetarian dishes.

I'm a vegetarian.
mah *o*-len *tai*-me-toyt-lah-ne   *Ma olen taimetoitlane.*

I don't eat ...	**mah ay serr ...**	*Ma ei söö ...*
meat	*li*-hah	*liha*
chicken	*kah*-nah	*kana*
fish	*kah*-lah	*kala*
ham	*sin*-ki	*sinki*
pork	*sea*-li-hah	*sealiha*

Breakfast

Estonians usually start the day with coffee. In the country, milk and buttermilk are also served. Porridge, eggs and open sandwiches with cheese, fish or sausages are also popular.

Rye bread (*leib*) is very much a part of Estonian culture and is eaten at every meal. *Jätku leiba!* – 'May the bread never run out!'.

breakfast	*hom*-mi-ku-serrk	*hommikusöök*

Would you like ...?	**kahs te *saw*-vi-te ...?**	*Kas te soovite ...?*
coffee	*koh*-vi	*kohvi*
tea	teed	*teed*
milk	*pee*-mah	*piima*
juice	*mah*-lah	*mahla*

barley porridge	*krroo*-bi-pu-derr	*kruubipuder*
bread (white)	sai	*sai*
cheese	yoost	*juust*
cornflakes	*mai*-si-hel-bed	*maisihelbed*
egg	*mu*-nah	*muna*
ground wheat porridge	*mahn*-nah-pu-derr	*mannapuder*
mashed potato	*kahrr*-tu-li-pu-derr	*kartulipuder*
pancake	*pahn*-kawk	*pannkook*
rice porridge	*rree*-si-pu-derr	*riisipuder*
riceflakes/puffed rice	*rri*-si-hel-bed	*riisihelbed*
rye bread	layb	*leib*
sausage	vorrst	*vorst*

ESTONIAN

Lunch & Dinner

There's no great distinction between lunch (*lõuna*) and dinner (*õhtusöök*) in Estonia. Either could be the main meal of the day. It typically consists of soup (*supp*), a main course (*praad*) and dessert (*magustoit*).

Meat, Poultry & Game

beef	*law*-mah-li-hah	*loomaliha*
boar meat	*mets*-sea-li-hah	*metssealiha*
chicken	*kah*-nah	*kana*
ham	sink	*sink*
lamb	*lahm*-bah-li-hah	*lambaliha*
pork	*sea*-li-hah	*sealiha*
turkey	*kahl*-kun	*kalkun*
veal	*vah*-si-kah-li-hah	*vasikaliha*

ESTONIAN

AT THE MARKET

Basics

bread	sai	*sai*
butter	vyi	*või*
cheese	yoost	*juust*
chocolate	*sho*-ko-lahd	*šokolaad*
cornflakes	*mai*-si-hel-bed	*maisihelbed*
egg	*mu*-nah	*muna*
margarine	*mahrr*-ga-rreen	*margariin*
marmalade	*mahrr*-me-lahd	*marmelaad*
milk	peem	*piim*
olive oil	*y*-li	*õli*
pasta	*pahs*-tah	*pasta*
rice	rrees	*riis*
sugar	*suh*-kurr	*suhkur*
water	*ve*-si	*vesi*
yogurt	*yo*-gurrt	*jogurt*

Meat & Poultry

beef	*law*-mah-li-hah	*loomaliha*
boar meat	*mets*-sea-li-hah	*metssealiha*
chicken	*kah*-nah	*kana*
ham	sink	*sink*
lamb	*lahm*-bah-li-hah	*lambaliha*
pork	*sea*-li-hah	*sealiha*
turkey	*kahl*-kun	*kalkun*
veal	*vah*-si-kah-li-hah	*vasikaliha*

Vegetables

beet	peht	*peet*
broad beans	oahd	*oad*
cabbage	*kahp*-sahs	*kapsas*
capsicum	*pap*-rri-kah	*paprika*
carrot	*porr*-gahnd	*porgand*
cauliflower	*lill*-kahp-sahs	*lillkapsas*
celery	*sel*-lerr	*seller*
cucumber	kurrk	*kurk*

AT THE MARKET

green beans	*aed*-oahd	*aedoad*
lettuce	*sah*-laht	*salat*
mushrooms	*seh*-ned	*seened*
onion	*si*-bul	*sibul*
peas	*herr*-ned	*herned*
potato	*kahrr*-tul	*kartul*
pumpkin	*kyrr*-vits	*kõrvits*
spinach	*spi*-naht	*spinat*
tomato	*to*-maht	*tomat*
turnip	*kaah*-li-kahs	*kaalikas*
vegetables	*yoorr*-vil-yahd	*juurviljad*
zucchini	*su*-vi-kyrr-vits	*suvikõrvits*

Seafood

Baltic herring	rraim	*räim*
cod	turrsk	*tursk*
crayfish	vahk	*vähk*
fish	*kah*-lah	*kala*
herring	*heh*-rrin-gahs	*heeringas*
lobster	*me*-rri-vahk	*merivähk*
mussels	*rran*-nah-karr-bid	*rannakarbid*
salmon	*ly*-he	*lõhe*

Fruit

apple	own	*õun*
apricot	*ahp*-rri-koos	*aprikoos*
banana	bah-*naahn*	*banaan*
berries	*mahrr*-yahd	*marjad*
fruit	*poo*-vil-yahd	*puuviljad*
grapes	*vee*-nah-mahrr-yahd	*viinamarjad*
lemon	*sid*-rrun	*sidrun*
orange	*ah*-pel-sin	*apelsin*
peach	*virr*-sik	*virsik*
pear	pirrn	*pirn*
plum	plawm	*ploom*
strawberry	*maah*-si-kahs	*maasikas*

ESTONIAN

ESTONIAN

Seafood

Baltic or small herring	rraim	*räim*
cod	turrsk	*tursk*
crayfish	vahk	*vähk*
fish	*kah*-lah	*kala*
herring	*heh*-rrin-gahs	*heeringas*
lobster	*me*-rri-vahk	*merivähk*
mussels	*rran*-nah-karr-bid	*rannakarbid*
oysters	*ahust*-rrid	*austrid*
salmon	*ly*-he	*lõhe*
shrimp	krre-*ve*-tid	*krevetid*
sprats	*ki*-lud	*kilud*

Vegetables & Salads

beet	peht	*peet*
broad beans	oahd	*oad*
cabbage	*kahp*-sahs	*kapsas*
capsicum	*pap*-rri-kah	*paprika*
carrot	*porr*-gahnd	*porgand*
cauliflower	*lill*-kahp-sahs	*lillkapsas*
celery	*sel*-lerr	*seller*
cucumber	kurrk	*kurk*
green beans	*aed*-oahd	*aedoad*
lettuce	*sah*-laht	*salat*
mushrooms	*seh*-ned	*seened*
onion	*si*-bul	*sibul*
peas	*herr*-ned	*herned*
pickle	*hah*-pu-kurrk	*hapukurk*
potato	*kahrr*-tul	*kartul*
potato salad	*kahrr*-tu-li-sah-laht	*kartulisalat*
pumpkin	*kyrr*-vits	*kõrvits*
spinach	*spi*-naht	*spinat*
tomato	*to*-maht	*tomat*
turnip	*kaah*-li-kahs	*kaalikas*
vegetables	*yoorr*-vil-yahd	*juurviljad*
zucchini	*su*-vi-kyrr-vits	*suvikõrvits*

Fruit

apple	own	õun
apricot	*ahp*-rri-koos	aprikoos
banana	bah-*naahn*	banaan
berries	*mahrr*-yahd	marjad
fruit	*poo*-vil-yahd	puuviljad
grapes	vee-nah-mahrr-yahd	viinamarjad
lemon	*sid*-rrun	sidrun
nuts	*pahk*-lid	pähklid
orange	ah-pel-sin	apelsin
peach	*virr*-sik	virsik
pear	pirrn	pirn
plum	plawm	ploom
strawberry	*maah*-si-kahs	maasikas
watermelon	ahrr-*boos*	arbuus

Desserts

biscuits	*küp*-si-sed	küpsised
cake	kawk	kook
fruit preserve	kom-*pott*	kompott
ice cream	*jaa*-tis	jäätis
whipped cream	vah-hu-kawrr	vahukoor

Condiments, Herbs & Spices

butter	vyi	või
dill	till	till
honey	*me*-si	mesi
jam	maws	moos
mustard	*si*-nep	sinep
oil	*y*-li	õli
pepper	*pi*-pahrr	pipar
salt	sawl	sool
sauce	*kahs*-te	kaste
sour cream	hah-pu-kawrr	hapukoor
sugar	*suh*-kurr	suhkur
vinegar	aa-di-kahs	äädikas

ESTONIAN

Cooking Methods

baked	*küp*-se-tah-tud	*küpsetatud*
boiled	*keh*-de-tud	*keedetud*
fried	*prrae*-tud	*praetud*
raw	*taw*-rres	*toores*

Non-Alcoholic Drinks

bottled mineral water	*ahl*-li-kah-ve-si	*allikavesi*
buttermilk	*keh*-firr	*keefir*
juice	mahhl	*mahl*
milk	peem	*piim*
water	*ve*-si	*vesi*

Alcoholic Drinks

champagne	*sham*-pus	*šampus*
cocktail	kok-*tayl*	*kokteil*
cognac	*kon*-yahk	*konjak*
home-brewed beer	*ko*-du-y-lu	*koduõlu*
mulled wine	*hyyg*-vayn	*hõõgvein*
squash	morrs	*morss*
vodka	veen	*viin*
wine	vayn	*vein*

SHOPPING

The big malls and grocery stores are usually open seven days a week but most other shops have reduced hours on Saturdays and are closed on Sundays. Estonians do not bargain when they go shopping, although they may haggle a bit at the colourful outdoor markets.

Shoppers usually bring their own bags, but plastic bags are available for a small fee from the cashier or checkout.

Where's a/an/the ...?	kus on ...?	*Kus on ...?*
antique shop	ahn-tik-vah-rri-*aaht*	*antikvariaat*
bakery	*lay*-vah-pawd	*leivapood*
bookshop	rraah-mah-tu-pawd	*raamatupood*
clothes shop	*rryi*-vah-pawd	*rõivapood*
department store	kau-bah-mah-yah	*kaubamaja*
pharmacy/ chemist	*ahp*-tehk	*apteek*
florist	*lil*-le-pawd	*lillepood*
food shop	*toy*-du-pawd	*toidupood*
gift shop	*kin*-gi-tus-te pawd	*kingituste pood*
hairdresser	*yook*-surr	*juuksur*
market	turrg	*turg*
shoe shop	*kin*-gah-pawd	*kingapood*
shop	pawd/*kaup*-lus	*pood/kauplus*

ESTONIAN

Making a Purchase

In pharmacies and some other stores you must pay for your goods at the cashier's desk and then present your receipt to collect them.

May I have ...?	*pah*-lun ...?	*Palun ...?*
I'd like to buy ...	mah *tah*-hahk-sin *os*-tah ...	*Ma tahaksin osta ...*
Please show it to me.	*pah*-lun *nai*-dah-ke *mul*-le se-dah	*Palun näidake mulle seda.*
I'll take it.	mah *vy*-tahn *sel*-le	*Ma võtan selle.*
I won't take it.	mah ay *vy*-tah se-dah	*Ma ei võta seda.*
What size is this?	mis *soo*-rrus see on?	*Mis suurus see on?*
I'd like to try this.	mah *tah*-hahks se-dah *prraw*-vi-dah	*Ma tahaks seda proovida.*
It fits.	seh on *pah*-rrahs	*See on paras.*
It's too ...	see on *lee*-gah ...	*See on liiga ...*
big	soorr	*suur*
small	*vai*-ke	*väike*
long	pikk	*pikk*
short	*lü*-hi-ke	*lühike*

Have you anything else like this?
    kahs tayl on *mi*-dah-gi muud
    tao-list?   *Kas teil on midagi muud*
                                       taolist?

It's too expensive.
    see on *lee*-gah *kahl*-lis   *See on liiga kallis.*

Does it have a guarantee?
    kahs *sel*-lel on *gah*-rrahn-tee?   *Kas sellel on garantii?*

Can I pay by credit card?
    kahs tayl saahb *mahks*-tah
    krre-*deet*-kaahrr-di-gah?   *Kas teil saab maksta*
                                       krediitkaardiga?

Please wrap it in paper.
    pah-lun *pahk*-ki-ge seh
    pah-be-rris-se   *Palun pakkige see*
                                       paberisse.

Do you have a plastic bag?
    kahs tayl on *ki*-le-kot-ti?   *Kas teil on kilekotti?*

Essential Groceries

batteries	*pah*-tah-rrayd	*patareid*
bread (white)	sai	*sai*
butter	vyi	*või*
candles	*küün*-lahd	*küünlad*
cheese	yoost	*juust*
chocolate	*sho*-ko-laahd	*šokolaad*
egg	*mu*-nah	*muna*
flour	*yah*-hu	*jahu*
gas cylinder	*maht*-kah-gaahs	*matkagaas*
ham	sink	*sink*
honey	*me*-si	*mesi*
jam	*keh*-dis/maws	*keedis/moos*
margarine	*mahrr*-gah-rreen	*margariin*
marmalade	*mahrr*-me-laahd	*marmelaad* (also
(orange)		means a type
		of sweet)
matches	*ti*-kud	*tikud*
milk	peem	*piim*

pasta	*pahs*-tah	*pasta* (older people may say *makaronid*)
pepper	*pi*-pahrr	*pipar*
rice	rrees	*riis*
salt	sawl	*sool*
shampoo	shahm-*poon*	*šampoon*
soap	sehp	*seep*
sugar	*suh*-kurr	*suhkur*
toilet paper	tua-*lett*-pah-berr	*tualettpaber*
toothpaste	*hahm*-bah-pahs-tah	*hambapasta*
washing powder	*pe*-su-pul-berr	*pesupulber*
yogurt	*yo*-gurrt	*jogurt*

ESTONIAN

Souvenirs

Where can I buy ...?	kust mah saahn *os*-tah ...?	*Kust ma saan osta ...?*
a traditional brooch	*sy*-le	*sõle*
Estonian handicrafts	*ehs*-ti *ka*-si-terrd	*eesti käsitööd*
folk costumes	rrah-vah-rryi-vahd	*rahvarõivad*
paintings	*maah*-le	*maale*
rugs and wall hangings	*vai*-pu	*vaipu*
souvenirs	su-ve-*neerr*-e	*suveniire*

ESTONIAN

Clothing

blouse	ploos	*pluus*
coat	*mahn*-tel	*mantel*
dress	klayt	*kleit*
gloves	*kin*-dahd	*kindad*
hat	*kü*-bahrr/	*kübar/*
	kaah-bu	*kaabu*
jacket	yahkk	*jakk*
scarf	sahll	*sall*
shirt	sarrk	*särk*
shoes	*kin*-gahd	*kingad*
skirt	*seh*-lik	*seelik*
socks	*so*-kid	*sokid*
suit (woman's)	kos-*tüüm*	*kostüüm*
(man's)	*ü*-li-kond	*ülikond*
trousers/pants	*pük*-sid	*püksid*

Materials

brass	vahsk	*vask*
cotton	*poo*-vill	*puuvill*
gold	kuld	*kuld*
handmade	*ka*-si-terr	*käsitöö*
leather	nahk	*nahk*
silk	seed	*siid*
silver	*hy*-be	*hõbe*
woollen	*vil*-lah-ne	*villane*

Toiletries

comb	kahmm	*kamm*
condoms	kon-*daw*-mid	*kondoomid*
deodorant	deo-do-*rrant*	*deodorant*
disinfectant	*peerr*-i-tus	*piiritus*
nappies	*mahk*-med	*mähkmed*
razor	zhi-*lett*	*žilett*
sanitary napkins	hü-gi-*eh*-ni-si-de-med	*hügieenisidemed*
shampoo	shahm-*poon*	*šampoon*
shaving cream	*hah*-be-me-ah-yah-mis-krrehm	*habemea jamiskreem*
soap	sehp	*seep*
sunblock cream	*paeh*-vi-tus-krrehm	*päevituskreem*
tampons	tahm-*paw*-nid	*tampoonid*
toilet paper	tua-*lett*-pah-berr	*tualettpaber*
toothbrush	*hahm*-bah-hah-rri	*hambahari*
toothpaste	*hahm*-bah-pahs-tah	*hambapasta*

Stationery & Publications

Newspapers and magazines are sold in small roadside kiosks. Larger shops and hotels often also carry some foreign language publications.

Do you have (a/an) ...?	kahs tayl on ...?	*Kas teil on ...?*
books about Estonia	*rraah*-mah-tuyd *ehs*-tist	*raamatuid Eestist*
Estonian text book	*ehs*-ti *keh*-le y-pi-kut	*eesti keele õpikut*
English-Estonian dictionary	*ing*-li-se – *ehs*-ti sy-nah-rraah-mah-tut	*inglise-eesti sõnaraamatut*
Tallinn guidebook	*tahl*-lin-nah *yuh*-ti	*Tallinna juhti*
map of Tallinn	*tahl*-lin-nah kaahrr-ti	*Tallinna kaarti*
books in English	*rrah*-mah-tuyd *ing*-li-se *keh*-les	*raamatuid inglise keeles*

ESTONIAN

ESTONIAN

envelope	*ümb*-rrik	*ümbrik*
magazine	*a*-yah-ki-rri	*ajakiri*
newspaper	*a*-yah-leht	*ajaleht*
notebook	*vi*-hik	*vihik*
paper	*pah*-berr	*paber*
pen	*pahs*-ta-plee-ahts	*pastapliiats*
wrapping paper	*pahk*-ke-pah-berr	*pakkepaber*

Photography

I'd like to buy some ... film.	ma *saw*-vin *os*-tah ... *fil*-mi	*Ma soovin osta ... filmi.*
B&W	*must*-vahl-get	*mustvalget*
colour	*varr*-vi	*värvi*
print	*ne*-gah-teev	*negatiiv*
slide	*slai*-di	*slaidi*

Do you develop film?
    kahs te *il*-mu-tah-te *fil*-me?   *Kas te ilmutate filme?*
When will it be ready?
    mil-al seh *vahl*-mis saahb?   *Millal see valmis saab?*

Smoking

Smoking isn't allowed in shops. It's permitted in cafes and bars, but in restaurants guests usually don't light up until the end of the meal.

A pack of cigarettes and
matches, please.
    pah-lun pahkk *si*-gah-rret-te   *Palun pakk sigarette*
    yah *ti*-kud   *ja tikud.*
May I smoke?
    kas mah *to*-hin   *Kas ma tohin*
    suyt-se-tah-dah?   *suitsetada?*

Colours

beige	behzh	*beež*
black	must	*must*
blue	*si*-ni-ne	*sinine*
brown	prroon	*pruun*
green	*rro*-he-li-ne	*roheline*
grey	hahll	*hall*
purple	*lil*-lah	*lilla*
red	*pu*-nah-ne	*punane*
white	*vahl*-ge	*valge*
yellow	*kol*-lah-ne	*kollane*

Sizes & Comparisons

big	soorr	*suur*
small	*vai*-ke	*väike*
heavy	*rrahs*-ke	*raske*
light	*kerr*-ge	*kerge*
more	*rroh*-kem	*rohkem*
less	va-hem	*vähem*
many	*pahl*-yu	*palju*
too much	*leh*-gah *pahl*-yu	*liiga palju*
enough	*ai*-tahb	*aitab*

ESTONIAN

HEALTH

Since regaining independence in 1991, Estonia has been working to raise standards of health and medicine. However, most visitors turn to privately-run medical and dental clinics for their health needs. Pharmacies are able to recommend over-the-counter medicines and toiletries, but visitors should bring prescription medicines with them. There's a 24-hour pharmacy in Tallinn. And when in the countryside, one should guard against ticks.

At the Doctor

I'm ill.
    mah *o*-len *hai*-ge   *Ma olen haige.*
My friend is ill.
    mu *sy*-berr on *hai*-ge   *Mu sõber on haige.*
I need a doctor who speaks English.
    ma *vah*-yan *ahrrs*-ti kes   *Ma vajan arsti, kes*
    rraa-gib *ing*-li-se kehlt   *räägib inglise keelt.*

Where's the nearest ...?	kus on *la*-him ...?	*Kus on lähim ...?*
chemist	ap-tehk	apteek
dentist	hahm-bah-ahrrst	hambaarst
doctor	ahrrst	arst
hospital	haig-lah	haigla

Ailments

I'm ill.	mah *o*-len *hai*-ge	*Ma olen haige.*
I've been vomiting.	mah *o*-len ok-sen-dah-nud	*Ma olen oksendanud.*
I feel nauseous.	mul on *ee*-vel-dus	*Mul on iiveldus.*
I can't sleep.	mah ay sah mah-gah-dah	*Ma ei saa magada.*

I feel ...	mul on ...	*Mul on ...*
dizzy	*pea*-perr-ri-tus	*peapööritus*
shivery	*kül*-mah-vah-rri-nahd	*külmavärinad*
weak	*nyrr*-kus	*nõrkus*

I have (a/an) ...	mul on ...	*Mul on ...*
allergy	ahl-*lerr*-gi-ah	*allergia*
bronchitis	brron-*heet*	*bronhiit*
burn	*py*-le-tus	*põletus*
cold	*kül*-me-tus	*külmetus*
constipation	*ky*-hu-kin-ni-sus	*kõhukinnisus*
cough	*ker*-hah	*köha*
diarrhoea	*ky*-hu-lah-ti-sus	*kõhulahtisus*
fever	*pah*-lah-vik	*palavik*
glandular fever	*naarr*-me-pah-lah-vik	*näärmepalavik*
hayfever	*hay*-nah-pah-lah-vik	*heinapalavik*
headache	*peah*-vah-lu	*peavalu*
infection	in-fekt-*siawn*	*infektsioon*
migraine	mig-*rrehn*	*migreen*
pain	*vah*-lud	*valud*
stomachache	*ky*-hu-vah-lu	*kõhuvalu*
thrush	*soo*-vahl-ge	*suuvalge*
travel sickness	*syi*-dust *sü*-dah *pah*-hah	*sõidust süda paha*
urinary infection	*urr*-i-naahrr-in-fekt-siawn	*urinaar infektsioon*
venereal disease	*su*-gu-hai-gus	*suguhaigus*

ESTONIAN

Useful Phrases

It hurts there.
    mul *vah*-lu-tahb seet   *Mul valutab siit.*
I feel better/worse.
    mul on *pah*-rrem/ *hahl*-vem   *Mul on parem/halvem.*
This is my usual medicine.
    seh on mu   *See on mu tavaline*
    tah-vah-li-ne *rro*-hi   *rohi.*

I don't want a blood transfusion.
  mah ay *tah*-hah   *Ma ei taha*
  ve-rre-ü-le-kahn-net   *vereülekannet.*
Can I have a receipt for my insurance?
  kahs mah *saahk*-sin   *Kas ma saaksin*
  kvee-tun-gi o-mah   *kviitungi oma*
  kind-lus-tu-se yaoks?   *kindlustuse jaoks?*

Parts of the Body

My ... hurts.	mu ... *vah*-lu-tahb	*Mu ... valutab.*
I have a pain in my ...	mul on ... *vah*-lu	*Mul on ... valu.*
I can't move my ...	mah ay saah *lee*-gu-tah-dah o-mah ...	*Ma ei saa liigutada oma ...*
ankle	*pahk*-lood	*pahkluud*
arm	ka-si-varrt	*käsivart*
back	*sel*-gah	*selga*
bone	loo	*luu*
chest	rrind	*rind*
ears	*kyrr*-vahd	*kõrvad*
eye	silm	*silm*
foot	*jah*-lah-lah-bah	*jalalaba*
head	peah	*pea*
knee	*pylv*	*põlv*
leg	yahlg	*jalg*
lungs	*kop*-sud	*kopsud*
mouth	soo	*suu*
nose	*ni*-nah	*nina*
shoulders	*y*-lahd	*õlad*
skin	nahk	*nahk*
spine	*selg*-rrawg	*selgroog*
stomach	kyht	*kõht*
teeth	*hahm*-bahd	*hambad*
throat	kurrk	*kurk*

ESTONIAN

At the Chemist

Is there an all-night chemist nearby?

kahs seen *lah*-he-dahl on
err-paeh-vah-rring-set
ahp-teh-ki?

*Kas siin lähedal on
ööpäevaringset
apteeki?*

I have a prescription.

mul on *rret*-sept

Mul on retsept.

How many times a day?

mi-tu *korr*-dah paeh-vahs?

Mitu korda päevas?

with food	kaws *toi*-du-gah	*koos toiduga*
antibiotics	*ahn*-ti-bi-aw-ti-ku-mid	*antibiootikumid*
Band-Aids	*plahst*-rrid	*plaastrid*
contraceptives	rrah-ses-tu-mis-vahst-tah-sed *vah*-hen-did	*rasestumisvastased vahendid*
cough medicine	*ker*-hah-rro-hi	*köharohi*
laxatives	*lah*-tis-ti	*lahtisti*
painkillers	vah-lu-vai-gis-ti	*valuvaigisti*

ESTONIAN

At the Dentist

I have a toothache.

mul on *hahm*-bah-vah-lu

Mul on hambavalu.

My gums hurt.

mu *i*-ge-med *vah*-lu-tah-vahd

Mu igemed valutavad.

I don't want my tooth extracted.

mah ay *tah*-hah *hahm*-mahst
val-yah *tym*-mah-tah

*Ma ei taha hammast
välja tõmmata.*

Please give me an anaesthetic.

pah-lun *teh*-ke *mul*-le
tuy-mes-tus

*Palun tehke mulle
tuimestus.*

Ouch!

ai!

Ai!

Useful Words & Phrases

I'm ...	mul on ...	*Mul on ...*
diabetic	*suhk*-rru-hai-gus	*suhkruhaigus*
asthmatic	*ahst*-mah	*astma*
anaemic	*ah*-neh-miah	*aneemia*

addiction	*ai*-ne-syl-tu-vus	*ainesõltuvus*
bite	*hahm*-mus-tus	*hammustus*
blood test	*ve*-rre-prrawv	*vereproov*
contraceptive	*rrah*-ses-tu-mis-vahs-tah-ne *vah*-end	*rasestumisvastane vahend*
injection	süst	*süst*
injury	*vi*-gahs-tus	*vigastus*
vitamins	*vi*-tah-mee-nid	*vitamiinid*
wound	haahv	*haav*

ESTONIAN

THEY MAY SAY ...

kus tayl *vah*-lu-tahb?	Where does it hurt?
kuy *kau*-ah seh on nee *ol*-nud?	How long have you been like this?
kahs te *vy*-tah-te *rroh*-tu?	Are you on medication?
kahs tayl on *mil*-le-gi *vahs*-tu ahl-*lerr*-gi-aht?	Are you allergic to anything?
kahs te o-le-te *rrah*-se?	Are you pregnant?

SPECIFIC NEEDS
Disabled Travellers

I'm disabled/handicapped.
　　mah *o*-len *poo*-de-gah
　　i-ni-me-ne
*Ma olen puudega
inimene.*

I need assistance.
　　mah *vah*-yan *ah*-bi
Ma vajan abi.

What services do you have
for disabled people?
　　mis *ah*-bi-va-hen-dayd
　　sah-vahd *kah*-su-tah-dah
　　poo-e-te-gah *i*-ni-me-sed?
*Mis abivahendeid saavad
kasutada puuetega
inimesed?*

Is there wheelchair access?
　　kahs *sin*-nah sahb kah
　　rrah-tahs-taw-li-gah?
*Kas sinna saab ka
ratastooliga?*

I'm partly deaf.
　　mah *koo*-len *hahl*-vahs-ti
Ma kuulen halvasti.

Speak more loudly, please.
　　pah-lun *rraa*-ki-ge
　　vahl-ye-mi-ni
Palun rääkige valjemini.

I have a hearing aid.
　　mul on *kool*-de-ah-pah-rraaht
Mul on kuuldeaparaat.

I'm blind.
　　mah *o*-len *pi*-me
Ma olen pime.

Are guide dogs permitted?
　　kahs mah *to*-hin *kaah*-sah
　　vyt-tah *yuht*-koe-rrah?
*Kas ma tohin kaasa
võtta juhtkoera?*

I'm mute.
　　mah *o*-len tumm
Ma olen tumm.

library for the	*pi*-me-dah-te	*pimedate*
blind	*rraah*-mah-tu-ko-gu	*raamatukogu*
disabled person	*poo*-de-gah *i*-ni-me-ne	*puudega inimene*
guide dog	*yuht*-koerr	*juhtkoer*
wheelchair	*rrah*-tahs-tawl	*ratastool*

ESTONIAN

ESTONIAN

A NATION OF MUSIC

In few other countries in the world is music such an integral part of the culture as in Estonia. From the birth of national identity in the mid-19th century to the regaining of freedom from the Soviet Union, music has played a vital role in the nation's history. Today Estonian musicians continue to exert world-wide influence. Best-known abroad are Neeme Järvi, the Musical Director of the Detroit Symphony, and the modern composer Arvo Pärt.

The oral tradition of folk singing in Estonia goes back probably thousands of years, and consists of long narrative songs based on mythological tales. In the mid-19th century, as part of the 'national awakening', these songs started to be written down. Much later, starting in the 1920's, they were also recorded. By the 1980's there were 41,000 melodies collected, and many more with written text only.

Estonian choir singing began early in the century and led to one of the earliest public manifestations of national identity, a Song Festival in Tartu in 1869. Later moved to Tallinn, the two-day song festival continues to be held every five years, and is perhaps the largest event of its kind in the world. The Song Festival grounds on the outskirts of Tallinn, with an enormous half-dome stage facing a sweeping natural amphitheatre, hosts choruses of up to 28,000 voices singing to an audience which can number 250,000 people, or one-quarter of all the Estonians in the world. Student and children's song festivals are held in the years between the big ones.

Estonia takes its turn with Latvia and Lithuania to host the Baltika festival every three years, in mid-July. Music, art and dance are included in the week-long event. Exhibitions and parades celebrate the nation's folklore heritage.

TIME & DATES

Telling the time in Estonian is very simple. Just state the hour and then the minutes. See pages 93-94 for a list of numbers.

Excuse me, what time is it?
    vah-**bahn**-dah-ge mis kell on?   *Vabandage, mis kell on?*

It's ...	kell on ...	*Kell on ...*
3.25	kolm *kahks*-küm-	*kolm kaksküm-*
(three twenty-five)	mend vees	*mend viis*
5.15	vees *vees*-tayst	*viis viisteist*
11.48	*üks*-tayst *ne*-li-küm-	*üksteist*
	mend	*nelikümmend*
8.00	*kah*-hek-sah	*kaheksa*
1.00	üks	*üks*

ESTONIAN

Take note of the following expressions:

12.30	pawl üks	*pool üks*
		(lit: half one)
12.15	*veh*-rrahnd üks	*veerand üks*
		(lit: quarter one)
12.45	*kolm*-veh-rrahnd üks	*kolmveerand üks*
		(lit: three-
		quarters one)

To indicate 'am' and 'pm', Estonians use the expressions *enne lõunat* ('before midday') and *pärast lõunat* ('after midday'):

It's 5 am.	kell on vees *en*-ne	*Kell on viis enne*
	lyu-nat	*lõunat.*
It's 6 pm.	kell on kuus *pa*-rrast	*Kell on kuus*
	lyu-nat	*pärast lõunat.*

ESTONIAN

second	se-kund	sekund
minute	mi-nut	minut
hour	tund	tund
in the morning	hom-mi-kul	hommikul
in the evening	yh-tul	õhtul

Days of the Week

Monday	es-mahs-paehv	esmaspäev
Tuesday	tay-si-paehv	teisipäev
Wednesday	kol-mah-paehv	kolmapäev
Thursday	nel-yah-paehv	neljapäev
Friday	rreh-de	reede
Saturday	lau-paehv	laupäev
Sunday	pü-hah-paehv	pühapäev

Months

January	yaah-nuahrr	jaanuar
February	vehb-rruahrr	veebruar
March	marrts	märts
April	ahp-rrill	aprill
May	mai	mai
June	joo-ni	juuni
July	joo-li	juuli
August	au-gust	august
September	sep-tem-berr	september
October	ok-taw-berr	oktoober
November	no-vem-berr	november
December	det-sem-berr	detsember

Seasons

spring	ke-vahd	kevad
summer	su-vi	suvi
autumn	sü-gis	sügis
winter	tahlv	talv

Dates

What's the date today?	mis *koo*-paehv *ta*-nah on?	*Mis kuupäev täna on?*
Today is ...	*ta*-nah on ...	*Täna on ...*
24 February	*kah*-he-küm-ne *nel*-yahs *veeb*-rruahrr	*kahekümne neljas veebruar*
9 March	*ü*-hek-sahs marrts	*üheksas märts*
16 August	kooe-*tayst*-küm-nes *au*-gust	*kuueteist- kümnes august*

Present

today	*ta*-nah	*täna*
this ...	sel ...	*sel ...*
year	*aah*-stahl	*aastal*
month	kool	*kuul*
week	*na*-dah-lahl	*nädalal*

Past

yesterday	ay-le	*eile*
day before yesterday	*ü*-le-ay-le	*üleeile*
last week	*merr*-du-nud *na*-dah-lahl	*möödunud nädalal*

Future

tomorrow	*hom*-me	*homme*
day after tomorrow	*ü*-le-hom-me	*ülehomme*
next week	*tu*-le-vahl *na*-dah-lahl	*tuleval nädalal*

ESTONIAN

ESTONIAN

During the Day

It's early.	aeg on *vah-rrah*-ne	*Aeg on varane.*
It's late.	aeg on *hi*-li-ne	*Aeg on hiline.*
afternoon	*pa*-rrahst-lyu-nah	*pärastlõuna*
dawn	koit	*koit*
day	paehv	*päev*
early	*vah*-rrah	*vara*
evening	*yh*-tu	*õhtu*
lunchtime	*lyu*-nah	*lõuna*
midnight	*sü*-dah-err	*südaöö*
morning	*hom*-mik	*hommik*
night	err	*öö*
noon/midday	*lyu*-nah	*lõuna*
sunrise	*paik*-se-tyus	*päiksetõus*
sunset	*law*-yang	*loojang*

Useful Words

a year ago	*aahs*-tah ehst	*aasta eest*
always	*ah*-lah-ti	*alati*
at once	*ko*-he	*kohe*
at the moment/now	*prrae*-gu	*praegu*
early	*vah*-rrah	*vara*
earlier	*vah*-rrem	*varem*
every day	*i*-gah paehv	*iga päev*
late	*hil*-yah	*hilja*
later	*hil*-yem	*hiljem*
never	*mit*-te *ku*-nah-gi	*mitte kunagi*
not yet	vehl *mit*-te	*veel mitte*
sometimes	*my*-ni-korrd	*mõnikord*
soon	*vahrrs*-ti	*varsti*
still	*ik*-kah	*ikka*

FESTIVALS & HOLIDAYS
National Holidays

Uusaasta	1 Jan	New Year's Day
Vabariigi aastapäev	24 Feb	Independence Day
Ülestõusmispühad	March/April	Easter
Võidupüha	23 Jun	Victory Day
Jaanipäev	24 Jun	St John's Day (Midsummer)
Jõulud	24-26 Dec	Christmas
Jõululaupäev	24 Dec	Christmas Eve
Jõulu esimene püha	25 Dec	First Christmas Day
Jõulu teine püha	26 Dec	Second Christmas Day

ESTONIAN

Festivals

New Year   *Uusaasta*

As Christmas was prohibited during the Soviet occupation, New Year's Eve served as a substitute and good children received presents from a Santa Claus-like figure called Father Frost. Nowadays, New Year's Eve is a time for champagne and fireworks and a time for friends to visit. As elsewhere, New Year's Day is for recuperation.

Independence Day – February 24 *Vabariigi aastapäev*

On this day in 1918, the Estonian Republic was proclaimed. It's marked by parades, speeches, flag ceremonies, concerts, and the President's reception on TV.

Easter – Spring   *Ülestõusmispühad*

Also called *Lihavõttepühad*, this was another holiday repressed during the Soviet period. Only old people who had little to fear from the government dared to go to church. But in the home eggs were painted and they still are. Some people send Easter cards.

ESTONIAN

THE SINGING REVOLUTION

During the Soviet era, the Song Festivals (see 'A Nation of Music' on page 86) continued, and were a rallying point for the Estonian national spirit, even though they had to include Russian and other pan-Soviet music. In 1980, the festival ended with an Estonian patriotic song, and the audience kept on singing it over and over and over, sending a clear message to the Soviets. In 1985, the authorities chose for the final song one which would not lead to a repeat of this.

In June of 1988, a festival in Tallinn's historic Old Town stirred up a wave of nationalist fervor. As it ended, a large part of the audience wanted to continue, and headed out to the Song Festival grounds where they stood in the twilight and sang Estonian patriotic songs. The following night an even larger crowd showed up. They broke into the maintenance buildings and turned the lights and sound system on. And the blue, black and white Estonian flag, forbidden for over forty years, appeared and was run up a flagpole. Each night more flags appeared, and the cheering crowds grew to over 200,000, with well-known popular singers leading them in song after patriotic song.

In addition to old anthems and traditional songs they sang new ones written by the young composer Alo Mattiisen. His 'Five Patriotic Songs' incorporated older musical elements and included 'Estonian I am'. It was sung over and over again during those fervent nights at the Song Festival grounds, and in the cafes and on the streets during the following months. The 'Singing Revolution' had replaced violence with music, and the overwhelming impact of the entire nation demonstrating forcefully but peacefully sent a signal to the Soviet authorities that their demand for freedom would not be repressed.

That year the Soviet Estonian legislature was the first in the USSR to declare sovereignty, and in 1990 it declared a transition to independence. In January 1991 the Soviets threatened a crackdown, but by August Estonia was free again.

Victory Day – June 23   *Võidupüha*

After the proclamation of the republic in 1918, Estonia had to fight both German and Soviet armies in the country. A decisive battle on this date in 1919 ensured the new nation's independence, so this day honours all who fought for Estonian freedom. Not surprisingly, the holiday was prohibited during the Soviet occupation but, conveniently, the following day was St John's Day. So for Estonians the bonfires of St John's Eve burned also for freedom and independence.

St John's Day – June 24   *Jaanipäev*

For Estonians, this is the biggest holiday after Christmas, and its ancient pagan roots mark the longest day of the year. All over Estonia on St John's Eve bonfires, both public and private, burn late into the short night. Jumping over the fire brings good luck, but that's hardly possible with the great fires towns put up nowadays. Often folk song or dance groups perform in traditional costume. Games like tug-of-war and sack races take place. More interesting for lovers is the custom of going into the forest to search for the fern flower, said to bloom only on this night. The search often takes a long time. Meanwhile around the fire people sing, dance, eat and drink, right up to dawn.

Souls' Visiting Day – November 2   *Hingedepäev*

The souls of forefathers are expected home on this day, and in olden times a set table was left for them. The holiday largely disappeared during the Soviet occupation but lately there's been a revival. Visits are made to the graves of relatives in the afternoon, and a lit candle is placed in the window of the home.

ESTONIAN

ESTONIAN

St Martin's Day – November 10   *Mardipäev*
St Catherine's Day – November 25 *Kadripäev*

These two holidays are for Estonian kids what Halloween is for American kids. They're most popular in rural areas. Although originally pagan festivals related to the start of winter which were taken over by the church, they're now occasions when children go door to door in costume. On St Martin's Eve boys dress in rough clothes and sing the associated songs (if they know them). On St Catherine's Eve it's the girls' turn (some cross-dressing may occur) and they go around in clean and light-coloured clothes. In both cases they're rewarded with sweets. Some families serve beans and roast goose on St Catherine's Day.

Christmas – December 25   *Jõulud*

Christmas really starts on Christmas Eve, when Santa Claus (*jõuluvana*) arrives and presents are given out. Children are expected to perform, reciting a verse or singing a song they have learned for the occasion. There's also a newer tradition of invisible elves (*päkapikk*) leaving sweets in children's slippers, which are left on the window sill for the night. Children often dress up as elves or at least wear a pointed red hat.

On December 24 the President of Estonia, following a 350-year tradition, declares Christmas Peace and attends a Christmas service. December 25 and 26 are called first and second Christmas day, and are a time for visiting friends and relatives.

The Christmas tree is a fir tree and is decorated with candles, ornaments and sweets. An older tradition is to bring a large pile of straw (as in Jesus' manger) into the main room for children to play in. The making of Christmas crowns, another old tradition, has had a revival in recent years. Made from straw, they're hung with ornaments and ribbons.

Food, and lots of it, is part of Christmas, and it symbolises enough food for the coming year. The traditional Christmas dinner features pork with sauerkraut, potatoes, potato salad with red beets and barley sausages, usually made with cows' blood. A bowl of ginger snaps is never absent from the coffee table. The traditional Christmas drink is home-brewed beer or mead, but store-bought beer is more common nowadays.

Happy Holiday!	haid *pü*-hi!	*Häid pühi!*
Happy New Year!	head oot *aahs*-taht!	*Head uut aastat!*
Happy Easter!	haid ü-les-yus-mis-*pü*-hahd!	*Häid ülestõus-mispühad!*
Merry Christmas!	haid *yow*-lu-pü-hi!	*Häid jõulupühi!*

ESTONIAN

NUMBERS & AMOUNTS
Cardinal Numbers

0	null	*null*
1	üks	*üks*
2	kahks	*kaks*
3	kolm	*kolm*
4	*ne*-li	*neli*
5	vees	*viis*
6	koos	*kuus*
7	*sayt*-se	*seitse*
8	*kah*-hek-sah	*kaheksa*
9	*ü*-hek-sah	*üheksa*
10	*küm*-me	*kümme*

ESTONIAN

11	*üks*-tayst	*üksteist*
12	*kahks*-tayst	*kaksteist*
13	*kolm*-tayst	*kolmteist*
14	*ne*-li-tayst	*neliteist*
15	*vees*-tayst	*viisteist*
16	*koos*-tayst	*kuusteist*
17	*sayt*-se-tayst	*seitseteist*
18	*kah*-hek-sah-tayst	*kaheksateist*
19	*ü*-hek-sah-tayst	*üheksateist*
20	*kahks*-küm-mend	*kakskümmend*
21	*kahks*-küm-mend-üks	*kakskümmend üks*
30	*kolm*-küm-mend	*kolmkümmend*
40	*ne*-li-küm-mend	*nelikümmend*
50	*vees*-küm-mend	*viiskümmend*
60	*koos*-küm-mend	*kuuskümmend*
70	*sayt*-se-küm-mend	*seitsekümmend*
80	*kah*-hek-sah-küm-mend	*kaheksakümmend*
90	*ü*-hek-sah-küm-mend	*üheksakümmend*
100	*sah*-dah	*sada*
1000	*tu*-haht	*tuhat*

Ordinal Numbers

1st	*e*-si-me-ne	*esimene*
2nd	*tay*-ne	*teine*
3rd	*kol*-mas	*kolmas*
4th	*nel*-jas	*neljas*
5th	*vee*-es	*viies*
6th	*koo*-es	*kuues*
7th	*sayts*-mes	*seitsmes*
8th	*kah*-hek-sahs	*kaheksas*
9th	*ü*-hek-sahs	*üheksas*
10th	*küm*-nes	*kümnes*
20th	*kah*-he-küm-nes	*kahekümnes*
21st	*kah*-he-küm-ne *e*-si-me-ne	*kahekümne esimene*

Fractions

1/4	*veh*-rrahnd	*veerand*
1/2	pawl	*pool*
3/4	*kolm*-veh-rrand	*kolmveerand*
1 1/2	*pawl*-tayst	*poolteist*

Useful Words

a little (amount)	*nah*-tu-ke	*natuke*
double	*to*-pelt	*topelt*
less	*va*-hem	*vähem*
many	*pahl*-yu	*palju*
more	*rroh*-kem	*rohkem*
percent	*prrot*-sent	*protsent*
some	*my*-ni	*mõni*
too much	*lee*-gah *pahl*-yu	*liiga palju*

ESTONIAN

SETU PEOPLE

The Setu are a Finno-Ugric people native to the area of Setumaa. This politically unrecognised territory straddles part of Estonia and Russia. The Setu never fully assimilated into Russian culture and have retained many of their old traditions. One of the most important of these is the day of the Setu kingdom which usually falls around 20 August every year. On this day, a representative of the Setu king (who according to folklore sleeps all day and night in his sand cave) is found. Competitions are held to find the king's royal singer and strongman, and the Setu kingdom is declared for another year.

The Setu are known for their songs, called *leelo*, which consist of solo spoken verses, followed by a refrain chanted by the whole group. *Leelo* are particularly the domain of women folk singers, who improvise new words every time they chant a verse.

ABBREVIATIONS

AS	*(aktsiaselts)*	Ltd or Inc
E	*(esmaspäev)*	Monday
e. l.	*(enne lõunat)*	am
e-post		email
hr	*(härra)*	Mr
jne	*(ja nii edasi)*	and so on/etc
jt	*(ja teised)*	and others/etc
K	*(kolmapäev)*	Wednesday
kl	*(kell)*	at (about time)
kr, EEK, s	*(kroon, sent)*	(Estonian currency)
L	*(laupäev)*	Saturday

ESTONIAN

lk	*(lehekülg)*	page
n	*(näiteks)*	eg
N	*(neljapäev)*	Thursday
P	*(pühapäev)*	Sunday
p. l.	*(pärast lõunat)*	pm
pr	*(proua)*	Mrs
prl	*(preili)*	Miss
R	*(reede)*	Friday
T	*(teisipäev)*	Tuesday
Tln		Tallinn
Trt		Tartu

EMERGENCIES

Help!
    ahp-pi!   *Appi!*

Watch out!
    ol-ge *et*-te-vaaht-lik!   *Olge ettevaatlik!*

Go away!
    min-ge *a*-rrah!   *Minge ära!*

Stop it!
    ly-pe-tah-ge!   *Lõpetage!*

Help, thief!
    ahp-pi *vah*-rrahs!   *Appi, varas!*

There's been an accident.
    seen *yuh*-tus *yn*-ne-tus   *Siin juhtus õnnetus.*

Call a doctor!
    kut-su-ge ahrrst!   *Kutsuge arst!*

Call an ambulance!
    kut-su-ge *keerr*-ah-bi!   *Kutsuge kiirabi!*

I'm ill/lost.
    mah *o*-len *hai*-ge/*ek*-si-nud *Ma olen haige/eksinud.*

I've been raped.
    mind *va*-gis-tah-ti   *Mind vägistati.*

I've been robbed.
    mind *rrerr*-vi-ti   *Mind rööviti.*

I'm sorry.
    vah-bahn-dah-ge   *Vabandage.*

I didn't realise I was doing
anything wrong.
    mah ay *tead*-nud et mah   *Ma ei teadnud, et ma*
    teen *mi*-dah-gi *vah*-les-ti *teen midagi valesti.*

I didn't do it.
    mah *po*-le *se*-dah *tay*-nud *Ma pole seda teinud.*

I want to call my embassy/
consulate.
    mah *tah*-hahn *he*-lis-tah-dah *Ma tahan helistada*
    o-mah *rree*-gi *saaht*-kon-dah/ *oma riigi saatkonda/*
    kon-su-laah-ti   *konsulaati.*

ESTONIAN

Could I use the telephone?
    kas mah vyin *kah*-su-tah-dah
    te-le-fo-ni?
                Kas ma võin kasutada
                telefoni?

I have medical insurance.
    mul on
    terr-vi-se-kind-lus-tus
                Mul on
                tervisekindlustus.

I've lost my ...	mah *kao*-tah-sin ...	*Ma kaotasin ...*
bag	*ko*-ti	*koti*
money	*rrah*-hah	*raha*
passport	*pahs*-si	*passi*

ESTONIAN

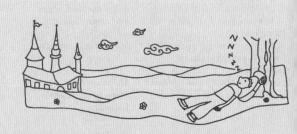

LATVIAN

LATVIAN

QUICK REFERENCE

Hello.	*svay*-kuh/svayks	Sveika/Sveiks. (f/m)
Goodbye.	uz *redz*-eh-shuhn-aws	Uz redzēšanos.
Yes./No.	yah/neh	Jā./Nē.
Excuse me/	*uht*-vai-naw-yeat/	Atvainojiet/
Sorry.	*pea*-dawd-eat	Piedodiet.
Thank you.	puhl-*deas*	Paldies.
You're welcome.	*loo*-dzu	Lūdzu.

I want to buy a ...	es *vaa*-laws *naw*-	Es vēlos nopirkt
ticket.	pirkt ... *bi*-lyet-i	... biļeti.
one-way	*vean*-virz-ean-uh	vienvirziena
return	turp *uht*-puh-kuhly	turp-atpakaļ

I don't understand.
es *ne*-suh-praw-tu   Es nesaprotu.

Do you speak English?
vai yoos *run*-ah-yuht
uhn-glis-ki?   Vai jūs runājat
                            angliski?

Where is ...?
kur *uht*-raw-duhs ...?   Kur atrodas ...?

Go straight ahead.
uz *preak*-shu   Uz priekšu.

Turn left/right.
puh *kray*-si/luh-bi   Pa kreisi/labi.

Do you have any rooms
available?
vai yums ir *bree*-vuhs
is-tuh-buhs?   Vai jums ir brīvas
                            istabas?

Where's the toilet?
kur ir *tu*-uh-le-tes?   Kur ir tualetes?

Help!
pah-lee-gah!   Palīgā!

1	veans	*viens*	6	sesh-i	*seši*
2	*di*-vi	*divi*	7	sep-ti-nyi	*septiņi*
3	trees	*trīs*	8	uhs-taw-nyi	*astoņi*
4	*chet*-ri	*četri*	9	de-vi-nyi	*deviņi*
5	*peats*-i	*pieci*	10	des-mit	*desmit*

INTRODUCTION

Latvian is the official language of the Republic of Latvia, which regained independence from the Soviet Union on 21 August 1991 after 50 years of occupation. With just under 2.5 million inhabitants, Latvian is the first language for approximately only 55% of the population (even fewer in the capital, Riga). Although Russian is spoken by just about everyone, Latvians are sensitive towards this fact, as the preservation of their nation's language is vital to their sense of identity and independence.

Latvian is one of the two surviving Baltic Indo-European languages – Lithuanian is the other. There are many similar words in both languages, but not sufficient to make them mutually intelligible. In Latvia there are dialect variations from east to west and this book covers what is known as 'High Latvian', which is the standard language originating from central Latvia.

English is a popular foreign language in Latvia so you may find that local people will be more than pleased to practise their language skills with you. If you manage to grasp at least some basic phrases in Latvian you'll be received warmly.

Latvian uses feminine and masculine forms of words. The feminine form appears first throughout this book and is separated from the masculine form by a slash. All phrases in this book are in the polite form unless otherwise indicated.

Help!

Take the time to learn the following everyday Latvian words and phrases, in order to make your stay more enjoyable:

Hello.	*svay*-kuh	*Sveika.* (to a female)
	svayks	*Sveiks.* (to a male)
Good day/afternoon.	luhb-*dean*	*Labdien.* (also serves as a general 'hello')

Goodbye.	uz *redz*-eh-shuhn-aws	*Uz redzēšanos.*
Yes./No.	yah/neh	*Jā./Nē.*
Please./	*loo-dzu*	*Lūdzu.*
You're welcome.		
Thank you.	puhl-*deas*	*Paldies.*
Pardon?	kuh *loo-dzu*?	*Kā, lūdzu?*
Do you speak	vai yoos *run*-ah-yuht	*Vai jūs runājat*
English?	*uhn*-glis-ki?	*angliski?*
Cheers!	*prea*-kah!	*Priekā!*

See pages 113-119 for all kinds of small talk phrases to help you get to know the Latvians a little better.

PRONUNCIATION

There's a consistent relationship between spelling and pronunciation in Latvian. Each letter and each vowel combination has its own constant sound.

Vowels

Latvian uses short and long vowels. As a rule, long and short vowels have the same sound; one is just an extended version of the other. A line above a vowel (called a macron) indicates that it has a long sound. It's important to make the distinction between short and long sounds as they can change the meaning of a word. For example, *istaba* ('a/the room') and *istabā* ('in a/the room'). Note that there are two different ways of pronouncing *e*, *ē* and *o*, so follow the pronunciation guide carefully.

LATVIAN

Latvian	Transliteration	Sounds
a	uh	as the 'u' in 'fund'
ā	ah	as the 'a' in 'father'
e	e	as the 'e' in 'bet'
	a	as the 'a' in 'fat'
ē	eh	as the 'ai' in 'fair'
	aa	as the 'a' in 'sad', but longer
i	i	as the 'i' in 'in'
ī	ee	as the 'ee' in 'beet'
o	o	as the 'o' in 'pot'
	aw	as the 'oa' in 'oar'
u	u	as the 'u' in 'pull'
ū	oo	as the 'u' in 'rule'

Diphthongs

Latvian	Transliteration	Sounds
ai	ai	as the 'i' in 'dive'
au	ow	as the 'ow' in 'now'
ei	ay	as the 'ay' in 'may'
ie	ea	as the 'ea' in 'fear'
oi	oy	as the 'oy' in 'toy'
ui	uy	similar to the 'ui' in 'ruin' (a combination of oo + y, but short)

LATVIAN

DID YOU KNOW ...

Latvian and Lithuanian are the only two surviving Baltic languages in the Indo-European language family. Neither of these languages bears much resemblance to Estonian, which is more closely related to Finnish.

Consonants

Consonants are pronounced as in English with the following exceptions:

Latvian	Transliteration	Sounds
c	ts	as the 'ts' in 'lots'
č	ch	as the 'ch' in 'chew'
dz	dz	as the 'ds' in 'beds'
dž	j	as the 'j' in 'job'
ģ	jy	a 'dy' sound, as the 'd' in British English 'duty'
j	y	as the 'y' in 'yellow'
ķ	ky	as the 'c' in 'cute'
ļ	ly	as the 'll' in 'million'
ņ	ny	as the 'n' in 'onion'
r	r	as the 'r' in 'bring' (slightly rolled)
š	sh	as the 'sh' in 'shop'
ž	zh	as the 's' in 'pleasure'

Stress

In Latvian, the stress is almost always on the first syllable. One notable exception is the word for 'thank you' *paldies* (puhl-*deas*).

Pronunciation Practice

Here are some sentences with transliterations for you to practise your Latvian pronunciation:

He went to the forest.
> vinysh *aiz*-gah-yuh uz *mezh*-u   *Viņš aizgāja uz mežu.*

We eat lunch at a restaurant.
> mehs *aa*-duhm *pus*-dea-nuhs   *Mēs ēdam pusdienas*
> res-to-rah-nah   *restorānā.*

The water in the sea is warm today.
> *shaw*-dean *yoo*-rah   *Šodien jūrā*
> ir silts *oo*-dens   *ir silts ūdens.*

I'd like to change my ticket.
    es *vaa*-laws *uhp*-main-eet   *Es vēlos apmainīt*
    suh-vu *bi*-lye-ti   *savu biļeti.*

Here's my passport.
    shayt ir *muh*-nuh *puh*-se   *Šeit ir mana pase.*

GRAMMAR

The purpose of this section is to give you a brief outline of Latvian grammar so that you'll be able to string together your own simple sentences. Note that in Latvian the endings of nouns, pronouns and adjectives change depending on their use within a sentence and whether or not they are masculine or feminine.

Word Order

The usual word order in Latvian is subject-verb-object, ie, the same as in English. Note that verbs almost always come second in a sentence and that there are no articles (a/an/the) in Latvian.

Nouns

In Latvian nouns can have up to seven different case endings depending on their relationship to other words in the sentence, ie, whether they're the subject, direct object, indirect object, etc. All nouns are either feminine (usually end with a vowel) or masculine (usually end with a consonant). To make a noun plural, the general rule is to add the letter 's' to feminine nouns and the letter 'i' to masculine nouns.

LATVIAN

Adjectives

Like pronouns, adjectives precede nouns and adopt the same gender and case.

big	*liels*
I have a big house.	*Man ir liela māja.*
	(lit: to-me is big house)
They live in a big house.	*Viņi dzīvo lielā mājā.*
	(lit: they live big house)
You see a big house.	*Jūs redzat lielu māju.*
	(lit: you see big house)
She sees the big house.	*Viņa redz lielo māju.*
	(lit: she sees big house)

Pronouns

Pronouns adopt the gender, number and case of the nouns they precede. Here they're listed in the nominative case (see page 20 for an explanation of case).

PRONOUNS		
PERSONAL		
I	es	*es*
you (sg & inf)	tu	*tu*
she	*viny*-uh	*viņa*
he	vinysh	*viņš*
we	mehs	*mēs*
you (pl & pol)	yoos	*jūs*
they	*viny*-uhs/*viny*-i	*viņas/viņi* (f/m)
POSSESSIVE		
my	*muh*-nuh/*muhns*	*mana/mans* (f/m)
your (sg & inf)	*tuh*-vuh/*tuhvs*	*tava/tavs* (f/m)
her	*viny*-uhs	*viņas*
his	*viny*-uh	*viņa*
our	*moos*-u	*mūsu*
your (pl & pol)	*yoos*-u	*jūsu*
their	*viny*-u	*viņu*

LATVIAN

Verbs
Present

I run to the station.	*Es skrienu līdz stacijai.*
	(lit: I run to station)
He reads the newspaper.	*Viņš lasa avīzi.*
	(lit: he reads newspaper)
We see the cat.	*Mēs redzam kaķi.*
	(lit: we see cat)

Past

I ran in the woods.	*Es skrēju pa mežu.*
	(lit: I ran through/in woods)
He reads a book.	*Viņš lasīja grāmatu.*
	(lit: he read book)
We saw the monument.	*Mēs redzējam pieminekli.*
	(lit: we saw monument)

LATVIAN

Future

I shall run to town.	*Es skriešu līdz pilsētai.*
	(lit: I shall-run to town)
She will read the letter.	*Viņa lasīs vēstuli.*
	(lit: she will-read letter)
We shall see a/the film.	*Mēs skatīsimies filmu.*
	(lit: we shall/will-see film)

TO BE

I am	es *as*-mu	*es esmu*
you are (sg & inf)	tu *es*-i	*tu esi*
she/he is	*viny*-uh/vinysh ir	*viņa/viņš ir*
we are	mehs *as*-uhm	*mēs esam*
you are (pl & pol)	yoos *as*-uht	*jūs esat*
they are	*viny*-uhs/	*viņas/*
	viny-i ir	*viņi ir* (f/m)

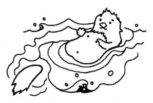

TO HAVE

There is no verb meaning 'to have' in Latvian. Instead, Latvians use subject pronouns with the third person of the verb 'to be'. Only one form of the verb is used for each of the present, past and future tenses, irrespective of the subject. Note that it's the subject pronoun that changes.

PRESENT – *ir*
I have a ticket.

Man ir biļete.
(lit: to-me is ticket)

PAST – *bija*
He had a ticket.

Viņam bija biļete.
(lit: to-him was ticket)

FUTURE – *būs*
They will have tickets.

Viņām/viņiem būs biļetes. (f/m)
(lit: to-them will-be tickets)

Questions

Who is there?	*Kas tur ir?*
	(lit: who there is?)
Why did you leave?	*Kāpēc jūs aizgājat?*
	(lit: why you left?)
How shall I dress?	*Kā lai es ģērbjos?*
	(lit: how shall I dress?)

Used at the start of a sentence, *vai* creates a question. It roughly translates as 'do' or 'may' in English.

Do you have a dictionary?	*Vai jums ir vārdnīca?*
	(lit: *vai* to-you is dictionary?)
May I ask you?	*Vai es drīkstu jums uzprasīt?*
	(lit: *vai* I may to-you ask?)

QUESTION WORDS

how?	kaah?	kā?
what?	kahs?	kas?
who?	*kur*-ah/kursh?	kura/kurš? (f/m)
why?	*kaah*-pehts/*kaah*-dehly?	kāpēc/kādēļ?
when?	kahd?	kad?
where?	kur?	kur?

LATVIAN

Negatives

To make a sentence negative in Latvian, place *ne-* in front of the verb.

He didn't arrive.	*Viņš neatbrauca.*
	(lit: he not-arrive)
I'm not coming with you.	*Es neiešu ar jums.*
	(lit: I not-will-come with you)

Prepositions

with	ahr	*ar*
without	bez	*bez*
at	pea(h)	*pie*
on	uz	*uz*
under	zem	*zem*
next to	*blah*-kus	*blakus*
above	virs	*virs*

Conjunctions

and	un	*un*
because	yaw	*jo*
but	bet	*bet*
or	vai	*vai*
therefore	*taah*-pets	*tāpēc*

Useful Words

far	*taah*-luh	tālu
here	shayt	šeit
near	*tu*-vu	tuvu
that (accusative case)	taw	to
that (nominative case)	taah/tahs	tā/tas (f/m)
there	tur	tur
these	shees/shea	šīs/šie (f/m)
this (accusative case)	shaw	šo
this (nominative case)	shee/shis	šī/šis (f/m)
those	taahs/tea	tās/tie (f/m)

LATVIAN

GREETINGS & CIVILITIES

Latvians are seen as good-natured, friendly people. They give flowers at almost every opportunity; however, on social occasions flowers should always be given in odd numbers, as an even number of flowers is for funerals. When you're invited to someone's home, you should remove your outdoor shoes and your host will hand you a pair of slippers to wear.

Greetings & Goodbyes

Hello. (inf)	svay-kuh/svayks	Sveika./Sveiks. (f/m)
Good morning.	luhb-reet	Labrīt.
Good day/afternoon.	luhb-dean	Labdien. (also serves as a general 'hello')
Good evening.	luhb-vuh-kuhr	Labvakar.
Goodbye.	uz-redz-eh-shuhn-aws	Uz redzēšanos.
All the best.	vis-u luh-bu	Visu labu.
See you tomorrow.	leedz reet-uhm	Līdz rītam.
Say hello to ...	puh-svayts-in-eat ...	Pasveiciniet ...
Good night.	uhr luh-bu nuhkt-i	Ar labu nakti.

LATVIAN

DON'T MENTION IT

If someone thanks you, you should respond with *lūdzu* (*loo-dzu*). This word not only means 'please', but also serves as 'don't mention it' or 'my pleasure'. You'll find that people also use it when handing you something and when addressing you in shops.

Civilities

How are you?	kah yums *klah*-yuhs?	*Kā jums klājas?*
Fine, thank you.	*luh*-bi puhl-*deas*	*Labi, paldies.*
And you?	un yums?	*Un jums?*
It was nice to meet you.	*biy*-uh puh-teek-uhm-i ea-puhz-eet-eas	*Bija patīkami iepazīties.*

Forms of Address

Miss	*yown*-kundz-e	*jaunkundze*
Madam/Mrs	*kundz*-e	*kundze*
Sir/Mr	kungs	*kungs*

UH-AH!

Remember, in the transliterations uh sounds like the 'u' in 'fund', and ah sounds like the 'a' in 'father'.

LATVIAN

Useful Words & Phrases

Yes.	yah	*Jā.*
No.	neh	*Nē.*
Please./ You're welcome.	loo-dzu	*Lūdzu.*
Thank you (very much).	(leals) puhl-*deas*	*(Liels) paldies.*
Excuse me.	*uht*-vai-naw-yeat	*Atvainojiet.*
May I?	vai es *dreekst*-u?	*Vai es drīkstu?*
Pardon?	*pea*-doad-eat?	*Piedodiet?*
Sorry/I apologise.	*pea*-doad-eat/ es *uht*-vain-aw-yaws	*Piedodiet/ Es atvainojos.*

SMALL TALK

When meeting people for the first time, always use the polite form of 'you' (*jūs*), except when speaking to children.

Meeting People

What's your name?	
kah yoos sowts?	*Kā jūs sauc?*
My name is ...	
muhn-i sowts ...	*Mani sauc ...*
I'd like to introduce you to ...	
vaa-laws yoos	*Vēlos jūs*
ea-puhz-eest-in-aht uhr ...	*iepazīstināt ar ...*
I'm pleased to meet you.	
preaks ea-puhz-eet-eas	*Prieks iepazīties.*

Nationalities

Where are you from?	
naw *kur*-ean-es yoos as-uht?	*No kurienes jūs esat?*

I'm from ...	es as-mu naw ...	*Es esmu no ...*
Africa	ah-fri-kuhs	*Āfrikas*
Australia	ow-strah-li-yuhs	*Austrālijas*
Canada	kuhn-ah-duhs	*Kanādas*
China	kyeen-uhs	*Ķīnas*
Denmark	dah-ni-yuhs	*Dānijas*
England	uhn-gli-yuhs	*Anglijas*
Finland	saw-mi-yuhs	*Somijas*
France	fruhn-tsi-yuhs	*Francijas*
Germany	vah-tsi-yuhs	*Vācijas*
Holland	ho-luhn-des	*Holandes*
Ireland	ee-ri-yuhs	*Īrijas*
Israel	iz-ruh-eh-luhs	*Izraēlas*
New Zealand	yown-zeh-luhn-des	*Jaunzēlandes*
Norway	nor-veh-jyi-uhs	*Norvēģijas*
Spain	spahn-i-yuhs	*Spānijas*
Sweden	zvea-dri-yuhs	*Zviedrijas*
the USA	uh-me-ri-kuhs	*Amerikas*

LATVIAN

Age

How old are you?	tsik yums ir *guh*-du?	*Cik jums ir gadu?*
I'm ... years old.	muhn ir ... *guh*-du	*Man ir ... gadu.*
When's your birthday?	kuhd ir *yoos*-u *dzim*-shuhn-uhs *dean*-uh?	*Kad ir jūsu dzimšanas diena?*

Occupations

What do you do?	uhr kaw yoos *naw*-duhrb-aw-yuht-eas?	*Ar ko jūs nodarbojaties?*
I'm (a/an) ...	es *as*-mu ...	*Es esmu ...*
artist	*mahk*-sl-neats-e	*mākslniece* (f)
	mahk-sl-neaks	*mākslnieks* (m)
business person	*biz*-nes-men-is	*biznesmenis*
doctor	*ahrs*-te	*ārste* (f)
	ahrsts	*ārsts* (m)
engineer	*in*-zhen-ear-e	*inženiere* (f)
	in-zhen-ear-is	*inženieris* (m)
factory worker	*roop*-neets-uhs *strahd*-neats-e	*rūpnīcas strādniece* (f)
	roop-neets-uhs *strahd*-neaks	*rūpnīcas strādnieks* (m)
farmer	*lowk*-saim-neats-e	*lauksaimniece* (f)
	lowk-saim-neaks	*lauksaimnieks* (m)
journalist	*zhur*-nah-list-e	*žurnaliste* (f)
	zhur-nah-lists	*žurnalists* (m)
lawyer	*yur*-is-te	*juriste* (f)
	yu-rists	*jurists* (m)
mechanic	*me*-hah-ni-kyis	*mehāniķis*
musician	*mooz*-i-kye	*mūziķe* (f)
	moo-i-kyis	*mūziķis* (m)
nurse	*med*-mah-suh	*medmāsa*
office worker	*bi*-raw-yuh *duhrb*-in-eats-e	*biroja darbiniece* (f)
	bi-raw-yuh *duhrb*-in-eaks	*biroja darbinieks* (m)

scientist	*zin*-aht-neats-e	*zinātniece* (f)
	zin-aht-neaks	*zinātnieks* (m)
student	*stud*-en-te	*studente* (f)
	stud-ents	*students* (m)
teacher	*skaw*-law-tah-yuh	*skolotāja* (f)
	skaw-law-tahys	*skolotājs* (m)
unemployed	*bez*-duhrb-neats-e	*bezdarbniece* (f)
	bez-duhrb-neaks	*bezdarb-nieks* (m)
waiter	*of*-its-i-uhn-te	*oficiante* (f)
	of-its-i-uhnts	*oficiants* (m)
writer	*ruhkst*-neats-e	*rakstniece* (f)
	ruhkst-neaks	*rakstnieks* (m)

THE SINGING REVOLUTION

The song and dance festivals which took place in 1990 were particularly significant events during the 'Singing Revolution', which resulted in Latvia regaining its independence from the Soviet Union in August 1991. For the first time since the end of World War II, Latvians from around the globe were reunited as one nation, with exile-Latvian choirs and dance groups singing and dancing alongside their Latvian peers. At the close of the 1990 Dance Festival the compere announced 'That was the first dance festival in Independent Latvia. Until next time, in a free Latvia!' which sums up the political climate and mood of optimism prevalent at the time.

LATVIAN

Religion

What's your religion?
　　kah-duh ir *yoos*-u *tits*-ee-buh?　　*Kāda ir jūsu ticība?*

I'm not religious.
　　es *ne*-as-mu *tits*-eeg-uh/　　*Es neesmu ticīga/*
　　tits-eegs　　*ticīgs.* (f/m)

I'm ...	es *as*-mu ...	*Es esmu ...*
Buddhist	*bud*-is-te	*budiste* (f)
	bud-ists	*budists* (m)
Catholic	*kuht*-aw-lea-te	*katoliete* (f)
	kuht-aw-lis	*katolis* (m)
Christian	*krist*-ea-te	*kristiete* (f)
	krist-ea-tis	*kristietis* (m)
Hindu	*in*-dea-te	*indiete* (f)
	in-deat-is	*indietis* (m)
Jewish	*e*-brey-eat-e	*ebrejiete* (f)
	e-breys	*ebrejs* (m)
Lutheran	*lut*-er-tits-ee-guh	*luterticīga* (f)
	lut-er-tits-eegs	*luterticīgs* (m)
Muslim	*mus*-ul-muhn-eat-e	*musulmaniete* (f)
	mus-ul-muhn-is	*musulmanis* (m)
Russian	*puhr*-ayz-tits-ee-guh	*pareizticīga* (f)
Orthodox	*puhr*-ayz-tits-eegs	*pareizticīgs* (m)

Family

Are you married?	vai yoos *as*-uht *prets*-eh-yus-eas/ *prets*-eh-yeas?	*Vai jūs esat precējusies/ precējies?* (f/m)

I'm ...	es *as*-mu ...	*Es esmu ...*
married	*prets*-eh-yus-eas	*precējusies* (f)
	prets-eh-yeas	*precējies* (m)
single	ne-*prets*-aa-tuh	*neprecēta* (f)
	ne-*prets*-aats	*neprecēts* (m)
divorced	*shkyee*-ru-seas	*šķīrusies* (f)
	shkyee-reas	*šķīries* (m)
widowed	*uht*-rait-ne	*atraitne* (f)
	uht-rait-nis	*atraitnis* (m)
lesbian/gay	*lez*-bea-te/gays	*lezbiete/gejs*

Do you have any children?
vai yums ir *baar*-ni?   *Vai jums ir bērni?*
I don't have any children.
muhn nuhv *baar*-nu   *Man nav bērnu.*
I have a daughter/son.
muhn ir *may*-tuh/daals   *Man ir meita/dēls.*
How many sisters/
brothers do you have?
tsik yums ir *mah*-su/ *brah*-lyu?   *Cik jums ir māsu/brāļu?*
Is your wife/
husband here?
vai *yoo*-su *sea*-vuh/veers   *Vai jūsu sieva /vīrs*
uht-raw-duhs shayt?   *atrodas šeit?*
Do you have a
girlfriend/boyfriend?
vai yums ir *drow*-dzen-e/   *Vai jums ir draudzene/*
drowgs?   *draugs?*

brother	*brah*-lis	*brālis*
children	*baar*-ni	*bērni*
family	*jyim*-en-e	*ģimene*
father	taavs	*tēvs*
friend	*drow*-dzen-e	*draudzene* (f)
	drowgs	*draugs* (m)
grandfather	*vats*-taavs	*vectēvs*
grandmother	*vats*-mah-miny-uh	*vecmāmiņa*
mother	*mah*-te	*māte*
sister	*mah*-suh	*māsa*

Kids' Talk

When talking to children, use the familiar form of you (*tu*).

How old are you?
  tsik tev ir *guh*-du?   *Cik tev ir gadu?*
When's your birthday?
  kuhd ir *tuh*-vuh   *Kad ir tava*
  dzim-shuhn-uhs dea-nuh?   *dzimšanas diena?*
What do you do after school?
  kaw tu *duh*-ri pehts *skaw*-luhs?   *Ko tu dari pēc skolas?*
Do you have a pet at home?
  Vai tev *mah*-yahs ir dzeev-neaks?   *Vai tev mājās ir dzīvnieks?*

I have a ...	muhn ir ...	*Man ir ...*
bird	*put*-ns	*putns*
canary	*kuhn*-ah-riy-put-ns	*kanārijputns*
cat	*kuh*-kyis	*kaķis*
dog	suns	*suns*
duck	*pee*-le	*pīle*
fish	zivs	*zivs*
frog	*vuhr*-de	*varde*
guinea pig	*yoo*-ruhs tsoo-tsiny-uh	*jūras cūciņa*
hamster	*kah*-mee-tis	*kāmītis*
horse	zirgs	*zirgs*
parrot	*puh*-puh-gai-lis	*papagailis*
tortoise	*bru*-nyu-ru-pu-tsis	*bruņrupucis*

Expressing Feelings

The verb 'to be' is not always used to express feelings. The Latvian equivalent of 'I have' (*man ir*) is often used instead.

I'm ...	muhn ir ...	*Man ir ...*
cold	*owk*-sti	*auksti*
hot	*kuhr*-sti	*karsti*
right	*tais*-nee-buh	*taisnība*
well	*luh*-bi	*labi*

The verb 'to be' is used with the following expressions, however.

I'm ...	es *as*-mu ...	*Es esmu ...*
angry	*dus*-mee-guh	*dusmīga* (f)
	dus-meegs	*dusmīgs* (m)
grateful	*puh*-tay-tsee-guh	*pateicīga* (f)
	puh-tay-tseegs	*pateicīgs* (m)
happy	*preats*-ee-guh	*priecīga* (f)
	preats-eegs	*priecīgs* (m)
hungry	*iz*-suhl-ku-si	*izsalkusi* (f)
	iz-suhl-tsis	*izsalcis* (m)
in a hurry	*stay*-gah	*steigā*
sad	*beh*-dee-guh	*bēdīga* (f)
	beh-deegs	*bēdīgs* (m)
sleepy	*mea*-gai-nuh	*miegaina* (f)
	mea-gains	*miegains* (m)
tired	*naw*-gu-ru-si	*nogurusi* (f)
	naw-gu-ris	*noguris* (m)
worried	*suh*-trowk-tuh	*satraukta* (f)
	suh-trowkts	*satraukts* (m)

Expressing Opinions

In my opinion ...	*muh*-nu-praht ...	*Manuprāt ...*
I think (believe)	es *daw*-mah-yu	*Es domāju*
that ...	(*tits*-u) kuh ...	*(ticu), ka ...*
Do you like ...?	vai yums *puh*-teek ...?	*Vai jums patīk ...?*
I like ...	muhn *puh*-teek ...	*Man patīk ...*
I agree.	es *pea*-kree-tu	*Es piekrītu.*
I disagree.	es *ne*-pea-kree-tu	*Es nepiekrītu.*

LATVIAN

BODY LANGUAGE

In Latvia there are no significant differences from any other European country as far as the interpretation of body language goes. Latvians shake hands when greeting each other and when saying goodbye, although you should be aware that shaking hands over the threshold is considered unlucky. Social kissing is also the norm nowadays. Women should note that chivalry is very much predominant in Latvia, so don't be surprised when a man helps you on with your coat, pours your drinks and lights your cigarettes for you.

BREAKING THE LANGUAGE BARRIER

Do you speak English?
  vai yoos *run*-ah-yuht
  uhn-gli-ski?

Vai jūs runājat angliski?

I don't speak ...
  es *ne*-run-ah-yu ...

Es nerunāju ...

I understand.
  es *suh*-praw-tu

Es saprotu.

I don't understand.
  es *ne*-suh-praw-tu

Es nesaprotu.

Could you speak more slowly please?
  run-ah-yeat *loo-dzu* laan-ahk

Runājiet lūdzu lēnāk.

Could you repeat that please?
  loo-dzu uht-kahr-taw-yeat

Lūdzu atkārtojiet.

What does that mean?
  kaw tuhs *naw*-zee-meh?

Ko tas nozīmē?

Please write that down.
  loo-dzu pea-ruhk-steat taw

Lūdzu pierakstiet to.

I speak ...	es *run-ah-yu* ...	*Es runāju ...*
English	*uhn-gli-ski*	*angliski*
French	*fruhn-tsis-ki*	*franciski*
German	*vah-tsis-ki*	*vāciski*
Polish	*paw-lis-ki*	*poliski*
Russian	*krea-vis-ki*	*krieviski*

Sports & Interests

I want to go ...	es *vaa-laws* ...	*Es vēlos ...*
bird watching	*vaa-rawt put-nus*	*vērot putnus*
bobsleighing	*browkt uhr bob-slay-u*	*braukt ar bobsleju*
canoeing	*ai-reht uhr kuh-nu*	*airēt ar kanoe*
cycling	*browkt uhr div-rit-e-ni*	*braukt ar divriteni*
gliding	*li-dawt uhr pluhn-ea-ri*	*lidot ar planieri*
hiking	eat *pahr-gah-yean-ah*	*iet pārgājienā*
horse riding	*yaht uhr zir-gu*	*jāt ar zirgu*
ice fishing	*naw-duhr-baw-teas ar zem-lad-us muhk-shkye-reh-shuh-nu*	*nodarboties ar zemledus makšķerēšanu*
jogging	*skreat*	*skriet*
skating	*sli-dawt*	*slidot*
skiing	*sleh-pawt*	*slēpot*
swimming	*pel-deht*	*peldēt*
tobogganing	*browkt uhr kuh-muh-niny-ahm*	*braukt ar kamaniņām*
yachting	*bu-raht*	*burāt*

I play ...	es *speh-leh-yu* ...	*Es spēlēju ...*
basketball	*buh-ske-tu*	*basketu*
cards	*kahr-tis*	*kārtis*
chess	*shuh-hu*	*šahu*
guitar	*jyi-tah-ri*	*gitāri*
soccer	*fut-bo-lu*	*futbolu*
tennis	*ten-i-su*	*tenisu*

I play winter sports.
es *naw*-duhr-baw-jaws uhr   *Es nodarbojos ar ziemas*
zea-muhs *spor*-tuh vay-deam   *sporta veidiem.*

Do you like ...?	vai yums *puh*-teek ...?	*Vai jums patīk ...?*
art	*mahk*-sluh	*māksla*
ballet	*buh*-lets	*balets*
the cinema	*ki*-no	*kino*
(classical) music	(*kluhs*-is-kah)	(*klasiskā*)
	mooz-i-kuh	*mūzika*
exhibitions	*iz*-stah-des	*izstādes*
opera	*o*-per-uh	*opera*
reading	*luh*-seet	*lasīt*
the theatre	*te*-ah-tris	*teātris*
travelling	*tse*-lyot	*ceļot*

LATVIAN

Useful Words & Phrases

Of course.	*praw*-tuhms	*Protams.*
Just a minute.	*uhts*-u-mir-kli	*Acumirkli.*
It's important.	ir *svuh*-ree-gi	*Ir svarīgi.*
It's not important.	nuhv *svuh*-ree-gi	*Nav svarīgi.*
It's not possible.	nuhv *ea*-speh-yams	*Nav iespējams.*
Wait!	*puh*-gai-deat!	*Pagaidiet!*

GETTING AROUND
Directions

Where's the ...?	kur *uht*-raw-duhs ...?	*Kur atrodas ...?*
airport	*lid*-aw-stuh	*lidosta*
bus station	*ow*-to-aws-tuh	*autoosta*
ferry terminal	*puh*-suh-zhea-ru *aw*-stuh	*pasažieru osta*
harbour	*aw*-stuh	*osta*
ticket office(s)	*bi*-lye-shu *kuh*-ses	*biļešu kases*
train station	*dzelz*-ce-lyuh *stuhts*-i-ya	*dzelzceļa stacija*
tram/	*truhm*-vuh-yuh/	*tramvaja/*
trolleybus stop	*trol*-ey-bu-suh *pea*-tu-ruh	*trolejbusa pietura*

STREETS AHEAD

IELA	STREET
LAUKUMS	SQUARE
PROSPEKTS/BULVĀRIS	AVENUE/BOULEVARD
CEĻŠ	ROAD
LIELCEĻŠ/ŠOSEJA	HIGHWAY
TILTS	BRIDGE

LATVIAN

How do I get to ...?
   kah es *tea*-ku leedz ...?   *Kā es tieku līdz ...?*
Is it far from here?
   vai tuhs *uht*-raw-duhs *tah*-lu?   *Vai tas atrodas tālu?*
Can I walk there?
   vai leedz *tur*-ea-ni vuhr   *Vai līdz turieni var*
   aiz-stai-gaht?   *aizstaigāt?*
Could you show me
(on the map) please?
   loo-dzu puhr-ah-deat muhn   *Lūdzu parādiet man*
   (uz *kuhrt*-es)   *(uz kartes)*

Go straight ahead.	uz *preak*-shu	*Uz priekšu.*
Turn left/right at the ...	puh *kray*-si/luh-bi pea ...	*Pa kreisi/labi pie ...*
corner	*krus*-taw-yum-uh	*krustojuma*
traffic lights	*luks*-o-for-eam	*luksoforiem*

Buying Tickets

Where can I buy a ticket to ...?	kur es vuh-ru naw-pirkt *bi*-lyet-i leedz ...?	*Kur es varu nopirkt biļeti līdz ...?*
How much does it cost?	tsik *muhk*-sah?	*Cik maksā?*

I want to buy a ... ticket.	es *vaa*-laws *naw*-pirkt ... *bi*-lyet-i	*Es vēlos nopirkt ... biļeti.*
one-way	*vean*-virz-ean-uh	*vienvirziena*
return	turp *uht*-puh-kuhly	*turp-atpakaļ*
student/child	*stud*-en-tu/ *baar*-nu	*studentu/bērnu*

1st class	*pir*-mah *kluh*-se	*pirmā klase*
2nd class	*aw*-trah *kluh*-se	*otrā klase*

ticket office(s)	*bi*-lye-shu *kuh*-ses	*biļešu kases*
local train	*pea*-pil-saat-uhs	*piepilsētas*
ticket office	kuh-ses	*kases*
international train	*stuhrp*-tow-tis-kahs	*starptautiskās*
ticket office	kuh-ses	*kases*

LATVIAN

Air

Riga International airport has recently undergone a revamp and is now a modern user-friendly airport, with English-speaking staff, signs in both Latvian and English and plenty of bars, cafes and duty free shops.

Is there a flight to ...?
    vai ir *lid*-aw-yums uz ...?   *Vai ir lidojums uz ...?*
What's the flight number?
    kahds ir *ray*-suh *num*-urs?   *Kāds ir reisa numurs?*

Bus, Tram & Trolleybus

Tickets are required for buses, trams and trolleybuses and are bought from the conductor on board. Monthly season tickets can be bought from newspaper kiosks.

Does this tram go to ...?
    vai shis *truhm*-vuhys browts   *Vai šis tramvajs brauc*
    leedz ...?   *līdz ...?*
Are you getting off?
    vai yoos *iz*-kahp-seat?   *Vai jūs izkāpsiet?*
Could you let me know
when to get off?
    vai yoos *vuhr*-aa-tu muhn   *Vai jūs varētu man*
    puh-taykt kuhd muhn ir   *pateikt, kad man ir*
    jah-iz-kahpy?   *jāizkāpj?*
I want to get off.
    es *vaa*-laws *iz*-kahpt   *Es vēlos izkāpt.*

What time is	*tsik*-aws *uht*-eat ...	*Cikos attiet ...*
the ... bus to ...?	*ow*-taw-bus uz ...?	*autobuss uz ...?*
next	*nah*-kuhm-ais	*nākamais*
first	*pirm*-ais	*pirmais*
last	*peh*-deh-yais	*pēdējais*

LATVIAN

Train

The train leaves from ...
> *vilts-eans uht-eat naw ...* — *Vilciens attiet no ...*

Is this the right train for ...?
> *vai shis ir puh-rayz-ais* — *Vai šis ir pareizais*
> *vilts-eans uz ...?* — *vilciens uz ...?*

dining car	*res-to-rah-nuh* *vuh-gons*	*restorāna* *vagons*
express	*eks-pres-is*	*ekspresis*
local	*pea-pil-saa-tuhs*	*piepilsētas*
platform	*pe-rawns*	*perons*
sleeping car	*kup-eh-yuh*	*kupēja*
timetable	*vilts-ea-nu suh-ruhksts*	*vilcienu saraksts*
track	*tselysh*	*ceļš*

Boat

Where does the
boat leave from?
> *naw ku-rea-nes uht-eat ku-gyis?* — *No kurienes attiet kuģis?*

What time does
the boat arrive?
> *tsi-kaws pea-nahk ku-gyis?* — *Cikos pienāk kuģis?*

Which boat goes to ...?
> *kursh ku-gyis ir leedz ...?* — *Kurš kuģis ir līdz ...?*

Which harbour is next?
> *kuhs ir nah-kuhm-ah aws-tuh?* — *Kas ir nākamā osta*

Is this the ferry for ...?
> *vai shis ir prah-mis leedz ...?* — *Vai šis ir prāmis līdz ...?*

boat (ship)	*ku-gyis*	*kuģis*
ferry	*prah-mis*	*prāmis*
harbour	*aws-tuh*	*osta*
Riga Passenger Terminal	*ree-guhs puh-suh-zhee-ru aws-tuh*	*Rīgas pasažieru osta*

Taxi

Licensed taxis in Latvia are distinguishable by the white sign on the roof and yellow-number-plates with the prefix TH. There are different tariffs for day and night rides. If the driver does not turn on the meter, make sure you agree on a price to avoid being ripped off.

taxi   *tuhks-ow-met-rs*   *taksometrs*

How much does it
cost to go to ...?
    tsik muhk-sah aiz-vest leedz ...?   *Cik maksā aizvest līdz ...?*
I want to go to the
next corner, please.
    leedz nah-kuhm-ah-yuhm   *Līdz nākamājam*
    krus-taw-yum-uhm loo-dzu   *krustojumam, lūdzu.*
Here is fine, thank you.
    te boos luh-bi puhl-deas   *Te būs labi, paldies.*
Please slow down.
    brow-tseat loo-dzu laa-nahk   *Brauciet lūdzu lēnāk.*
Please stop.
    loo-dzu uhp-staht-eas   *Lūdzu apstāties.*
Please wait.
    loo-dzu uz-gai-deat   *Lūdzu uzgaidiet.*

Car

Where can I rent a car/motorcycle?
    kur es vuh-ru naw-ee-reht   *Kur es varu noīrēt mašīnu/*
    muh-shee-nu/ mo-to-tsik-lu?   *motociklu?*
How much is it daily/weekly?
    tsik muhk-sah dea-nah/   *Cik maksā dienā/nedēļā?*
    ned-eh-lyah?
Is insurance included?
    vai uhp-draw-shin-ah-shuhn-uh   *Vai apdrošināšana ir*
    ir ea-skai-tee-tuh?   *ieskaitīta?*

Where's the next
petrol station?
   kur ir *tuv*-ah-kah *dag*-veal-uhs   *Kur ir tuvākā degvielas*
   uz-*pil*-des *stats*-i-yuh?   *uzpildes stacija?*
Please fill the tank.
   pil-nu *bah*-ku *loo-dzu*   *Pilnu bāku, lūdzu.*

air	gais	*gaiss*
battery	*uh*-ku-mu-luh-tors	*akumulators*
brakes	*brem*-zes	*bremzes*
clutch	*suh*-yoogs	*sajūgs*
engine	*mo*-tors	*motors*
lights	*gais*-muhs	*gaismas*
oil	*ely*-lyuh	*eļļa*
road map	*tse*-lyuh *kuhr*-te	*ceļa karte*
tyre	*rea*-puh	*riepa*
windscreen	*preak*-sheh-yais *stik*-ls	*priekšējais stikls*

I need a mechanic.
   muhn ir *vuhy*-uh-dzeegs
   me-hah-ni-kyis
   Man ir vajadzīgs
   mehāniķis.

> ### DON'T STRESS OUT!
> Stress is almost always on the first syllable in Latvian.

The car is overheated.
   muh-shee-nuh ir *pahr*-kuhr-   *Mašīna ir pārkarsēta.*
   saa-tuh
The radiator is leaking.
   ruhd-i-uh-tors tak   *Radiators tek.*
The battery is flat.
   uh-ku-mu-luh-tors ir *iz*-lah-   *Akumulators ir izlādējies.*
   deh-yeas
I have a puncture.
   rea-puh ir *pahr*-sprah-gu-si   *Riepa ir pārsprāgusi.*

LATVIAN

ACCOMMODATION
Finding Accommodation

I'm looking for a ...	es *mek*-leh-yu ...	*Es meklēju ...*
cheap hotel	*laa*-tu *veas*-neets-u	*lētu viesnīcu*
clean hotel	*tee*-ru *veas*-neets-u	*tīru viesnīcu*
good hotel	*luh*-bu *veas*-neets-u	*labu viesnīcu*
youth hostel	*yow*-nea-shu *meet*-ni	*jauniešu mītni*

At the Hotel

Do you have any rooms available?
  vai yums ir *bree*-vuhs
  is-tuh-buhs? — *Vai jums ir brīvas istabas?*

Sorry, we're full.
  es *uht*-vai-naw-yaws mums
  nuhv *vea*-tu — *Es atvainojos, mums nav vietu.*

I have a reservation.
  muhn ir *puh*-soo-teets — *Man ir pasūtīts.*

I'd like a ...	es *vaa*-laws ...	*Es vēlos ...*
single room	*vean*-vea-tee-gu *is*-tuh-bu	*vienvietīgu istabu*
double room	*div*-vea-tee-gu *is*-tuh-bu	*divvietīgu istabu*
room with a shower/bath	*is*-tuh-bu uhr *du*-shu/*vuhn*-nu	*istabu ar dušu/vannu*
room with a balcony	*is*-tuh-bu uhr *buhl*-ko-nu	*istabu ar balkonu*

I'm going to stay for ...	es *puh*-lik-shu ...	*Es palikšu ...*
one night	*vea*-nu *nuhk*-ti	*vienu nakti*
two nights	*di*-vuhs *nuhk*-tis	*divas naktis*
a week	*ne*-deh-lyu	*nedēļu*

How much is it per night?
  tsik *muhk*-sah *dean*-nuhk-tee? — *Cik maksā diennaktī?*

LATVIAN

Is there (a) ...?	vai ir ...?	*Vai ir ...?*
bathroom	*vuhn*-nuhs is-tuh-buh	*vannas istaba*
hot water	kuhrsts *oo*-dens	*karsts ūdens*
sauna	pirts	*pirts*
shower	*du*-shuh	*duša*
telephone	te-le-fons	*telefons*
television	te-le-vi-zors	*televizors*

Can I see the ...?	vai es *vuh*-ru *uhp*-skuh-teet ...?	*Vai es varu apskatīt ...?*
room	is-tuh-bu	*istabu*
bathroom	*vuhn*-nuhs is-tuh-bu	*vannas istabu*

Fine, I'll take it.
   luh-bi es taw *nyem*-shu   *Labi, es to ņemšu.*
I'd like a different room.
   es *vaa*-laws *tsi*-tu is-tuh-bu   *Es vēlos citu istabu.*
Is there a reduction for
students/children?
   vai ir *uht*-lai-de *stud*-en-team/   *Vai ir atlaide studentiem/*
   baar-neam?   *bērniem?*
Does it include breakfast?
   vai *braw*-kuhs-tis ir *ea*-skai-   *Vai brokastis ir ieskaitītas?*
   teet-uhs?
Is there a lift?
   vai ir lifts?   *Vai ir lifts?*
Is there hot water all day?
   vai ir *kuhrst*-ais oo-dens   *Vai ir karstais ūdens*
   vi-su *dea*-nu?   *visu dienu?*
Do you have a safe?
   vai yums ir sayfs?   *Vai jums ir seifs?*
May I have the bill please?
   loo-dzu reh-kyin-u   *Lūdzu rēķinu.*

LATVIAN

Requests & Complaints

Please wake me up at ...
    loo-dzu puh-maw-din-eat   *Lūdzu pamodiniet*
    muh-ni pulks-tens ...   *mani pulkstens ...*
The ... doesn't work.
    ... ne-strah-dah   *... nestrādā.*
I can't open the window.
    es ne-vuh-ru uht-vehrt law-gu   *Es nevaru atvērt logu.*
I can't flush the toilet.
    es ne-vuh-ru naw-rowt oo-den-i   *Es nevaru noraut ūdeni*
    tu-uh-le-teh   *tualetē.*

It's too ...	*ir puhr ...*	*Ir par ...*
cold	*owk-stu*	*aukstu*
hot	*kuhr-stu*	*karstu*
noisy	*skuh-lyu*	*skaļu*

Laundry

Can you please	*vai yoos vuh-reh-tu*	*Vai jūs varētu*
... this?	*sho ... loo-dzu?*	*šo ... lūdzu?*
clean	*iz-tee-reet*	*iztīrīt*
iron	*iz-glud-in-aht*	*izgludināt*
mend	*suh-lah-peet*	*salāpīt*
wash	*iz-maz-gaht*	*izmazgāt*

I need it ...	*muhn ir*	*Man ir*
	vay-uh-dzeegs ...	*vajadzīgs ...*
today	*shaw-dean*	*šodien*
tomorrow	*ree-tah*	*rītā*
as soon as	*tsik vean aht-ri*	*cik vien ātri*
possible	*ea-speh-yuhms*	*iespējams*

Useful Words

name	vahrds	*vārds*
surname	uz-vahrds	*uzvārds*
room number	is-tuh-buhs num-urs	*istabas numurs*
address	uh-dre-se	*adrese*
air-conditioning	gai-suh kon-dits-i-on-aa-tahys	*gaisa kondicionētājs*
balcony	buhl-kons	*balkons*
bathroom	vuhn-nuhs is-tuh-buh	*vannas istaba*
bed	gul-tuh	*gulta*
bill	reh-kyins	*rēķins*
blanket	sa-guh	*sega*
chair	kraa-sls	*krēsls*
clean	teers	*tīrs*
dark	tumsh	*tumšs*
dirty	ne-teers	*netīrs*
key	uht-slaa-guh	*atslēga*
lift (n)	lifts	*lifts*
light bulb	spul-dze	*spuldze*
lock (n)	sleh-dze	*slēdze*
mattress	muh-druh-tsis	*madracis*
pillow	spil-vans	*spilvens*
quiet	klus	*kluss*
sheet	puh-luhgs	*palags*
shower	du-shuh	*duša*
soap	zea-pes	*ziepes*
suitcase	ko-fer-is	*koferis*
table	guhlds	*galds*
toilet	tu-uh-le-te	*tualete*
toilet paper	tu-uh-le-tes puh-peers	*tualetes papīrs*
towel	dvea-lis	*dvielis*
(hot/cold) water	(kuhr-stais/auk-stais) oo-dens	*(karstais/aukstais) ūdens*

AROUND TOWN

Where's the ...?	kur uht-raw-duhs ...?	*Kur atrodas ...?*
art gallery	*muhk-sluhs*	*mākslas*
	guh-le-ri-yuh	*galerija*
bank	*buhn-kuh*	*banka*
city/town centre	*pil-saa-tuhs tsent-rs*	*pilsētas centrs*
... embassy	... *vehst-nea-tsee-buh*	... *vēstniecība*
hotel	*veas-nee-tsuh*	*viesnīca*
library	*bib-lio-te-kuh*	*biblioteka*
market	*tir-gus*	*tirgus*
museum	*muz-eys*	*muzejs*
old town	*vats-pil-saa-tuh*	*vecpilsēta*
post office	*puhsts*	*pasts*

Is there a tourist office here?
vai shayt ir	*Vai šeit ir*
too-ris-muh bi-rawys?	*tūrisma birojs?*

At the Bank

Money can be changed into *lats* at currency exchange booths (*valūtas maiņa*), where exchange rates are posted on the window. It's also possible to withdraw money on your credit card, transfer money and exchange foreign currency and travellers cheques in banks. Be aware that notes that are crumpled, torn or have any writing on them will generally not be accepted – or may be accepted on payment of a surcharge. If you don't wish to bother with exchange booths and banks, simply use your credit card to withdraw money from one of the many cash machines.

I'd like to	es vaa-laws	*Es vēlos*
change ...	iz-mai-neet ...	*izmainīt ...*
this into lats	shaw luh-taws	*šo latos*
a travellers	tsely-aw-yum-uh	*ceļojuma*
cheque	che-ku	*čeku*

Can I have money transferred
here/abroad?
    vai ir *ea*-speh-yuhms
    pahr-soo-teet *now*-du uz
    shay-ea-ni/uz *ahr*-zem-ehm?

Vai ir iespējams
pārsūtīt naudu uz
šejieni/uz ārzemēm?

How long will it take?
    tsik *il*-gah *lai*-kah?

Cik ilgā laikā?

Has my money arrived yet?
    vai *muh*-nuh *now*-duh ir
    pea-nah-ku-si?

Vai mana nauda ir
pienākusi?

coins	*mo*-neh-tuhs	*monētas*
currency exchange booth	*vuh*-loo-tuhs *mai*-nyuh	*valūtas maiņa*
exchange rate	*vuh*-loo-tuhs kurs	*valūtas kurss*
money	*now*-duh	*nauda*
notes	*puh*-peer-*now*-duh	*papīrnauda*

At the Post Office

Signs above each counter in the post office indicate what you can
do at that particular counter, such as send registered letters and
buy stamps. Post offices also sell newspapers, and telephone cards.

I'd like to send a ...	es *vaa*-laws *naw*-soo-teet ...	*Es vēlos nosūtīt ...*
I'm expecting a ...	es *gai*-du ...	*Es gaidu ...*
fax	*fuhks*-u	*faksu*
letter	*vaa*-stu-li	*vēstuli*
postcard	*uht*-klaht-ni	*atklātni*
parcel	*puh*-ku	*paku*
telegram	*te*-le-*gruhm*-mu	*telegrammu*
I'd like to send this (by) ...	es *vaa*-laws *naw*-soo-teet shaw ...	*Es vēlos nosūtīt šo ...*
airmail	uhr *gai*-su *puhst*-u	*ar gaisa pastu*
express	uhr *eks*-pre-si	*ar ekspresi*
ordinary post	uhr *puh*-ruh-staw *puhst*-u	*ar parasto pastu*
registered mail	*ea*-ruhk-stee-tu	*ierakstītu*

LATVIAN

I'd like a stamp, please.

es *vaa*-laws *puhst*-muhr-ku loodz-u   *Es vēlos pastmarku, lūdzu.*

Has any post arrived for me?

vai muhn ir *pea*-nah-tsis kahds *puhst*-uh *soo*-tee-yums?   *Vai man ir pienācis kāds pasta sūtījums?*

Telephone & Internet

The telephone system in Latvia has undergone significant modernisation over the last few years and most telephone lines are now digital, enabling users to make national and international telephone calls easily. In order to use the public telephone booths, you have to buy a telephone card from a newspaper kiosk or post office. Public telephone booths provide instructions in a number of languages (including English) on how to use the phone system. Making calls from your hotel or someone's home is just as simple. The Internet and email are used widely throughout Latvia, and there are many Internet cafes providing Internet access for a small fee.

SIGNS

IESNIEGŠANA and **IZSNIEGŠANA** – here you can hand in and collect parcels and registered letters at larger post-offices.

APDROŠINĀTAS PAKAS	INSURED PARCELS
BANDROLES	PRINTED MATTER
IERAKSTĪTAS PAKAS	REGISTERED PARCELS
IERAKSTĪTAS SĪKPAKAS	REGISTERED PACKETS
IERAKSTĪTAS VĒSTULES	REGISTERED LETTERS
KOMERCPRECES	COMMERCIAL GOODS
PASTMARKAS	STAMPS
PAKU DAĻA	PARCEL SECTION
TELEGRAMMAS	TELEGRAMS
TELEKARTES	TELEPHONE CARDS
VĒSTULES	LETTERS

LATVIAN

A telephone card, please.
  *te-*le-kuhr-ti *loo-dzu* *Telekarti, lūdzu.*
How much does it cost?
  tsik tuhs *muhk-*sah? *Cik tas maksā?*
I was cut off.
  *muh-*ni *uht-*vea-naw-yuh *Mani atvienoja.*
It was the wrong number.
  *bi-*yuh *ne-*puh-ray-zais
  *num-*urs *Bija nepareizais numurs.*
The number is engaged.
  *num-*urs ir *aiz-*nyemts *Numurs ir aizņemts.*

international	*stuhrp-*tow-tis-kahs	*starptautiskās*
phone calls	*suh-*ru-nuhs	*sarunas*
local phone calls	*vea-*teh-yahs	*vietējās sarunas*
	*suh-*ru-nuhs	
mobile phone	*mo-*bee-lais *te-*le-fons	*mobīlais telefons*
telephone	*te-*le-fons	*telefons*
telephone booth	*te-*le-fo-nuh	*telefona automāts*
	*ow-*to-mahts	
telephone number	*te-*le-fo-nuh *num-*urs	*telefona numurs*

I need to use the Internet.
  es *vaa-*laws *lea-*tawt *Es vēlos lietot*
  *in-*ter-ne-tu *internetu.*
I need to check my email.
  es *vaa-*laws *pahr-*bow-deet *Es vēlos pārbaudīt*
  *suh-*vu e-*puhst-*u *savu e-pastu.*

Sightseeing

Do you have a guidebook?
  vai yums ir *cely-*ved-is? *Vai jums ir ceļvedis?*
What's worth seeing?
  kaw ir vaarts *uhp-*skuh-teet? *Ko ir vērts apskatīt?*
What time does it open?
  naw tsik-eam ir *uht-*vaarts? *No cikiem ir atvērts?*
What time does it close?
  tsik-aws slaadz? *Cikos slēdz?*

LATVIAN

I'm interested in ...	muh-ni in-te-re-she ...	Man interesē ...
architecture	uhr-hi-tek-too-ruh	arhitektūra
art	mahk-sluh	māksla
history	vaas-tu-re	vēsture

I want to go	es vaa-laws	Es vēlos
to the ...	uhp-me-kleht ...	apmeklēt ...
botanical	bo-tah-nis-kaw	botānisko
gardens	dahr-zu	dārzu
castle	pi-li	pili
cathedral	kuht-e-drah-li	katedrāli
cemetery	kuh-pus	kapus
church	buhz-neets-u	baznīcu
concert hall	konts-er-tu zah-li	koncertu zāli
exhibition	iz-stah-di	izstādi
Freedom	bree-vee-buhs	Brīvības
Monument	pea-mi-ne-kli	pieminekli
... national park	... nats-i-o-nah-law	... nacionālo
	puhr-ku	parku
opera house	o-per-u	operu
park	puhr-ku	parku
ruins	dru-puhs	drupas
stadium	stuhd-i-aw-nu	stadionu
synagogue	sin-uh-go-gu	sinagogu
university	un-i-versi-tah-ti	universitāti
zoo	zo-o-lo-jyis-kaw	zooloģisko
	dahr-zu	dārzu

Useful Words

boulevard	*bul*-vah-ris	*bulvāris*
bridge	tilts	*tilts*
building	*tselt*-ne	*celtne*
monument	*pea*-mi-nek-lis	*piemineklis*
road	tselysh	*ceļš*
statues	*stuht*-u-yuhs	*statujas*
street	ea-luh	*iela*
square	*low*-kums	*laukums*

Going Out

What's there to do in the evenings?

kaw shayt vuhr	*Ko šeit var*
duh-reet *vuh*-kuh-raws?	*darīt vakaros?*

Is there a ...?	vai ir ...?	*Vai ir ...?*
bar	bahrs	*bārs*
cafe	*kaf*-ey-neets-uh	*kafejnīca*
casino	*kuh*-zi-no	*kazino*
cinema	*ki*-no	*kino*
concert	*konts*-erts	*koncerts*
disco	*dis*-ko-teh-kuh	*diskotēka*
nightclub	*nuhkts*-klubs	*nakstklubs*
theatre	te-ah-tris	*teātris*

How much is it to get in?

tsik *muhk*-sah ea-ey-uh?	*Cik maksā ieeja?*

Two tickets, please.

di-vuhs *bily*-e-tes *loo*-dzu	*Divas biļetes, lūdzu.*

LATVIAN

SIGNS

In accordance with the Latvian language laws all signs should be in Latvian, although you do come across the occasional sign in Russian and sometimes English.

SIGNS

AIZŅEMTS	ENGAGED
APSTĀTIES	STOP
APVEDCEĻŠ	DIVERSION
ATVĒRTS	OPEN
BIĻEŠU KASES	TICKET OFFICE
BRĪVS	VACANT
CEĻA REMONTS	ROADWORKS
IEBRAUKT AIZLIEGTS	NO ENTRY
IEEJA AIZLIEGTA	ENTRY PROHIBITED
IEEJA	ENTRANCE
IEKĀPŠANA	DEPARTURES
IELIDOŠANA	ARRIVALS
INFORMĀCIJA	INFORMATION
IZEJA	EXIT
IZEJAS NAV	NO ENTRY
MAKSAS TUALETES	PUBLIC TOILETS
MUITA	CUSTOMS
NESMĒĶĒT/	NO SMOKING
SMĒĶĒT AIZLIEGTS	
NESTRĀDĀ	OUT OF ORDER
PASU KONTROLE	PASSPORT CONTROL
POLICIJAS IECIRKNIS	POLICE STATION
REĢISTRĀCIJA (BIĻEŠU)	CHECK-IN
REMONTS	UNDER REPAIR
REZERVĒTS	RESERVED
SIEVIEŠU TUALETES	WOMEN'S TOILETS
SLĒGTS	CLOSED
STĀVĒT AIZLIEGTS	NO STANDING
STĀVVIETA	PARKING
TAKSOMETRS	TAXI
UZMANĪBU	CAUTION
VĪRIEŠU TUALETES	MEN'S TOILETS
VIETU NAV	NO SEATS/FULL

LATVIAN

PAPERWORK

name	*vahrds*	*vārds*
surname	*uz*-vahrds	*uzvārds*
address	*uh*-dre-se	*adrese*
age	*vats*-ums	*vecums*
border	*raw*-be-zhuh	*robeža*
car registration	*muh*-sheen-uhs	*mašinas*
	do-ku-men-ti	*dokumenti*
date	*duh*-tums	*datums*
date of birth	*dzim*-shuhn-uhs	*dzimšanas*
	duh-tums	*datums*
driver's licence	*browk*-shuhn-uhs	*braukšanas*
	uht-lyow-yuh	*atļauja*
	(*tea*-see-buhs)	(*tiesības*)

LATVIAN

marital status	*jyim*-en-es *stah*-vaw-klis	*ģimenes stāvoklis*
passport	*puh*-se	*pase*
passport number	*puh*-ses *num*-urs	*pases numurs*
place of birth	*dzim*-shuhn-uhs *vea*-tuh	*dzimšanas vieta*
sex/gender	*dzim*-ums	*dzimums*
signature	*puh*-ruhksts	*paraksts*
visa	*vee*-zuh	*vīza*

IN THE COUNTRY
Weather

What's the weather
like today?

    kahds *shaw*-dean ir laiks?   *Kāds šodien ir laiks?*

Will it/there be	vai reet boos ...?	*Vai rīt būs ...?*
... tomorrow?		
cloudy	*mah*-kaw-nyains	*mākoņains*
cold	owksts	*auksts*
foggy	*mig*-lains	*miglains*
frost	*suhl*-nuh	*salna*
hot	kuhrsts	*karsts*
icy	*lad*-ains	*ledains*
rain	lea-tus	*lietus*
snow	sneags	*sniegs*
sunny	*sow*-lains	*saulains*
warm	silts	*silts*
windy	*veh*-yains	*vējains*

Directions

How far is it?

    tsik *tah*-lu?   *Cik tālu?*

Can we walk/drive there?

    vai ir ea-speh-yuhms leedz   *Vai ir iespējams līdz*
    tu-rea-ni *aiz*-browkt/   *turieni aizbraukt/*
    aiz-stai-gaht?   *aizstaigāt?*

north	zea-me-lyi	*ziemeļi*
south	*dean*-vi-di	*dienvidi*
east	*ow*-stru-mi	*austrumi*
west	*rea*-tu-mi	*rietumi*

LATVIAN

Animals, Birds & Insects

beaver	*be*-brs	bebrs
bird	*put*-ns	putns
boar	*me*-zhuh *tsoo*-kuh	meža cūka
cat	*ka*-kyis	kaķis
chicken	*vis*-tuh	vista
cow	gaws	govs
dog	suns	suns
elk	*uhl*-nis	alnis
fish	zivs	zivs
deer	*stir*-nuh	stirna
horse	zirgs	zirgs
lynx	*loo*-sis	lūsis
mouse	*pe*-le	pele
otter	*oo*-drs	ūdrs
pig	*tsoo*-kuh	cūka
pigeon	*buh*-law-dis	balodis
sheep	*ai*-tuh	aita
spider	*zir*-ne-klis	zirneklis
wild animals	*me*-zhuh *dzeev*-nea-ki	meža dzīvnieki
wolf	vilks	vilks

Plants

tree	kawks	koks
birch	baarzs	bērzs
fir	*eg*-le	egle
flower	*pu*-kye	puķe
oak	*aw*-zawls	ozols
pine	*prea*-de	priede

Camping

There aren't many camp sites in Latvia. The solution is to ask a farmer if you may pitch a tent on his or her land. However, please bear in mind that amenities may be somewhat dilapidated and running water will probably be unavailable.

May we ... here?	vai mehs *dreek*-stuhm shayt ...?	*Vai mēs drīkstam šeit ...?*
camp	*uz*-stah-deet	*uzstādīt*
	suh-vu tel-ti	*savu telti*
light a fire	*kur*-in-aht	*kurināt*
	u-guns-ku-ru	*ugunskuui*
camp site	*kemp*-ings	*kempings*
can opener	(kon-ser-vu *kahr*-bu)	*(konservu kārbu)*
	uht-var-uhm-ais	*atveramais*
compass	*kom*-pas	*kompass*
drinking water	dzar-uhm-ais oo-dens	*dzeramais ūdens*
gas cylinder	*gah*-zes *buh*-lawns	*gāzes balons*
insect repellent	pret aw-du *leedz*-ek-lis	*pret odu līdzeklis*
matches	*saar*-kaw-tsiny-i	*sērkociņi*
saucepan	*kuh*-stro-lis	*kastrolis*
sleeping bag	*guly*-uhm-mais	*guļammaiss*
torch	(*kuh*-buh-tuhs)	*(kabatas)*
	buh-ter-i-yuh	*baterija*
tent	telts	*telts*

Useful Words

beach	*plud*-muh-le	*pludmale*
country house	*low*-ku *mah*-yuh	*lauku māja*
farm	*low*-ku *saa*-tuh	*lauku sēta*
farmer	*lowk*-saim-neaks	*lauksaimnieks*
field	lowks	*lauks*
forest	mezhs	*mežs*
lake	a-zars	*ezers*
river	u-pe	*upe*
sea	*yoo*-ruh	*jūra*
tree	kawks	*koks*
well	*uh*-kuh	*aka*
windmill	*dzir*-nuh-vuhs	*dzirnavas*

LATVIAN

FOOD

Over the last few years there's been a terrific boom in the number and variety of bars, cafes and restaurants in Latvia serving authentic food from around the world, with multilingual menus. Riga has become a gourmet's paradise and you'll be hard pressed not to be able to find something to suit both your pocket and palate. The dishes described below are ones you'll come across in places serving traditional Latvian food. Tipping is not generally expected in Latvia, although this depends to some extent on the 'class' of restaurant you go to.

Can you recommend a good ...?	vai yoos muhn *vuh*-ruht *ea*-taykt *luh*-bu ...?	*Vai jūs man varat ieteikt labu ...?*
bar	*bah*-ru	*bāru*
cafe	*kuh*-fey-neets-u	*kafejnīcu*
restaurant	*res*-to-rah-nu	*restorānu*

Is it possible to get something to eat?
    vai shayt ir *ea*-speh-yuhms *puh*-ehst?   *Vai šeit ir iespējams paēst?*

At the Restaurant

I have a reservation.
    muhn ir *puh*-soo-teets   *Man ir pasūtīts.*
A table for ... people please.
    ***loo*-dzu *guhl*-du ... per-so-nahm**   *Lūdzu galdu ... personām.*
Do you have a menu?
    vai yums ir *eh*-dean-kuhrt-e?   *Vai jums ir ēdienkarte?*
What do you recommend?
    kaw yoos *ea*-suh-kuht?   *Ko jūs iesakat?*
What's this dish?
    kuhs ir shis *eh*-deans?   *Kas ir šis ēdiens?*
I'd like ...
    es *vaa*-laws ...   *Es vēlos ...*
We'd like ...
    mehs *vaa*-luhm-eas ...   *Mēs vēlamies ...*

LATVIAN

Please may I have a/an ...?	vai *vuh*-raa-tu *puh*-loogt ...?	*Vai varētu palūgt ...?*
ashtray	*pal*-nu *trow*-ku	*pelnu trauku*
fork	*duhk*-shu	*dakšu*
glass	*glah*-zi	*glāzi*
glass of water	*glah*-zi *oo*-dens	*glāzi ūdens*
knife	*nuh*-zi	*nazi*
plate	*shkyee*-vi	*šķīvi*
spoon	*kuh*-raw-ti	*karoti*

This dish is too ...	shis *eh*-deans ir puhr ...	*Šis ēdiens ir par ...*
cold	*owk*-stu	*aukstu*
hot	*kuhr*-stu	*karstu*
salty	*sah*-lee-tu	*sālītu*
sweet	*suhl*-du	*saldu*

This isn't what I ordered.
   es shaw *ne*-puh-soo-tee-yu   *Es šo nepasūtīju.*
Nothing else, thank you.
   tuhs boos vis *puhl*-deas   *Tas būs viss, paldies.*
That was delicious.
   tuhs *bi*-yuh *guhr*-sheegs   *Tas bija garšīgs.*
The bill, please.
   loo-dzu *reh*-kyi-nu   *Lūdzu rēķinu.*

Can I pay ...?	vai es *vuh*-ru *muhk*-saht ...?	*Vai es varu maksāt ...?*
by credit card	uhr *kred*-eet-*kuhr*-ti	*ar kredītkarti*
with foreign currency	*ahr*-zehm-yu *vuhl*-oo-tah	*ārzemju valūtā*

LATVIAN

MENU DECODER

Starters

desa	da-suh	sausage (usually smoked)
kūpināts/ sālīts lasis	koo-pin-ahts/ sah-leets luh-sis	smoked/ salted salmon
marinētas sēnes	muh-rin-aa-tuhs seh-nes	pickled mushrooms
mēle majonēzē	meh-le muhy-o-neh-zeh	tongue in mayonnaise
siļķe kažokā	sil-kye kuh-zhaw-kah	pickled herring with sour cream, egg and beetroot
šprotes	shpro-tes	smoked sprats in vegetable oil
žāvēts zutis	zhah-vaats zu-tis	smoked eel

Soup

biešu zupa	bea-shu zu-puh	beetroot soup (similar to borscht)
buljons ar pīradziņiem	bul-yawns uhr pee-ruhdz-iny-eam	clear broth with meat-filled buns
frikadeļu zupa	fri-kuh-de-lyu zu-puh	clear broth with meatballs
kāpostu zupa	kah-paw-stu zu-puh	cabbage soup
soļanka	so-lyan-kuh	tomato soup with sausage and pickles
zivju zupa	ziv-yu zu-puh	fish soup

Meat

karbonāde ar piedevām	kuhr-bo-nah-de uhr pea-dev-ahm	fried pork chop with potatoes, pickled and fresh vegetables
kotletes	kot-le-tes	meatballs
kurzemes stroganovs	kur-zem-es stro-guh-novs	'Courland' stroganoff

MENU DECODER

mednieku desiņas	*med-nea-ku de-siny-uhs*	'Hunter's' sausages (pork)
pelēkie zirņi ar speķi	*pa-laa-kea zir-nyi uhr spe-kyi*	grey peas with pork fat and onions (best washed down with a glass of buttermilk)
sīpolu sitenis	*see-paw-lu si-ten-is*	beefsteak with fried onions
šašliks	*shuh-shliks*	shish kebab (usually lamb)

Seafood

cepts lasis ar piedevām	tsapts *luh-sis uhr pea-dev-ahm*	fried salmon with potatoes, pickled and fresh vegetables
lasis poļu mērcē	*luh-sis paw-lyu mehrts-eh*	salmon in cream sauce
lasis sēņu un diļļu mērcē	*luh-sis seh-nyu un dily-lyu mehrts-eh*	salmon in mushroom and dill sauce

Salads

biešu salāti	*bea-shu suh-lah-ti*	grated beetroot in sour cream
dārzeņu salāti	*dahr-ze-nyu suh-lah-ti*	diced vegetable salad in sour cream and mayonnaise
kokteiļu salāti	*kok-tay-lyu suh-lah-ti*	diced mixture of sausages, peas and cucumber in sour cream and mayonnaise
kāpostu salāti	*kah-paw-stu suh-lah-ti*	fresh grated cabbage

LATVIAN

MENU DECODER

krevešu salāti	*kre*-ve-shu *suh*-lah-ti	diced mixture of shrimp and vegetables in sour cream and mayonnaise
siera salāti	*sea*-ruh *suh*-lah-ti	diced cheese and carrots in sour cream and mayonnaise
svaigo gurķu salāti	*svai*-gaw *gur*-kyu *suh*-lah-ti	fresh cucumbers with sour cream
svaigo tomātu salāti	*svai*-gaw *to*-mah-tu *suh*-lah-ti	fresh tomatoes with sour cream

Desserts & Cakes

putukrējums (ar riekstiem)	*pu*-tu-kray-yums (uhr *reak*-steam)	whipped cream (with nuts)
buberts ar augļu mērci	*bu*-berts uhr *ow*-glyu mehr-tsi	egg mousse with fruit sauce
debesmanna	*de*-bes-muhn-nuh	'manna from heaven' – a semolina and berry-based pudding with fruit sauce
ķīselis	*kyee*-se-lis	stewed fruit jelly

Vegetarian Meals

Despite the fact that meat is considered an important part of the meal in Latvia, dining opportunities for vegetarians have certainly improved over the last few years. If in doubt, ask if the chef would be willing to rustle you up something off-menu.

I'm a vegetarian.
es *as*-mu *ve*-jye-tah-rea-te/ *ve*-jye-tah-rea-tis

Es esmu veģetāriete/ veģetārietis. (f/m)

Do you have any vegetarian dishes?
vai yums ir *ve*-jye-tah-rea eh-dea-ni?

Vai jums ir veģetārie ēdieni?

I don't eat ...	es *ne*-aa-du ...	*Es neēdu ...*
chicken	*vis*-tu/ *vis*-tuhs *guh*-lyu	*vistu/vistas gaļu*
fish	zivs	*zivs*
meat	*guh*-lyu	*gaļu*
pork	*tsook*-guh-lyu	*cūkgaļu*

Breads

You may not automatically be served bread with your restaurant meal, but don't hesitate to ask the waiter for some – especially the dark rye bread.

rye bread	*ru*-dzu *mai*-ze	*rudzu maize*
sour-sweet bread	*suhld*-skahb-mai-ze	*saldskābmaize*
white bread	*buhlt*-mai-ze	*baltmaize*

Dairy Produce

butter	*sveasts*	*sviests*
buttermilk	*ke-*feers	*kefīrs*
cheese	*sears*	*siers*
cottage cheese	*beaz-*peans/	*biezpiens/*
	*mah-*yuhs sears	*mājas siers*
cream	*kray-*yums	*krējums*
ice cream	*suhl-*day-yums	*saldējums*
milk	*peans*	*piens*
boiled eggs	*vah-*ree-tuhs	*vārītas*
	*aw-*luhs	*olas*
fried eggs	*tsep-*tuhs	*ceptas*
	*aw-*luhs	*olas*

Meat

beef	*leal-*law-pu	*liellopu*
	*guh-*lyuh	*gaļa*
ham	*shkyiny-*kyis	*šķiņķis*
lamb	*yaar-*guh-lyuh	*jērgaļa*
pork	*tsook-*guh-lyuh	*cūkgaļa*
sausage (sliced)	*da-*suh	*desa*
sausages	*tsee-*siny-i	*cīsiņi*
veal	*te-*lyuh *guh-*lyuh	*teļa gaļa*

Seafood

carp	*kuhr-*puh	*karpa*
cod	*mants-*uh	*menca*
eel	*zu-*tis	*zutis*
herring	*sil-*kye	*silķe*
mackerel	*skum-*bri-yuh	*skumbrija*
plaice	*bu-*te	*bute*
salmon	*luh-*sis	*lasis*
shrimp	*guhr-*ne-le	*garnele*
trout	*fo-*re-le	*forele*

LATVIAN

Poultry & Game

chicken	*vis*-tuh	*vista*
elk meat	*uhl*-nyu *guh*-lyuh	*aļņu gaļa*
turkey	*tee*-tuhrs	*tītars*
wild boar	*mezh*-tsoo-kuh	*mežcūka*

Vegetables

beans	*pu*-piny-uhs	*pupiņas*
beetroot	*bea*-tes	*bietes*
cabbage	*kah*-paw-sti	*kāposti*
capsicum	*suhl*-dea *pi*-puh-ri	*saldie pipari*
carrots	*bur*-kah-ni	*burkāni*
cauliflower	*puky-kah*-paw-sti	*puķkāposti*
cucumber	*gur*-kyis	*gurķis*
eggplant	*buhk*-luh-zhahns	*baklažāns*
lettuce	*suh*-lah-ti	*salāti*
mushrooms	*seh*-nes	*sēnes*
onions	*see*-paw-li	*sīpoli*
peas	*zir*-nyi	*zirņi*
pickled	*muhr*-in-aa-ti	*marinēti*
cucumbers	*gur*-kyi	*gurķi*
potatoes	*kuhr*-tu-pe-lyi	*kartupeļi*
spinach	*spin*-ah-ti	*spināti*
tomatoes	*to*-mah-ti	*tomāti*

Legumes

broad beans	*tsook*-pu-puhs	*cūkpupas*
grey peas	*pal*-aa-kea *zir*-nyi	*pelēkie zirņi*
pearl barley	*groo*-buhs	*grūbas*
semolina	*muhn*-nuh	*manna*

LATVIAN

AT THE MARKET

Basics

bread	*mai*-ze	maize
butter	sveasts	sviests
cereal	*braw*-kuhs-tu	brokastu
	pahr-sluhs	pārslas
cheese	sears	siers
chocolate	*sho*-ko-lah-de	šokolāde
eggs	*aw*-luhs	olas
flour	*mil*-ti	milti
margarine	*muhr*-guh-reens	margarīns
mineral water	*min*-er-uhl-oo-dens	minerālūdens
jam	*ea*-vah-ree-yums	ievārījums
milk	peans	piens
oil	*ely*-lyuh	eļļa
pasta	*muh*-kuh-raw-ni	makaroni
rice	*ree*-si	rīsi
sugar	*tsuk*-kurs	cukurs
yogurt	*yo*-gurts	jogurts

Meat & Poultry

beef	*leal*-law-pu *guh*-lyuh	liellopu gaļa
chicken	*vis*-tuh	vista
ham	*shkyiny*-kyis	šķiņķis
lamb	*yaar*-guh-lyuh	jērgaļa
sausage (sliced)	*da*-suh	desa
pork	*tsook*-guh-lyuh	cūkgaļa
turkey	*tee*-tuhrs	tītars
veal	*te*-lyuh -guh-lyuh	teļa gaļa

Vegetables

beans	*pu*-piny-uhs	pupiņas
beetroot	*bea*-tes	bietes
cabbage	*kah*-paw-sti	kāposti
carrots	*bur*-kah-ni	burkāni
cauliflower	*puky*-*kah*-paw-sti	puķkāposti
cucumber	*gur*-kyi	gurķi

AT THE MARKET

eggplant	*buhk*-luh-zhahn	*baklažāns*
lettuce	*suh*-lah-ti	*salāti*
mushrooms	*seh*-nes	*sēnes*
onions	*see*-paw-li	*sīpoli*
peas	*zir*-nyi	*zirņi*
potatoes	*kuhr*-tu-pe-lyi	*kartupeļi*
spinach	*spin*-ah-tai	*spināti*
tomatoes	*to*-mah-ti	*tomāti*

Seafood

carp	*kuhr*-puh	*karpa*
cod	*mants*-uh	*menca*
eel	*zu*-tis	*zutis*
herring	*sil*-kyeh	*siļķe*
mackerel	*skum*-bri-yuh	*skumbrija*
plaice	*bu*-te	*bute*
salmon	*luh*-sis	*lasis*
shrimp	*guhr*-ne-le	*garnele*
trout	*fo*-re-le	*forele*

Fruit

apples	*ah*-baw-li	*āboli*
apricot	*uhp*-ri-kawzs	*aprikozs*
bananas	*ban*-ah-ni	*banāni*
berries	aw-guhs	*ogas*
cherries	*kyir*-shi	*ķirši*
fruit	*ow*-glyi	*augli*
grapes	*veen*-aw-guhs	*vīnuogas*
lemon	*tsit*-rons	*citrons*
oranges	*uhp*-el-see-ni	*apelsīni*
peach	*per*-si-kyis	*persiķis*
pears	*bum*-bea-ri	*bumbieri*
plums	*ploom*-es	*plūmes*
raspberries	*uh*-ve-nes	*avenes*
strawberries	*ze*-me-nes	*zemenes*
watermelon	*uhr*-boozs	*arbūzs*

LATVIAN

LATVIAN

Fruit

apples	*ah*-baw-li	āboli
apricot	*uhp*-ri-kawzs	aprikozs
bananas	*ban*-ah-ni	banāni
berries	*aw*-guhs	ogas
blueberries	*mell*-en-es	mellenes
cherries	*kyir*-shi	ķirši
cranberries	*dzehr*-ve-nes	dzērvenes
fruit (pl)	*ow*-głyi	augļi
grapes	*veen*-aw-guhs	vīnogas
lemon	*tsit*-rons	citrons
oranges	*uhp*-el-see-ni	apelsīni
peach	*per*-si-kyis	persiķis
pears	*bum*-bea-ri	bumbieri
pineapple	*uhn*-uhn-uhs	ananass
plums	*ploom*-es	plūmes
quinces	*tsid*-o-ni-yuhs	cidonijas
raspberries	*uh*-ve-nes	avenes
red/white	*suhr*-kuhn-ahs/	sarkanās/
currants	*buhl*-tahs	baltās
	yahny-aw-guhs	jāņogas
strawberries	*ze*-me-nes	zemenes
watermelon	*uhr*-boozs	arbūzs

Desserts & Cakes

apple cake	*ah*-bawl-koo-kuh	ābolkūka
baked cheese cake	*beaz*-pea-nu *koo*-kuh	biezpienu kūka
biscuits	*tsap*-u-mi	cepumi
chocolate	*sho*-ko-lah-de	šokolāde
ice cream	*suhl*-day-yums	saldējums
pancakes	*puhn*-koo-kuhs	pankūkas
pastry	*smuhlk*-mai-zee-te	smalkmaizīte
poppyseed cake	*muh*-gaw-nyu *mai*-zee-te	magoņu maizīte

BUN IN THE OVEN

Recipe for *pīragi* (Buns filled with meat)
(Eaten at Latvian festivals, on Latvian holidays, at names days, birthdays etc. Every Latvian family has its own version of this recipe.)

Ingredients
approx 500g smoked bacon (diced)
1 onion (finely chopped)
1 cup of milk
100g butter or margarine
2 tablespoons sugar
half teaspoon salt
2 egg yolks
500g flour
1 packet dry yeast (dissolved in warm water)
seasoning (salt, pepper, nutmeg, caraway seeds) to taste
1 egg (beaten)

Melt the butter in the milk, add sugar and salt and leave to cool. Add about half a cup of the flour, egg yolks and yeast. Stir well and add the rest of the flour. Knead the mixture and then cover and leave it to rise in a warm place.

Mix the diced bacon with the onion and season according to taste.

Once the dough has risen, roll it out on a floured surface. Cut out circles of dough, put the bacon/onion filling on one side of each circle of dough, fold over, seal the edges and put on a greased baking tray with the sealed side underneath. Once prepared, leave to rise for around half an hour, brush with beaten egg. Bake for around 10 – 15 minutes at 400°F (205°C) until golden brown.

LATVIAN

Condiments

honey	*mad*-us	*medus*
horseradish	*mah*-rut-ki	*mārrutki*
jam	ea-vah-ree-yums	*ievārījums*
mustard	*sin*-e-pes	*sinepes*
oil	*ely*-lyuh	*eļļa*
pepper	*pi*-puh-ri	*pipari*
salt	sahls	*sāls*
sugar	*tsu*-kurs	*cukurs*
vinegar	e-ti-kyis	*etiķis*

Cooking Methods

baked	*krah*-snee tsapts	*krāsnī cepts*
boiled	vah-reets	*vārīts*
fried	tsapts	*cepts*
grilled	*gril*-aats	*grilēts*

Non-Alcoholic Drinks

Coffee and tea are usually served black, so if you want milk, you'll generally have to ask for it.

coffee	*kuh*-fi-yuh	*kafija*
(fruit) juice	(*ow*-glyu) *su*-luh	(*augļu*) *sula*
lemonade	*li*-mo-nah-de	*limonāde*
milk	peans	*piens*
mineral water	*min*-er-ahl-oo-dens	*minerālūdens*
tea (with lemon)	*teh*-yuh	*tēja*
	(uhr *tsit*-raw-nu)	(*ar citronu*)

Alcoholic Drinks

Aldaris beer is known worldwide and in Latvia the Aldaris brewery offers the largest selection of beers (and mineral water) to suit all tastes. Wine has grown in popularity over the last several years, but locally produced vodka, cognac, sparkling wine and other spirits remain firm favourites. Riga Black Balsam is very much an acquired taste, but well worth a try.

beer	*uh*-lus	*alus*
local beer	*vea*-teh-yais *uh*-lus	*vietējais alus*
cognac	*kon*-yuhks	*konjaks*
liqueur	*li*-kyear-is	*liķieris*
red wine	*suhr*-kuhn-veens	*sarkanvīns*
white wine	*buhlt*-veens	*baltvīns*
sparkling wine	*shuhm*-puhn-ea-tis	*šampanietis*
vodka	*shnyuh*-bis/*dag*-veens	*šņabis/degvīns*

BOTTOMS UP!

Rīgas Melnais Bālzams is a thick, jet-black alcoholic drink (very alcoholic – 45% proof!) that's been produced in Latvia since 1755. It was created by Abraham Kunze, a druggist, and was supposedly administered to Catherine the Great, when she was struck down in Riga by a mystery illness. The story goes that after drinking Riga Black Balsam, she made an instant recovery.

Useful Words

breakfast	*braw*-kuhs-tis	*brokastis*
lunch	*pus*-dea-nuhs	*pusdienas*
dinner	*vuh*-kuh-riny-uhs	*vakariņas*
canned	*kon*-ser-vaats	*konservēts*
food	*pahr*-ti-kuh	*pārtika*
fresh	*svaigs*	*svaigs*
pickled	*muh*-ri-naats	*marinēts*

| Bon appetit! | *luh*-bu *uh*-pe-tee-ti! | *Labu apetīti!* |
| Cheers! | *prea*-kah! | *Priekā!* |

SHOPPING

In Latvia you'll find everything your heart desires in small specialist shops, large department stores, supermarkets or the open-air markets. Be aware that prices of imported goods can often be higher than in Western countries, but the significant increase in choice allows you to be selective as to where you spend your money. Happily, the days of queuing and rationing are just a distant memory.

SIGNS

DIENNAKTS VEIKALS	24-HOUR SHOP
KASE	CASH REGISTER/ CHECK-OUT
SLĒGTS	CLOSED
ATVĒRTS	OPEN
DARBA LAIKS	OPENING HOURS
VILKT	PULL
GRŪST	PUSH
(CENU) ATLAIDE	SALE

Making a Purchase

In smaller shops goods are sometimes located on shelves behind the sales assistants and y ou have to ask them to show you what you are interested in. You may also have to pay a cashier first and then present your receipt to the sales assistant to pick up your goods.

May I help you?	*loo-dzu* yoos *vaa-luh-teas?*	*Lūdzu jūs vēlaties?*
Do you have ...?	vai yums ir ...?	*Vai jums ir ...?*
I'd like to buy ...	es *vaa-laws naw-*pirkt ...	*Es vēlos nopirkt ...*

| Please show me this/that ... | loo-dzu puh-rah-deat muhn shaw/taw ... | Lūdzu parādiet man šo/to ... |

Do you have a ... one?	vai yums ir kowt-kuhs ...?	Vai jums ir kautkas ...?
better	luhb-ahks	labāks
bigger	leal-ahks	lielāks
cheaper	laat-ahks	lētāks
different	tsits	cits
smaller	muhz-ahks	mazāks

Can I try it on?
    vai es *vuh*-ru *uz*-meh-jyin-aht?   *Vai es varu uzmēģināt?*
I don't like it.
    neh muhn tuhs *ne*-puh-teek   *Nē, man tas nepatīk.*
I don't want it.
    neh es taw *ne*-vaa-laws   *Nē, es to nevēlos.*
I'll take it.
    es taw *nyem*-shu   *Es to ņemšu.*
How much is it?
    tsik tuhs *muhk*-sah?   *Cik tas maksā?*
Can I pay by credit card?
    vai es *vuh*-ru *muhk*-saht uhr   *Vai es varu maksāt ar*
    kred-eet-kuhr-ti?   *kredītkarti?*
Could you wrap it please?
    vai *vuh*-raa-tu *loo*-dzu ea-sai-   *Vai varētu lūdzu iesaiņot?*
    nyawt?
Do you have a bag?
    vai yums ir *mais*-inysh?   *Vai jums ir maisiņš?*

When asking for a specific amount of something in Latvian, use the word *gabalu* (pieces/items) after the number.

One (piece/item), please.
    vea-nu *guh*-buh-lu *loo*-dzu   *Vienu gabalu, lūdzu.*

LATVIAN

Two (pieces/items), please.
    di-vus *guh*-buh-lus *loo*-dzu   *Divus gabalus, lūdzu.*
Five (pieces/items), please.
    peats-us *guh*-buh-lus *loo*-dzu   *Piecus gabalus, lūdzu.*

Shops

Window-shopping in Latvia can be a time-saver when the name
of the shop offers no clues as to what is for sale inside. Window-
shopping is also an enjoyable way to spend a few hours, especially
around midsummer and Christmas, when window dressers' artistic
talents and imaginations run wild.

bakery	*mai*-z-neets-uh	*maiznīca*
bookshop	*gruh*-muh-tu *vay*-kuhls	*grāmatu veikals*
chemist/pharmacy	*uhp*-tea-kuh	*aptieka*
clothing shop	*uhp*-jyaar-bu *vay*-kuhls	*apgērbu veikals*
department store	*un*-i-ver-sahl-vay-kuhls	*universālveikals*
drycleaners	*kyee*-mis-kah *tee*-ree-tuh-vuh	*ķīmiskā tīrītava*
electrical shop	*el*-ek-tro-pre-chu *vay*-kuhls	*elektropreču veikals*
food shop	*pahr*-ti-kuhs *vay*-kuhls	*pārtikas veikals*
greengrocer	*suhk*-nyu *vay*-kuhls	*sakņu veikals*
hairdresser	*friz*-aa-tuh-vuh	*frizētava*
jewellery shop	*yu*-vel-ear-iz-strah-dah-yum-i	*juvelieriz-strādājumi*
laundrette	*vely*-uhs *muhz*-gah-tu-ve	*veļas mazgātuve*
shoe shop	*uh*-puh-vu *vay*-kuhls	*apavu veikals*
souvenir shop	*su*-ven-ea-ru *vay*-kuhls	*suvenīru veikals*
stationers	*ruhk*-stahm-pea-dar-um-u *vay*-kuhls (*ruhk*-stahm-pea-dar-um-i)	*rakstāmpiederumu veikals (rakstāmpie-derumi)*

LATVIAN

Essential Groceries

batteries	*buh*-te-ri-yuhs	*baterijas*
bread	*mai*-ze	*maize*
butter	sveasts	*sviests*
candles	*sve*-tses	*sveces*
cereal	*braw*-kuhs-tu	*brokastu*
	pahr-sluhs	*pārslas*
cheese	sears	*siers*
chocolate	*sho*-ko-lah-de	*šokolāde*
eggs	*aw*-luhs	*olas*
flour	*mil*-ti	*milti*
gas cylinder	*gah*-zes	*gāzes*
	buh-lawns	*balons*
ham	*shkyiny*-kyis	*šķiņķis*
honey	*mad*-us	*medus*
insect repellent	pret *aw*-du	*pret odu*
	leedz-ek-lis	*līdzeklis*
jam	ea-vah-ree-yums	*ievārījums*
margarine	*muhr*-guh-reens	*margarīns*
matches	*saar*-kaw-tsiny-i	*sērkociņi*
milk	peans	*piens*
pepper	*pi*-puh-ri	*pipari*
pasta	*muh*-kuh-raw-ni	*makaroni*
rice	*ree*-si	*rīsi*
salt	sahls	*sāls*
shampoo	*shuhm*-poons	*šampūns*
soap	*zea*-pes	*ziepes*
sunblock cream	*sow*-les krehms	*saules krēms*
sugar	*tsu*-kurs	*cukurs*
toilet paper	*tu*-uh-le-tes	*tualetes*
	puh-peers	*papīrs*
toothpaste	*zaw*-bu *puhs*-tuh	*zobu pasta*
washing powder	*vely*-uhs *pul*-ve-ris	*veļas pulveris*
yogurt	*yo*-gurts	*jogurts*

Souvenirs

amber	*dzin*-tuhrs	*dzintars*
art work	*mahk*-sluhs *duhr*-bi	*mākslas darbi*
folk art (articles)	*tow*-tis-kea *preaksh*-mati	*tautiskie priekšmeti*
handicrafts	*raw*-ku *duhr*-bi	*roku darbi*
jewellery	*yu*-vel-ear-iz-strah-dah-yum-i	*juvelier-izstrādājumi*
leather goods	*ah*-duhs iz-strah-dah-yum-i	*ādas izstrādājumi*
Latvian mittens/ socks	*tow*-tis-kea *tsim*-di/ *tow*-tis-kahs ze-kyes	*tautiskie cimdi/ tautiskās zeķes*
linen	lins	*lins*
pottery	*ke*-ruh-mi-kuh	*keramika*
souvenirs	*su*-ve-nee-ri	*suvenīri*
tapestries	*go*-be-lah-ni	*gobelēni*
wood carvings	*kawk*-grea-zu-mi	*kokgriezumi*
weavings	*ow*-du-mi	*audumi*

Clothing

blouse	*bloo*-ze	*blūze*
clothing	*uhp*-jyaar-bi	*apģērbi*
coat	*meh*-te-lis	*mētelis*
dress	*klay*-tuh	*kleita*
hat	*tsa*-pu-re	*cepure*
jacket	*yuh*-kuh/ *zhuh*-ke-te	*jaka/ žakete*
jumper/ sweater	*jem*-per-is	*džemperis*
scarf	*shuhl*-le	*šalle*
shirt	*kra*-kls	*krekls*
shoes	*uh*-puh-vi	*apavi*
skirt	*svahr*-ki	*svārki*
socks	ze-kyes	*zeķes*
trousers	*bik*-ses	*bikses*

LATVIAN

Materials

cotton	*kawk*-vilnuh	*kokvilna*
gold	zalts	*zelts*
handmade	*raw*-ku duhrbs	*roku darbs*
leather	*ah*-duh	*āda*
linen	lins	*lins*
metal	*me*-tahls	*metāls*
silver	*su*-druhbs	*sudrabs*
wood	kawks	*koks*
wool	*vil*-nuh	*vilna*

Toiletries

comb	*kyem*-me	*ķemme*
condoms	*prez*-er-vuh-tee-vi	*prezervatīvi*
deodorant	*dez*-o-do-ruhnts	*dezodorants*
razor	*zhi*-le-te	*žilete*
sanitary napkins	*bin*-des	*bindes*
shampoo	*shuhm*-poons	*šampūns*
shaving cream	*skuy*-uhm-ahs	*skujamās*
	pu-tuhs	*putas*
soap	*zea*-pes	*ziepes*
sunblock cream	*sow*-les krehms	*saules krēms*
tampons	*tuhm*-po-ni	*tamponi*
toilet paper	*tu*-uh-le-tes *puh*-peers	*tualetes papīrs*
toothbrush	*zaw*-bu *su*-kuh	*zobu suka*
toothpaste	*zaw*-bu *puhs*-tuh	*zobu pasta*

IT'S NEWS TO ME

A large selection of Western newspapers and magazines are widely available in the well-stocked newspaper kiosks. Most kiosks also sell stamps, telephone cards, monthly transport tickets, cigarettes, confectionary and other items, too numerous to mention. For Baltic news and events get hold of a copy of 'The Baltic Times', published weekly in Riga. Failing that, you can always read the Internet version.

Stationery & Publications

Do you have ...?	vai yums ir ...?	*Vai jums ir ...?*
books/	*grah*-muh-tuhs/	*grāmatas/*
newspapers/	uh-vee-zes/	*avīzes/*
magazines in	zhur-nah-li	*žurnāli*
English	uhn-glyu	*angļu*
	vuh-*law*-dah	*valodā*
an English-	uhn-glyu	*angļu-*
Latvian	*luht*-vea-shu	*latviešu*
dictionary	*vahrd*-neets-uh	*vārdnīca*
a textbook	*luht*-vea-shu	*latviešu*
to learn	vuh-*law*-duhs	*valodas*
Latvian	*mahts*-ee-bu	*mācību*
	grah-muh-tuh	*grāmata*

books	*gruh*-muh-tuhs	*grāmatas*
guidebook	*tsely*-ve-dis	*ceļvedis*
map	*kuhr*-te	*karte*
newspaper	*laik*-ruhksts/uh-vee-ze	*laikraksts/avīze*
pen	*pild*-spuhl-vuh	*pildspalva*
postcard	*uht*-klaht-ne	*atklātne*
writing paper	*ruhk*-stahm-puh-peers	*rakstāmpapīrs*

Photography

How much is it to process this film?	
tsik *muhk*-sah uh-*tees*-teet shaw *fil*-mu?	*Cik maksā attīstīt šo filmu?*
When will it be ready?	
kuhd boos *guh*-tuhvs?	*Kad būs gatavs?*

I'd like a ... film for this camera.	es *vaa*-laws ... *fil*-mu shim *fo*-to-uh-puh-rah-tuhm.	*Es vēlos ... filmu šim fotoaparātam.*
B&W	*maln*-buhl-tu	*melnbaltu*
colour	krah-sai-nu	*krāsainu*
slide	*di*-uh-poz-i-tee-vu	*diapozitīvu*

LATVIAN

Smoking

A packet of cigarettes, please.
pats-iny-u *tsig*-uh-re-tes *loo*-dzu   *Paciņu cigaretes, lūdzu.*

May I smoke?
vai es *dreek*-stu *smeh*-kyeht?   *Vai es drīkstu smēķēt?*

Do you have a light?
vai yums ir *u*-guns?   *Vai jums ir uguns?*

cigarettes	*tsig*-uh-re-tes	*cigaretes*
matches	*saar*-kaw-tsiny-i	*sērkociņi*
tobacco	*tuh*-buh-kuh	*tabaka*

Colours

black	malns	*melns*
blue	zils	*zils*
brown	broons	*brūns*
green	zuhlysh	*zaļš*
orange	*o*-ruhnzh	*oranžs*
pink	*ro*-zah	*rozā*
red	*suhr*-kuhns	*sarkans*
white	buhlts	*balts*
yellow	*dzal*-tans	*dzeltens*

Sizes & Comparisons

big	leals	*liels*
enough	*pea*-tea-kuhm-i	*pietiekami*
heavy	smuhgs	*smags*
less	*muh*-zahk	*mazāk*
light	veagls	*viegls*
a little	*muhz*-leat	*mazliet*
long	guhrsh	*garš*
many	dowdz	*daudz*
more	*vai*-rahk	*vairāk*
short	ees	*īss*
size	*lea*-lums	*lielums*
small	muhzs	*mazs*
too much	puhr dowdz	*par daudz*

HEALTH

Hotels and embassies in Riga will be able to provide you with lists of English speaking doctors in Latvia. Many Western brands of medicine are readily available, but make sure you bring any prescription medicines with you. Ticks can be a problem in rural areas and forests during the summer months, so if you plan to go hiking or camping you should make sure you're vaccinated prior to travelling to Latvia.

At the Doctor

Please call a doctor.	*loo-dzu iz-sow-tseat ahrs-tu*	*Lūdzu izsauciet ārstu.*
Where can I find a/an ...?	kur es *vuh-ru uht-ruhst* ...?	*Kur es varu atrast ...?*
chemist	*uhp-tea-ku*	*aptieku*
dentist	*zawb-ahr-stu*	*zobārstu*
doctor	*ahr-stu*	*ārstu*
English-speaking doctor	*ahr-stu kuhs ru-nah uhn-gli-ski*	*ārstu, kas runā angliski*
hospital	*slim-neets-u*	*slimnīcu*
I'd like to see a female doctor.	es *vaa-laws redz-eht ahr-stu-sea-vea-ti*	*Es vēlos redzēt ārstu-sievieti.*
I feel nauseous.	muhn ir *slik-tuh doo-shuh*	*Man ir slikta dūša.*
I've been vomiting.	muhn *bi-yuh yah-vemy*	*Man bija jāvemj.*
I feel dizzy.	muhn ir *ray-baw-nis*	*Man ir reibonis.*

Ailments

I'm sick.	
es *as-mu slim-uh/slims*	*Es esmu slima/slims.* (f/m)
My friend is sick.	
muhn-uh drow-dze-ne ir slim-uh	*Mana draudzene ir slima.* (f)
muhns drowgs ir slims	*Mans draugs ir slims.* (m)

Where does it hurt?
   ku-rah *vea*-tah sahp?   *Kurā vietā sāp?*
It hurts here.
   muhn sahp shayt   *Man sāp šeit.*

I have a/an ...	man sahp ...	*Man sāp ...*
earache	ows	*auss*
headache	*guhl*-vuh	*galva*
sore throat	*kuh*-kls	*kakls*
stomachache	vaa-dars	*vēders*

I have (a/an) ...	muhn ir ...	*Man ir ...*
She/He has (a/an) ...	*viny*-ai/*viny*-uhm ir ...	*Viņai/Viņam ir ...*
asthma	*uhst*-muh	*astma*
backache	*mu*-gur-sah-pes	*mugursāpes*
burn	*uhp*-dag-ums	*apdegums*
cold	eas-nuhs	*iesnas*
constipation	aiz-tsea-teh-yums	*aizcietējums*
cough	*klap*-us	*klepus*
cramps	*kruhmp*-yi	*krampji*
diabetes	*di*-uh-behts	*diabēts*
diarrhoea	*tsowr*-e-yuh	*caureja*
epilepsy	ep-i-lep-si-yuh	*epilepsija*
fever	*dru*-dzis	*drudzis*
food poisoning	suh-in-deh-shuhn-ahs	*saindēšanās*
	uhr eh-dea-nu	*ar ēdienu*
headache	*guhl*-vuhs *sah*-pes	*galvas sāpes*
hepatitis	*he*-puh-teets	*hepatīts*
high/low blood	owgsts/zams	*augsts/zems*
pressure	*uhs*-ins-spea-deans	*asinsspiediens*
indigestion	gram-aw-shuhn-uhs	*gremošanas*
	trau-tseh-yum-i	*traucējumi*
infection	ea-kai-sums	*iekaisums*
influenza	gri-puh	*gripa*
rash	*iz*-sit-um-i	*izsitumi*
sprain	*iz*-mezh-jyee-yums	*izmežģījums*
temperature	tem-pe-ruh-too-ruh	*temperatūra*
venereal disease	ven-e-ris-kah	*veneriskā*
	slim-ee-buh	*slimība*

Allergies

I have an allergy.

    muhn ir *uh*-ler-jyi-yuh   *Man ir alerģija.*

I'm allergic to penicillin.

    es *as*-mu *uh*-ler-jyis-kuh/   *Es esmu alerģiska/*
    uh-ler-jyisks pret   *alerģisks pret*
    pen-its-i-lee-nu   *penicilīnu.* (f/m)

Parts of the Body

ankle	*paw*-tee-te	*potīte*
arm	*raw*-kuh	*roka*
back	*mu*-gu-ruh	*mugura*
chest	*kroo*-tis	*krūtis*
ear	ows	*auss*
eye	uhts	*acs*
finger	pirksts	*pirksts*
foot	*paa*-duh	*pēda*
gums	*smuh*-guh-nuhs	*smaganas*
hand	*raw*-kuh	*roka*
head	*guhl*-vuh	*galva*
heart	sirds	*sirds*
knee	*tse*-lis	*celis*
leg	*kah*-yuh	*kāja*
mouth	*mu*-te	*mute*
nose	*da*-guns	*deguns*
shoulder	plats	*plecs*
throat/neck	*kuh*-kls	*kakls*
tongue	*meh*-le	*mēle*

At the Chemist

Do you have
something for ...?

    vai yums ir *kowt*-kuhs pret ...?   *Vai jums ir kaut kas pret ...?*

I have a prescription.

    muhn ir *rets*-ep-te   *Man ir recepte.*

At the Dentist

I have a toothache.
    muhn sahp zawbs   *Man sāp zobs.*

I've lost a filling.
    muhn ir *iz*-kri-tu-si *plom*-buh   *Man ir izkritusi plomba.*

I've broken a tooth.
    muhn ir *naw*-loo-zis zawbs   *Man ir nolūzis zobs.*

My gums hurt.
    muhn sahp *smuh*-guh-nuhs   *Man sāp smaganas.*

I don't want it extracted.
    loo-dzu ne-iz-row-yeat   *Lūdzu neizraujiet.*

Useful Words & Phrases

I've been vaccinated.
    es *as*-mu *paw*-taa-tuh/   *Es esmu potēta/*
    paw-taats   *potēts.* (f/m)

I haven't had my
period for ... months.
    muhn nuhv *bi*-yu-shuhs ray-zes *Man nav bijušas reizes*
    jow ... *meh*-ne-shus   *jau ... mēnešus.*

I have my own syringe.
    muhn *puh*-shai/*puh*-sham ir *Man pašai/pašam ir*
    suh-vuh shlir-tse   *sava šlirce.* (f/m)

I'm pregnant.
    es *as*-mu *stah*-vaw-klee   *Es esmu stāvoklī.*

I feel better/worse.
    muhn ir *luh*-bahk/*slik*-tahk   *Man ir labāk/sliktāk.*

accident	*ne*-lai-me/	*nelaime/*
	uh-vah-ri-yuh	*avārija*
animal bite	*kaw*-deans	*kodiens*
antibiotic	*uhn*-ti-bi-o-ti-kuh	*antibiotika*
aspirin	uhs-pi-reens	*aspirīns*
bleeding	uhs-i-nyaw-shuh-nuh	*asiņošana*
blood pressure	uhs-ins-spea-deans	*asinsspiediens*
blood test	uhs-ins-uhn-uh-lee-ze	*asinsanalīze*
cough medicine	*kla*-pus zah-les	*klepus zāles*
injury	ea-vai-naw-yums	*ievainojums*
insect bite	*dzeh*-leans	*dzēliens*
medicine	zah-les	*zāles*
menstruation	*men*-stru-ah-tsi-yuh	*menstruācija*
oxygen	*skah*-be-klis	*skābeklis*
vitamins	*vit*-uh-mee-ni	*vitamīni*

SPECIFIC NEEDS
Disabled Travellers

I'm disabled/handicapped.
es *as*-mu *in*-vuh-lee-de/   *Es esmu invalīde/*
in-vuh-leeds   *invalīds.* (f/m)

I need assistance.
muhn ir *vuhy*-uh-dzee-guh   *Man ir vajadzīga*
puh-lee-dzee-buh   *palīdzība.*

What services are there
for disabled people?
kah-di *puh*-kuhl-paw-yu-mi ir   *Kādi pakalpojumi ir*
in-vuh-lee-deam?   *invalīdiem?*

Is there wheelchair access?
vai tur vuhr *pea*-klyoot uhr   *Vai tur var piekļūt ar*
brauts-uhm-kraas-lu?   *braucamkrēslu?*

I'm deaf. Speak more loudly, please.
es *as*-mu *kur*-luh/kurls   *Es esmu kurla/kurls*
(*ne*-dzir-dee-guh/*ne*-dzir-deegs).   *(nedzirdīga/nedzirdīgs).*
loo-dzu *run*-ah-yeat *skuh*-lyahk   *Ludzu runājiet skaļāk.* (f/m)

LATVIAN

I have a hearing aid.
> muhn ir dzir-des uh-puh-rahts   *Man ir dzirdes aparāts.*

I'm blind.
> es *as*-mu *uh*-kluh/*uh*-kls   *Es esmu akla/akls.* (f/m)

I'm blind.
> es *as*-mu *ne*-re-dzee-guh/   *Es esmu neredzīga/*
> *ne*-re-dzeegs   *neredzīgs.* (f/m)

Are guide dogs permitted?
> vai shayt dreekst vest *su*-nyus   *Vai šeit drīkst vest suņus*
> *puh*-vuh-daw-nyus?   *pavadoņus?*

I'm mute.
> es *as*-mu maa-muh/maams   *Es esmu mēma/mēms.*(f/m)
>   (NB Colloquially this
>   means 'I'm lost for words'.)

Braille library	ne-re-dzee-gaw ruhk-stu bib-li-o-te-kuh	*Neredzīgo rakstu biblioteka.*
disabled person	in-vuh-lee-de/ in-vuh-leeds	*invalīde/ invalīds* (f/m)
guide dog	suns puh-vuh-daw-nis	*suns pavadonis*
wheelchair	brauts-uhm-kraa-sls	*braucamkrēsls*

TIME & DATES

The 24-hour clock is used in Latvia. You may find that Latvians also use it when speaking. The easiest way to tell the time in Latvian is to say the hour and then the minutes, eg, 'three-twenty'. However, there are a few simple rules to learn to be able to tell the time correctly.

hour	*stun*-duh	*stunda*
minute	*min*-oo-te	*minūte*
o'clock	*pulk*-sten-is	*pulkstenis*

What time (is it)?
    tsik (ir) *pulk*-sten-is?   *Cik (ir) pulkstenis?*
It's one o'clock.
    ir *pulk*-sten-is veans   *Ir pulkstenis viens.*

You'll find that the word *pulkstenis* is often omitted:

It's ...	ir ...	*Ir ...*
two o'clock	*di*-vi	*divi*
		(lit: it's two)
five o'clock	*peats*-i	*pieci*
ten o'clock	*des*-mit	*desmit*

To tell the time between the half-hour and the hour, use the word *bez* at the beginning of the phrase, which literally means 'without':

It's ...	ir ...	*Ir ...*
20 (minutes)	bez *div*-des-mit	*bez divdesmit*
to two	(*min*-oo-tehm) *di*-vi	*(minūtēm)*
		divi
10 (minutes)	bez *des*-mit	*bez desmit*
to seven	(*min*-oo-tehm)	*(minūtēm)*
	sep-ti-nyi	*septiņi*

LATVIAN

To tell the time between the hour and the half-hour, use the word *pāri* between the two numbers, which literally means 'over':

It's ...	ir...	Ir ...
25 past three	*div*-des-mit	*divdesmit*
	peats-i *pah*-ri	*pieci pāri*
	tri-yeam	*trijiem*
five past eight	*peats*-uhs	*piecas*
	(*min*-oo-tes)	(*minūtes*)
	pah-ri *uhs*-taw-nyeam	*pāri astoņiem*

To say 'half past ...', use the word *pus* ('half') with the next hour of the clock:

It's half past three.	ir pus *chet*-ri	*Ir pus četri.*
		(lit: half before four)

Days of the Week

Monday	*pirm*-dea-nuh	*pirmdiena*
Tuesday	*aw*-tr-dea-nuh	*otrdiena*
Wednesday	*tresh*-dea-nuh	*trešdiena*
Thursday	*tsat*-urt-dea-nuh	*ceturtdiena*
Friday	*peakt*-dea-nuh	*piektdiena*
Saturday	*sast*-dea-nuh	*sestdiena*
Sunday	*sveht*-dea-nuh	*svētdiena*

Months

January	*yuhn*-vah-ris	*janvāris*
February	*feb*-ru-ah-ris	*februāris*
March	muhrts	*marts*
April	*uhp*-ree-lis	*aprīlis*
May	maiys	*maijs*
June	*yoo*-niys	*jūnijs*
July	*yoo*-liys	*jūlijs*
August	*ow*-gusts	*augusts*
September	*sep*-tem-bris	*septembris*
October	*ok*-to-bris	*oktobris*
November	*no*-vem-bris	*novembris*
December	*dets*-em-bris	*decembris*

Seasons

summer	*vuh*-suh-ruh	*vasara*
autumn	*ru*-dens	*rudens*
winter	*zea*-muh	*ziema*
spring	*puh*-vuh-suh-ris	*pavasaris*

Dates

What's the date today?

    kahds *shaw*-dean ir duh-tums?   *Kāds šodien ir datums?*

It's 5 June.

    ir *peak*-tais yoo-niys   *Ir piektais jūnijs.*

It's 18 October.

    ir *uhs*-tawny-puhds-mi-tais   *Ir astoņpadsmitais oktobris.*
    ok-to-bris

Present

today	*shaw*-dean	*šodien*
this morning	*shaw*-reet	*šorīt*
this week	shaw *ne*-deh-lyu	*šo nedēļu*
this year	*shaw*-guhd	*šogad*
tonight	*shaw*-vuh-kuhr	*šovakar*
now	*tuh*-guhd	*tagad*

Past

yesterday	*vuh*-kuhr	*vakar*
day before yesterday	*aiz*-vuh-kuhr	*aizvakar*
yesterday morning	*vuh*-kuhr-reet	*vakarrīt*
last night	*vuh*-kuhr *vuh*-kuh-rah	*vakarvakarā*
last week	*puhg*-ah-yu-shah *ne*-deh-lyah	*pagājušā nedēļā*
last year	*puhg*-ah-yu-shah *guh*-dah	*pagājušā gadā*

IT'S A DATE

Latvians write the year first, then the day and then the month. However, where the situation is not particularly formal, the date will be the same as in British English, ie, day, month, year.

Future

tomorrow	reet	*rīt*
day after tomorrow	*puh*-reet	*parīt*
tomorrow morning	reet naw *ree*-tuh	*rīt no rīta*
tomorrow afternoon/ evening	*reet*-dean/ *reet*-vuh-kuhr	*rītdien/ rītvakar*
next week	*nuh*-kuhm *ned*-eh-lyu	*nākam nedēļu*
next year	*nah*-kuhm-guhd	*nākamgad*

During the Day

afternoon	*pehts*-pus-dea-nuh	*pēcpusdiena*
day	*dea*-nuh	*diena*
early	*uh*-gri	*agri*
midnight	*pus*-nuhkts	*pusnakts*
morning	reets	*rīts*
night	nuhkts	*nakts*
noon	*div*-puhds-mit *dea*-nah	*divpadsmit dienā*
sunset	*sowl*-reats	*saulriets*
sunrise	*sowl*-laakts	*saullēkts*

LATVIAN

LATVIAN

Useful Words

a year ago	pirms *guh*-duh	*pirms gada*
always	*vean*-maar	*vienmēr*
at the moment	*puhsh*-laik	*pašlaik*
century	*guhd*-simts	*gadsimts*
early	*uh*-gri	*agri*
every day	*kuh*-tru *dea*-nu	*katru dienu*
forever	*vean*-maar	*vienmēr*
just then	*ti*-kaw	*tikko*
late	vaa-lu	*vēlu*
later on	vaa-lahk	*vēlāk*
never	ne-*kuhd*	*nekad*
not yet	vehl neh	*vēl ne*
now	*tuh*-guhd	*tagad*
since	kawpsh	*kopš*
sometimes	*dazh*-rayz	*dažreiz*
soon	dreez	*drīz*
still	*vehl*-yaw-praw-yahm	*vēljoprojām*
straight away	too-*leet*	*tūlīt*

FESTIVALS & HOLIDAYS

An entire book could be devoted to the subject of festivals and holidays in Latvia. Suffice it to say that you're guaranteed to have a memorable time if you're lucky enough to spend midsummer, Easter or Christmas in the company of Latvians, as they love any excuse to sing, dance and celebrate.

The traditional Latvian calendar was divided into eight seasons to coincide with the farming year and there are many days, which are marked in the Latvian calendar – although not necessarily celebrated – to signify these points in the year.

You'll never forget a Latvian song festival if you're fortunate enough to be in Riga when one takes place. Latvia also has a number of historically significant public holidays, when all buildings throughout the country must display the Latvian flag.

National Holidays

New Year's Day (1 January)
  yown-guh-duh *dea*-nuh   *Jaungada diena*
Easter Sunday
  leal-dea-nuhs   *Lieldienas*
  (*leal*-dea-nu *sveht*-dea-nuh)   (*lieldienu svētdiena*)
Midsummer (23 June)
  lee-gaw *svaat*-ki   *Līgo svētki*
St John's Day (24 June)
  yah-nyi   *Jāņi*
Independence Day (18 November)
  ne-uht-kuhr-ee-buhs   *Neatkarības*
  prok-lo-meh-shuhn-uhs   *Proklomēšanas Diena*
  dea-nuh
Christmas (24, 25 & 26 December)
  zeam-uhs-svaat-ki   *Ziemassvētki*
                                      (lit: winter festival)

birthday	*dzim*-shuh-nuhs *dea*-nuh	*dzimšanas diena*
name day	*vahr*-duh *dea*-nuh	*vārda diena*
song festival	*dzeas*-mu *svaat*-ki	*dziesmu svētki*
dance festival	*de*-yu *svaat*-ki	*deju svētki*

Felicitations

Happy New Year!
  lai-mee-gu *yown*-aw *guh*-du!   *Laimīgu Jauno Gadu!*
Happy Easter!
  preats-ee-guhs *leal*-dea-nuhs!   *Priecīgas Lieldienas!*
Happy 'Līgo'!
  preats-ee-gus *lee*-gaw *svaat*-kus! *Priecīgus Līgo svētkus!*
Happy Midsummer!
  preats-ee-gus *yah*-nyus!   *Priecīgus Jāņus!*
Merry Christmas!
  preats-ee-gus   *Priecīgus*
  zeam-uhs-svaat-kus!   *Ziemassvētkus!*
Happy name day/birthday!
  dowdz lai-mes   *Daudz laimes*
  vuhr-da *dea*-nah/   *vārda diena/*
  dzim-shuh-nuhs *dea*-nah!   *dzimšanas diena!*

LATVIAN

HAPPY MIDSUMMER!

The greetings *Priecīgus Līgo svētkus!* 'Happy 'Līgo'!' and *Priecīgus Jāņus!* 'Happy Midsummer!' are pretty much interchangeable.

Festivals

Song & Dance Festivals   *Dziesmu Svētki/Deju Svētki*

The first song festival took place in 1873 as part of a European cultural phenomeon and they have continued to this day. Festivals now take place approximately once every four years (the 22nd Song Festival was in July 1998) and are a culmination of the Latvians' love for their culture and history. Choirs and Latvian folk-dance groups from every corner of Latvia and from overseas (totalling up to 30,000 singers and around 5,000 dancers) join forces to perform in several concerts over the course of approximately one week. This is a cultural event not to be missed!

Midsummer/St John's Night   *Līgo Svētki/Jāņi*

This is celebrated on the shortest night of the year – 23 June, the summer solstice. Latvians head out to the countryside and stay up all night singing songs and dancing around a bonfire.

Traditionally, buildings and livestock are decorated with garlands and women weave wreaths from grasses and flowers gathered in the fields. It is important to decorate the doors of the house in order to keep evil spirits away. Beer is brewed and a special St John's Night cheese with caraway seeds is eaten, along with other Latvian foods such as *pīrāgi* (see recipe, page 155). Young girls wear flower wreaths and men called Jānis (John) are honoured with a wreath made of oak leaves. Young couples head off to the forest to look for fern, which is said to blossom only on this night – those who find it (or at least try to!) are guaranteed happiness and love.

Baltica International Folk Festival

The first Baltica folk festival took place in 1987 and is held in each of the Baltic states in rotation. The 1987 festival was again a significant event in the Baltic states' move towards renewed independence, as the flag of the Republic of Latvia was carried openly in the festival parade for the first time in over 40 years.

This international festival continues to this day and aims to popularise traditional folk culture and its spiritual values.

18 November   *Neatkarības Proklomēšanas Diena*

18 November is the day on which Latvia proclaimed independence in 1918. This first period of independence lasted until 17 June 1940 when Latvia was invaded by Soviet troops. Today 18 November is a significant public holiday in Latvia.

Easter   *Lieldienas*

Many of the traditional Easter rituals which Latvians follow to this day relate to the Spring Equinox, *Lielā diena* (lit: big day), although these traditions are now mixed with the Christian festival of Easter.

Traditionally everyone gets up at sunrise and washes their face in running water. In the countryside men build swings and couples take it in turn to swing, so that they are not bitten by mosquitos during the summer. Eggs – which symbolise the sun – are coloured using onion skins, roots and grasses and are given as gifts. Eggs are also a significant part of the Easter breakfast and are the source of many rituals and superstitions. For example, when cracking hard-boiled eggs against other people around the breakfast table, the person whose egg remains intact is guaranteed fortune and happiness. And the person who eats a hard boiled egg without salt is a liar.

LATVIAN

Christmas   *Ziemassvētki*

Nowadays Christmas, like Easter, is a mixture of old and new. Preparations for the four days of Christmas involve decorating the house and lighting candles. Ancient traditions dictate that a fire is lit in the hearth, which should be kept burning. Logs are dragged around the house to ward off evil spirits. People wearing fancy dress go from house to house singing Christmas folk songs. By feeding these people evil spirits are driven away.

The most important day of Christmas is Christmas Eve, when Latvian families go to church and then return home to open presents and eat a traditional meal of pork, sauerkraut, potatoes and grey peas. The remaining days of Christmas are spent visiting relatives and friends.

NUMBERS & AMOUNTS
Cardinal Numbers

0	*nul*-le	*nulle*
1	veans	*viens*
2	*di*-vi	*divi*
3	trees	*trīs*
4	*chet*-ri	*četri*
5	*peats*-i	*pieci*
6	*sesh*-i	*seši*
7	*sep*-ti-nyi	*septiņi*
8	*uhs*-taw-nyi	*astoņi*
9	*de*-vi-nyi	*deviņi*
10	*des*-mit	*desmit*
11	vean-puhds-mit	*vienpadsmit*
12	*div*-puhds-mit	*divpadsmit*
13	trees-puhds-mit	*trīspadsmit*
14	*chet*-r-puhds-mit	*četrpadsmit*
15	*peats*-puhds-mit	*piecpadsmit*
16	sesh-puhds-mit	*sešpadsmit*
17	*sep*-tiny-puhds-mit	*septiņpadsmit*
18	*uhs*-tawny-puhds-mit	*astoņpadsmit*

19	de-viny-puhds-mit	deviņpadsmit
20	*div*-des-mit	divdesmit
21	*div*-des-mit-veans	divdesmitviens
30	trees-des-mit	trīsdesmit
40	chet-r-des-mit	četrdesmit
50	peats-des-mit	piecdesmit
60	sesh-des-mit	sešdesmit
70	sep-tiny-des-mit	septiņdesmit
80	uhs-tawny-des-mit	astoņdesmit
90	de-viny-des-mit	deviņdesmit
100	simts	simts
200	*di*-vi *sim*-ti	divi simti
500	peats-i *sim*-ti	pieci simti
1000	*tooks*-tawts	tūkstots
100,000	simts *tooks*-tawts	simts tūkstots
1 million	*mil*-yawns	miljons
2 million	*di*-vi *mil*-yaw-ni	divi miljoni

Ordinal Numbers

Ordinal numbers have different forms, depending on the gender of the noun they precede. The feminine ending is *-ā* and the masculine ending is *-ais*:

1st	*pir*-mah/ *pir*-mais	pirmā/pirmais (f/m)
2nd	awt-rah/ awt-rais	otrā/otrais (f/m)
3rd	tre-shah/ tre-shais	trešā/trešais (f/m)
4th	tsat-ur-tah/ tsat-ur-tais	ceturtā/ceturtais (f/m)
5th	peak-tah/ peak-tais	piektā/piektais (f/m)
6th	sas-tah/ sas-tais	sestā/sestais (f/m)
7th	sep-tee-tah/ sep-tee-tais	septītā/septītais (f/m)
8th	uhs-taw-tah/ uhs-taw-tais	astotā/astotais (f/m)
9th	dev-ee-tah/ dev-ee-tais	devītā/devītais (f/m)
10th	des-mit-ah/ des-mit-ais	desmitā/desmitais ((f/m)
20th	div-des-mit-ah/	divdesmitā/
	div-des-mit-ais	divdesmitais (f/m)
21st	*div*-des-mit pir-mah/	divdesmit pirmā/
	div-des-mit *pir*-mais	divdesmit pirmais (f/m)

Fractions

1/4	*tsat-urt-duh-lyuh*	*ceturtdaļa*
1/3	*tresh-duh-lyuh*	*trešdaļa*
1/2	*pu-se*	*puse*
3/4	trees *tsat-urt-duh-lyuhs*	*trīs ceturtdaļas*
1 1/2	*pus-aw-truh da-lyuh*	*pusotra daļa*

Useful Words

once	*vean-rayz*	*vienreiz*
twice	*div-rayz*	*divreiz*
a little	*drus-ku*	*drusku*
some	muhz-*leat*	*mazliet*
double	*du-bul-ti*	*dubulti*
few	*pah-ris*	*pāris*
less	*muh-zahk*	*mazāk*
much	*dowdz*	*daudz*
more	*vai-rahk*	*vairāk*

JŪS YOU TU

Always use *jūs*, the polite form of 'you' when talking to people you don't know. With children, you should use *tu*.

LATVIAN

ABBREVIATIONS

plkst	*pulkstens*	at (about time)
ls	*lats*	lats (Latvian currency)
PVN	*Pievienotās Vērtības Nodoklis*	sales tax
utt	*un tā tālāk*	and so on/etc
P/O/T/C/P/S/S	*pirmdiena/otrdiena/ trešdiena/ceturtdiena/ piektdiena/sestdiena/ svētdiena*	Monday/Tuesday/ Wednesday/ Thursday/Friday/ Saturday/Sunday

EMERGENCIES

Help!
   puh-lee-gah!   *Palīgā!*

There's been an accident!
   ir *naw*-ti-ku-si *ne*-lai-me/   *Ir notikusi nelaime/*
   uh-vah-ri-yuh!   *avārija!*

Call a/an/the ...!   *iz*-sowts-eat ...!   *Izsauciet ...!*
   ambulance   *ah*-traw   *ātro palīdzību*
                 puh-lee-dzee-bu
   doctor   *ahr*-stu   *ārstu*
   police   *pol*-its-i-yu   *policiju*

Where's the police station?
   kur ir *pol*-its-i-yuhs   *Kur ir policijas*
   ea-tsirk-nis?   *iecirknis?*

I've been raped/robbed.
   muh-ni *iz*-vuh-raw-yuh/   *Mani izvaroja/*
   uhp-zuh-guh   *apzaga.*

Go away!
   ay-eat *praw*-yam!   *Ejiet projam!*

I'll call the police!
   es *iz*-sowk-shu *pol*-its-i-yu!   *Es izsaukšu policiju!*

Thief!
   zuh-glis!   *Zaglis!*

I'm lost.
   es *as*-mu *uhp*-muhl-dee-yu-seas/   *Es esmu apmaldījusies/*
   uhp-muhl-dee-yeas   *apmaldījies. (f/m)*

Could I please use the telephone?
   vai es *vuh*-raa-tu *loo*-dzu   *Vai es varētu, lūdzu,*
   iz-muhn-tawt *te*-le-fo-nu?   *izmantot telefonu?*

Where are the toilets?
   kur ir *tu*-uh-le-tes?   *Kur ir tualetes?*

I'm sorry/I apologise.
   pea-daw-deat/   *Piedodiet/*
   es *uht*-vai-naw-yaws   *Es atvainojos.*

LATVIAN

I didn't realise I was doing
anything wrong.
    es *ne*-zin-ah-yu kuh tah
    ne-dreek-stu *duh*-reet
        Es nezināju, ka tā
        nedrīkstu darīt.

I didn't do it.
    es taw *ne*-iz-duh-ree-yu
        Es to neizdarīju.

I want to contact my
embassy/consulate.
    es vaa-laws *suh*-zin-ah-teas
    uhr *suh*-vu *vehst*-neats-ee-bu/
    kon-su-lah-tu
        Es vēlos sazināties
        ar savu vēstniecību/
        konsulātu.

I've lost my ...	es *as*-mu *puh*-zow- deh-yu-si/ *puh*-zow-deh-yis *suh*-vu ...	*Es esmu pazau- dējusi/pazaudējis savu ... (f/m)*
bag	*saw*-mu	*somu*
money	*now*-du	*naudu*
passport	*puh*-si	*pasi*

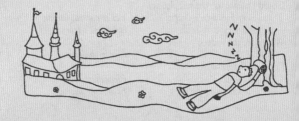

LITHUANIAN

QUICK REFERENCE

Hello.	svay-ki/*lah*-bahs	Sveiki/Labas. (pol/inf)
Goodbye.	su-*deah*	Sudie.
Yes./No.	tayp/na	Taip./Ne.
Excuse me/	aht-si-prah-*show*/	Atsiprašau/
Sorry.	aht-*lays*-ki-ta	Atleiskite.
Thank you.	deh-*kaw*-yu/	Dėkoju/
	ah-choo	Ačiū. (pol/inf)
You're welcome.	prah-*show*	Prašau.
I'd like a ...	ahsh naw-*reh*-chow ...	Aš norėčiau ...
one-way	*bil*-eah-tah i	bilietą į
ticket	*veah*-nah	vieną
	gah-lah	galą
return	*bil*-eah-tah i ah-*bu*	bilietą į abu
ticket	gah-*lus*	galus

I don't understand you.

ahsh *yoo*-soo	Aš jūsų
na-su-prahn-*tu*	nesuprantu.

Do you speak English?

ahr yoos *kahl*-bah-ta	Ar jūs kalbate
ahn-glish-kai?	angliškai?

Where is ...?

kur ee-*rah* ...?	Kur yra ...?

straight ahead	*teah*-say	tiesiai
to the left/right	i *kai*-ra/*dash*-na	į kairę/dešinę

Do you have any rooms available?

ahr *tu*-ri-ta lais-*voo*	Ar turite laisvų
kahm-bahr-yew?	kambarių?

Where's the toilet?

kur tu-ah-*lat*-ai?	Kur tualetai?

Help!

gal-beh-ki-te!	Gelbėkite!

1	*veah*-nahs	vienas	6	shash-*i*	šeši
2	du	du	7	sap-tee-*ni*	septyni
3	trees	trys	8	ahsh-tu-aw-*ni*	aštuoni
4	kat-u-*ri*	keturi	9	dav-ee-*ni*	devyni
5	pan-*ki*	penki	10	*dash*-imt	dešimt

LITHUANIAN

INTRODUCTION

Lithuania is the largest of the three Baltic countries and, in 1990, was the first to regain its independence after more than 50 years of forced annexation to the Soviet Union.

Standard Lithuanian is based on the High West dialect of the country and was declared the official language of Lithuania in 1918. Regional dialects in some provincial areas of Lithuania make communication more difficult, though not impossible. While other Indo-European languages have undergone various metamorphoses over time, Lithuanian, due to its isolation in the past, has preserved its homogeneity and has retained a more archaic character than most other contemporary Indo-European tongues. This makes it particularly interesting to linguists.

However, modernity, advances in technology, commerce and global communication in English are leaving their marks on the Lithuanian lexicon. Words with English roots are found in Lithuanian journalism and increasingly in everyday speech.

Traditionally, Lithuanians strive to accommodate and assist visitors. It's hoped that this phrasebook will provide users with a useful guide while visiting the country. Please note that Lithuanian has feminine and masculine forms of words, separated by a slash and indicated by (f) and (m), the feminine form first.

Help!

While you settle back on your plane, train, ferry or bus ride to Lithuania, take some time to learn a few necessary words to ensure that communication with the locals runs a little more smoothly. One of the phrases you may find yourself inclined to utter is, *Ar kas nors kalba angliškai?* (ahr kahs nors *kahl*-bah *ahn*-glish-kai?), which means 'Does anyone speak English?'.

PRONUNCIATION

Pronunciation in Lithuanian is unambiguous. Each letter denotes a particular sound. The sound may be short or long, depending on the surrounding letters. Vowel combinations, or diphthongs, also have short and long sounds.

Vowels

Lithuanian	Transliteration	Sounds
a, ą	ah	as the 'u' in 'cut' or longer, as the 'a' in 'arm'
e, ę	a	as the 'a' in 'cat' or longer, as the 'a' in 'amber'
ė	eh	as the 'e' in 'bed' but longer
i	i	as the 'i' in 'it'
y, į	ee	as the 'ee' in 'eel'
o	aw	as the 'aw' in 'law'
	o	as the 'o' in 'hot'
u	u	as the 'u' in 'put'
ū, ų	oo	long, as the 'oo' in 'poor'

Diphthongs

Lithuanian	Transliteration	Sounds
ai	ai	as the 'i' in 'bite' or longer as the 'ai' in 'aisle'
au	ow	as the 'ou' in 'ouch' or longer as the 'ow' in 'owl'
ei	ay	as the 'ay' in 'say'
ie	eah	as the 'ea' in 'ear'
ių	ew	as the 'ew' in 'new'
ui	wi	as the 'oui' in 'Louis'
uo	u-aw	as the 'wa' in 'wander'

Consonants

Lithuanian	Transliteration	Sounds
c	ts	as the 'ts' in 'ants'
č	ch	as the 'ch' in 'chicken'
ch	h	as the 'h' in 'hot'
dz	dz	as the 'ds' in 'roads'
dž	j	as the 'j' in 'jump'
g	g	as the 'g' in 'gas'
j	y	as the 'y' in 'you'
r	r	trilled like the Italian 'r'
s	s	soft, as the 's' in 'kiss'
š	sh	as the 'sh' in 'shop'
ž	zh	as the 's' in 'treasure'

The following sentences will help you to practise your pronunciation in Lithuanian:

How is this word pronounced?
kaip shis zhaw-dis
tahr-yah-mahs
Kaip šis žodis tariamas?

The sun is shining.
shveah-cha sow-leh
Šviečia saulė.

Would you please help me?
mah-law-neh-ki-ta mahn
pah-deh-ti
Malonėkite man padėti.

I'll be ready in about five minutes.
uzh pan-kew mi-nu-chew ahsh
boos-yu pah-si-ru-aw-sh(u-si/-as)
Už penkių minučių aš būsiu pasiruoš(usi/ęs). (f/m)

Stress

Stress and tone variations are very subtle and complex in Lithuanian. You'll be understood without having to worry about this too much. The best way to learn is by listening. Stressed syllables are indicated by italic in the transliterations.

GRAMMAR
Sentence Structure

In everyday speech, sentence structure is subject-verb-object, just as it is in English.

Articles

There are no articles (a/an/the) in Lithuanian. So, *gydytojas* can mean 'doctor', 'the doctor' or 'a doctor'.

Nouns

Nouns in Lithuanian have a more complex structure than in English due to their different forms. Here are two tables showing the different forms of the masculine noun *bičiulis* ('friend/mate') and the feminine noun *draugė* ('friend/girlfriend') for the nominative, genitive, dative and accusative cases:

MASCULINE NOUN	SINGULAR	PLURAL
Nominative	*bičiulis*	*bičiuliai*
Genitive	*bičiulio*	*bičiulių*
Dative	*bičiuliui*	*bičiuliams*
Accusative	*bičiulį*	*bičiulius*
FEMININE NOUN	SINGULAR	PLURAL
Nominative	*draugė*	*draugės*
Genitive	*draugės*	*draugių*
Dative	*draugei*	*draugėms*
Accusative	*draugę*	*drauges*

Gender

Nouns are either masculine or feminine. The range of noun endings in Lithuanian is large and varies for each noun depending on the declension used. Therefore, in general, there's no simple way by looking at the form of a noun in a sentence, to determine whether it's masculine or feminine. This will come gradually as you become more familiar with the language.

Adjectives

Adjectives in Lithuanian agree in number, gender and case with the nouns they describe but the suffixes of adjectives and nouns don't necessarily match letter for letter. Here's the adjective *didelis* ('large') in each of the four cases listed before in both masculine and feminine forms:

SINGULAR	MASCULINE	FEMININE
Nominative	*didelis*	*didelė*
Genitive	*didelio*	*didelės*
Dative	*dideliam*	*didelei*
Accusative	*didelį*	*didelę*

PLURAL	MASCULINE	FEMININE
Nominative	*dideli*	*didelės*
Genitive	*didelių*	*didelių*
Dative	*dideliems*	*didelioms*
Accusative	*didelius*	*didelias*

Comparatives

To form a comparative adjective drop the case ending of the nominative singular form of the adjective and add *-esnė* (f) or *-esnis* (m):

It's a nice day.	*Graži diena.* (lit: nice day)
Today is a nicer day.	*Šiandiena gražesnė diena.* (lit: today it-is-nicer day)
You have a handsome/pretty face.	*Jus turite gražų veidą.* (lit: you have handsome/ pretty face)
Your face is more handsome/prettier.	*Jūsų veidas gražesnis.* (lit: your face is-more-handsome/prettier)

Superlatives

To form a superlative adjective use the endings *-iausia* (f) or *-iausias* (m). If, after dropping the case endings, the word stem ends in *d* or *t*, replace these letters with *dž* and *č* respectively:

Today is the loveliest day.	*Šiandiena gražiausia diena.*
	(lit: today it-is-loveliest day)
Yours is the most handsome/ prettiest face.	*Jūsų yra gražiausias veidas.*
	(lit: yours is most-handsome/prettiest face)
This is the largest house.	*Šis yra didžiausias namas*
	(lit: this is largest house)

PRONOUNS

PERSONAL		
I	ahsh	*aš*
you (sg & inf)	tu	*tu*
she	yi	*ji*
he	yis	*jis*
we	mas	*mes*
you (pl & sg pol)	yoos	*jūs*
they	yaws/yeah	*jos/jie* (f/m)

POSSESSIVE		
my	*mah*-naw	*mano*
your (sg & inf)	*tah*-vaw	*tavo*
her	yaws	*jos*
his	yaw	*jo*
our	*moo*-soo	*mūsų*
your (pl & sg pol)	*yoo*-soo	*jūsų*
their	yoo	*jų*

LITHUANIAN

Verbs

The infinitive (dictionary form) of every verb in Lithuanian ends in *-ti*. Verbs belong to three different groups. Each of these groups has its own set of endings for each tense. Which endings to use for the present, past and future tenses, for example, is determined by the last letter of the verb in the third person, present tense. This ending will be either *-a*, *-o* or *-i*. To be able to use the correct tense endings (conjugations), you have to know whether the verb ends in *-a*, *-i* or *-o* in the third person, present tense.

He is going.	*Jis eina.*
	(lit: he goes/is-going)
She loves her daughter.	*Ji myli dukterį.*
	(lit: she loves her-daughter)
He is reading.	*Jis skaito.*
	(lit: he reads/is-reading)

The endings of verbs for each conjugation are consistent so, if you're given a verb stem, ie, the dictionary form of the verb minus the *-ti* ending, and the endings for a particular tense, the correct conjugation of a verb in Lithuanian is possible. It is, however, beyond the scope of this book to list all the possible conjugations.

Imperatives

There are three different forms of the imperative (command) in Lithuanian.

- When *tu* is the subject, drop *-ti* from the infinitive (dictionary form) and add k:

    skaityti 'to read' becomes *Skaityk!* 'Read!'

- When *jūs* is the subject, drop *-ti* from the infinitive and add *-kite*:

    dirbti 'to work' becomes *Dirbkite!* 'Work!'

- When *mes* is the subject, drop *-ti* and add *-kime*:

    daryti 'to do' becomes *Darykime!* 'Let's do it!'

TO BE	
I am	*aš esu*
you (sg & inf) are	*tu esi*
she/he is	*ji/jis yra*
we are	*mes esame*
you (pl & sg pol) are	*jūs esate*
they are	*jos/jie yra* (f/m)

TO HAVE	
I have	*aš turiu*
you (sg & inf) have	*tu turi*
she/he has	*ji/jis turi*
we have	*mes turime*
you (pl & sg pol) have	*jūs turite*
they have	*jos/jie turi* (f/m)

Questions

To turn a sentence into a question, you can place the word *ar* at the beginning of the sentence or just use rising intonation of your voice as you would in English.

You speak English.	*Jūs kalbate angliškai.*
	(lit: you speak English)
You speak English?	*Jūs kalbate angliškai?*
	(rising intonation)
	(lit: you speak English?)
Do you speak English?	*Ar jūs kalbate angliškai?*
	(lit: is-it-that you speak English?)

(Note: *Ar* at the beginning of a statement changes it into a question.)

She has change.	*Ji turi grąžos.*
	(lit: she has some-change)
Does she have change?	*Ar ji turi grąžos?*
	(lit: is-it-that she has some-change?)

LITHUANIAN

How do I get there?	*Kaip ten nuvažiuoti?*
	(lit: how there to-go?)
What's that?	*Kas tai yra?*
	(lit: what that is?)
Why have we stopped?	*Kodėl mes sustojome?*
	(lit: why we have-stopped?)

QUESTION WORDS		
how?	kaip?	*kaip?*
what?	kahs?	*kas?*
who?	kahs?	*kas?*
why?	kaw-*dehl*?	*kodėl?*
when?	kah-*dah*?	*kada?*
where?	kur?	*kur?*

Negatives

The word *ne-* is placed in front of nouns or joined to the word which it negates, ie, before a verb, adjective or adverb. When used with *ne-*, the verb *yra* ('is/are') is contracted to *nėra*.

She is a relative.	*Ji giminė.*
	(lit: she is relative)
She is not a relative.	*Ji ne giminė.*
	(lit: she is-not relative)

The ticket is legible.	*Bilietas aiškus.*
	(lit: ticket is-legible)
The ticket is not legible.	*Bilietas neaiškus.*
	(lit: ticket is-not-legible)

This has been done correctly.	*Čia gerai padaryta.*
	(lit: this well has-been-done)
This has not been done correctly.	*Čia negerai padaryta.*
	(lit: this not-well has-been-done)

Want & Need

To express desire for someone or something in Lithuanian, use the verb *norėti* ('to want'). In the present tense its forms are:

I want you.	*Aš tavęs noriu.*
	(lit: I of-you want)
Do you want a drink?	*Ar tu nori atsigerti?*
	(lit: is-it-that you want to-have-drink?)
We want to go home.	*Mes norime važiuoti namo.*
	(lit: we want to-go to-home)

To express need in Lithuanian the keywords in a sentence are *reikia* for the present tense, *reikėjo* for the past tense and *reikės* for the future tense:

I need some change.	*Man reikia grąžos.*
	(lit: for-me there-is-need of-some-change)
We needed help.	*Mums reikėjo pagalbos.*
	(lit: for-us there-was-need of-some-help)
He will need a doctor.	*Jam reikės daktaro.*
	(lit: for-him there-will-be-need of-doctor)

TO WANT

I want	*aš noriu*
you (sg & inf) want	*tu nori*
she/he wants	*ji/jis nori*
we want	*mes norime*
you (pl & pol) want	*jūs norite*
they want	*jos/jie nori* (f/m)

Prepositions

above	virsh	*virš*
on	ahnt	*ant*
next to	preah	*prie*
under	paw	*po*
with	su	*su*
without	ba	*be*

Conjunctions

and	ir	*ir*
because	nas	*nes*
but	bat	*bet*
or	*ahr*-bah	*arba*
therefore	taw-*dehl*	*todėl*

Useful Words

after (time)	paw *taw*/kai	*po to*/*kai*
after (place)	paw	*po*
before (time)	ahnks-*chow*	*anksčiau*
before (place)	preah-sh	*prieš*
here	cha	*čia*
far	taw-*li*	*toli*
from	nu-*aw*	*nuo*
near	ahr-*ti*	*arti*
that/this	shi-tah/shi-tahs	*šita*/*šitas* (f/m)
those/these	shi-teah	*šitie*
there	tan	*ten*
this much	teahk	*tiek*

GREETINGS & CIVILITIES
Greetings & Goodbyes

Hello.	*svay*-ki	*Sveiki.*
Hi.	*lah*-bahs	*Labas.*
Good morning.	*lah*-bahs *ree*-tahs	*Labas rytas.*
Good day.	*lah*-bah *deah*-nah	*Laba diena.*
Good evening.	*lah*-bahs *vah*-kah-rahs	*Labas vakaras.*
Welcome.	*svay*-ki aht-*vee*-ka	*Sveiki atvykę.*
Goodbye.	su-*deah*	*Sudie.*
All the best.	*vi*-saw *ga*-raw	*Viso gero.*
So long.	kawl kahs	*Kol kas.*
See you later.	i-ki pah-si-*mah*-tee-maw	*Iki pasimatymo.*
Good night.	*lah*-*baws* nahk-*teahs*	*Labos nakties.* (pol)
	lah-*bah*-nahk-tis	*Labanaktis.* (inf)
See you soon.	i-ki *gray*-taw pah-si-*mah*-tee-maw	*Iki greito pasimatymo.*

Until ...	i-ki ...	*Iki ...*
this afternoon	paw peah-*too*	*po pietų*
tomorrow	ree-*taw*-yows	*rytojaus*
next week	*sak*-ahn-chaws sah-*vai*-tehs	*sekančios savaitės*

Civilities

How are you?	kaip gee-*vu*-aw-yah-ta?	*Kaip gyvuojate?* (pol)
	kaip gee-*vu*-aw-yi?	*Kaip gyvuoji?* (inf)
How are things?	kaip *sak*-ah-si?	*Kaip sekasi?*
How are you going?	kaip yums *ay*-nah-si?	*Kaip jums einasi?* (i▸
Well, thanks.	ah-*choo* ga-*rai*	*Ačiū gerai.*
Glad to see you.	mah-*law*-nu yus mah-*tee*-ti	*Malonu jus matyti.*
Have a pleasant trip.	lai-*min*-gaw *kal*-yaw	*Laimingo kelio.*
You're welcome.	prah-*show*	*Prašau.*

Special Occasions

When people meet during a special holiday season such as Christmas or Easter, they greet each other with a handshake or a kiss, saying *Su šventėm!*

Season's greetings!	su *shvan*-tehm!	*Su šventėm!*

I/We wish you ...!	lin-*kyu*/lin-ki-ma ...!	*Linkiu/Linkime ...!*
happy birthday	il-*gyow*-syew *mat*-oo	*ilgiausių metų*
good health	svay-*kah*-taws	*sveikatos*
happiness	*lai*-mehs	*laimės*
success	sak-*mehs*	*sekmės*

Congratulations!	svay-ki-nu!	*Sveikinu!*
Merry Christmas!	*links*-moo kah-*leh*-doo!	*Linksmų Kalėdų!*
Happy New Year!	lai-*min*-goo now-yoo *mat*-oo!	*Laimingų Naujų Metų!*

Forms of Address

It's important to use the polite singular pronoun *jūs* when you're speaking to someone you don't know well, such as an official, a teacher, elders or the like. Children, family and friends address each other using *tu*.

Miss	pah-*nal*-eh	*Panelė*
Madam/Mrs	pawn-*ya*	*Ponia*
Sir/Mr	pawn-ahs	*Ponas*
Ladies and Gentlemen	pawn-yaws ir pawn-ai	*Ponios ir ponai*
Dear ...	brahn-goos ...	*Brangūs ...*
colleagues	ko-*lag*-ehs	*kolegės* (f)
	ko-*lag*-os	*kolegos* (m)
friends	drow-*gai*	*draugai*
guests	svach-*ay*	*svečiai*

LITHUANIAN

Useful Words & Phrases

Yes.	tayp	*Taip.*
No.	na	*Ne.*
No way!	yawk-yu *boo*-du!	*Jokiu būdu!*
Please.	prah-*show*	*Prašau.*
Thank you.	deh-*kaw*-yu	*Dėkoju.* (pol)
	ah-choo	*Ačiū.* (inf)
Excuse me.	aht-si-prah-*show*	*Atsiprašau.*
Sorry.	aht-*lays*-ki-ta	*Atleiskite.*
I see. (I understand.)	su-*prahn*-tu	*Suprantu.*

SMALL TALK

Lithuanians are generally considered very gregarious and self-confident. Meeting and talking with Lithuanians will undoubtedly be a warm and welcoming experience for you.

Meeting People

My name is ...
  mah-*naw* *vahr*-dahs ee-*rah* ...   *Mano vardas yra ...*
What's your name?
  kaip *yoo*-soo *vahr*-dahs?   *Kaip jūsų vardas?*
I'd like to introduce you to ...
  lays-ki-ta mahn yums   *Leiskite man jums*
  pri-stah-*tee*-ti ...   *pristatyti ...*
Pleased to meet you.
  mah-*law*-nu   *Malonu.*

LITHUANIAN

Nationalities

Where are you from?	ish kur yoos a-sah-ta?	*Iš kur jūs esate?*

I'm from ...	ahsh a-*su* ish ...	*Aš esu iš ...*
Africa	*ahf*-ri-kaws	*Akrikos*
Australia	ows-*trah*-li-yaws	*Australijos*
Canada	kah-*nah*-daws	*Kanados*
China	*ki*-ni-yaws	*Kinijos*
Denmark	*dah*-ni-yaws	*Danijos*
England	*ahn*-gli-yaws	*Anglijos*
Finland	*su*-aw-mi-yaws	*Suomijos*
France	prahn-tsoo-*zi*-yaws	*Prancūzijos*
Germany	vaw-keah-*ti*-yaws	*Vokietijos*
Holland	aw-*lahn*-di-yaws	*Olandijos*
Ireland	*ai*-ri-yaws	*Airijos*
Israel	iz-rah-*ehl*-yaw	*Izraėlio*
New Zealand	now-*yaws*	*Naujos*
	ze-*lahn*-di-yaws	*Zelandijos*
Norway	nor-*vag*-i-yaws	*Norvegijos*
Scotland	*shko*-ti-yaws	*Škotijos*
Spain	is-*pah*-ni-yaws	*Ispanijos*
Sweden	*shvad*-i-yaws	*Švedijos*
the USA	yung-*ti*-new	*Jungtinių*
	ah-*ma*-ri-kaws	*Amerikos*
	vahl-*sti*-yoo	*Valstijų*

Age

How old are you?	keahk yums *mat*-oo?	*Kiek jums metų?*
I'm ... years old.	mahn ... *mat*-oo	*Man ... metų.*

For numbers, see pages 274-275.

Occupations

What (work) do you do?	kawk-*yah* yoo-soo praw-*fas*-i-yah?	*Kokia jūsų profesija?*
I'm (a/an) ...	ahsh a-*su* ...	*Aš esu ...*
artist	*man*-in-in-keh	*menininkė* (f)
	man-in-in-kahs	*menininkas* (m)
business person	ko-mer-*sahn*-teh	*komersantė* (f)
	ko-mer-*sahn*-tahs	*komersantas* (m)
doctor	*gee*-dee-taw-yah	*gydytoja* (f)
	gee-dee-taw-yahs	*gydytojas* (m)
engineer	in-*zhi*-near-yus	*inžinierius*
farmer	*oo*-ki-nin-keh	*ūkininkė* (f)
	oo-ki-nin-kahs	*ūkininkas* (m)
journalist	zhur-nah-*lis*-teh	*žurnalistė* (f)
	zhur-nah-*lis*-tahs	*žurnalistas* (m)
lawyer	yoo-*ris*-the	*juristė* (f)
	yoo-*ris*-tahs/	*juristas* (m)/
	ahd-*vaw*-kah-teh	*advokatė* (f)
	ahd-*vaw*-kah-tahs	*advokatas* (m)
mechanic	ma-*hah*-ni-kahs	*mechanikas*
musician	mu-zi-*kahn*-tahs	*muzikantas*
nurse	*slow*-geh	*slaugė*
office worker	tahr-*now*-taw-yah	*tarnautoja* (f)
	tahr-*now*-taw-yahs	*tarnautojas* (m)
scientist	gahm-*taws* *mawks*-li-nin-keh	*gamtos mokslininkė* (f)
	gahm-*taws* *mawks*-li-nin-kahs	*gamtos mokslininkas* (m)
student	stu-*dan*-teh	*studentė* (f)
	stu-*dan*-tahs	*studentas* (m)
teacher	*maw*-kee-taw-yah	*mokytoja* (f)
	maw-kee-taw-yahs	*mokytojas* (m)
unemployed	bad-*ahr*-beh	*bedarbė* (f)
	bad-*ahr*-bis	*bedarbis* (m)
waiter	pah-dah-*veh*-yah	*padavėja* (f)
	pah-dah-*veh*-yahs	*padavėjas* (m)
writer	rah-*shee*-taw-yah	*rašytoja* (f)
	rah-*shee*-taw-yahs	*rašytojas* (m)

LITHUANIAN

Religion

What's your religion?
    ku-*ray* yoos ra-*li*-gi-yay   *Kuriai jūs religijai*
    pri-*klow*-saw-ta?   *priklausote?*
I'm not religious.
    ahsh na-*su* ra-li-*gin*-g(ah/ahs)   *Aš nesu religing(a/as).* (f/m)

I'm ...	ahsh a-*su* ...	*Aš esu ...*
Buddhist	bu-*dis*-teh	*budistė* (f)
	bu-*dis*-tahs	*budistas* (m)
Catholic	kah-tah-*li*-keh	*katalikė* (f)
	kah-tah-*li*-kahs	*katalikas* (m)
Christian	kriksh-*chaw*-neh	*krikščionė* (f)
	kriksh-*chaw*-nis	*krikščionis* (m)
Hindu	*in*-deh	*indė* (f)
	in-dahs	*indas* (m)
Jewish	zhee-deh	*žydė* (f)
	zhee-dahs	*žydas* (m)
Lutheran	lyew-ta-*raw*-neh	*liuteronė* (f)
	lyew-ta-*raw*-nahs	*liuteronas* (m)
Muslim	mu-sul-*maw*-neh	*musulmonė* (f)
	mu-sul-*maw*-nahs	*musulmonas* (m)
Russian Orthodox	stah-*chah*-ti-keh	*stačiatikė* (f)
	stah-*chah*-ti-kis	*stačiatikis* (m)

Family

Are you married?	ahr yoos ish-tak-*eh*-yu-si?	*Ar jūs ištekėjusi?* (to a female)
	ahr yoos *vad*-as?	*Ar jūs vedęs?* (to a male)
I'm ...	ahsh a-*su* ...	*Aš esu ...*
divorced	ish-si-*skee*-ru-si	*išsiskyrusi* (f)
	ish-si-*skee*-ras	*išsiskyręs* (m)
gay	laz-*beah*-teh	*lezbietė* (f)
	ho-mo-sak-swah-*lis*-tahs	*homoseksualistas* (m)
married	ish-tak-*eh*-yu-si	*ištekėjus* (f)
	vad-as	*vedęs* (m)
single	na-ish-tak-*eh*-yu-si	*neištekėjusi* (f)
	na-*vad*-as	*nevedęs* (m)
widowed	nahsh-*leh*	*našlė* (f)
	nahsh-*lees*	*našlys* (m)

How many children do you have?
keahk yoos tu-ri-ta vai-*koo*?   *Kiek jūs turite vaikų?*
I don't have any children.
ahsh na-tur-*yu* vai-*koo*   *Aš neturiu vaikų.*
I have a daughter/son.
ahsh tur-*yu* duk-ta-ri/*soo*-nu   *Aš turiu dukterį/sūnų.*
How many sisters/
brothers do you have?
keahk yoos *tu*-ri-ta sa-sa-*roo*/   *Kiek jūs turite seserų/*
brawl-yoo?   *brolių?*
Is your wife/husband here?
ahr *yoo*-soo zhmaw-*nah*/   *Ar jūsų žmona/vyras čia?*
vee-rahs cha?
Do you have a girlfriend/boyfriend?
ahr yoos *tu*-ri-ta *drow*-ga/   *Ar jūs turite draugę/*
drow-gah?   *draugą?*

baby	*koo*-di-kis	*kūdikis*
brother	*braw*-lis	*brolis*
child/children	*vai*-kahs/vai-*kai*	*vaikas/vaikai*
daughter	duk-*teh*	*duktė*
family	shay-*mah*	*šeima*
father	*teh*-vahs	*tėvas*
grandfather	san-*al*-is	*senelis*
grandmother	san-*al*-eh	*senelė*
mother	*maw*-ti-nah	*motina*
sister	sas-*u-aw*	*sesuo*
son	soo-*nus*	*sūnus*

Kids' Talk

How old are you?
  keahk tow *ma*-too? — *Kiek tau metų?*

When's your birthday?
  kah-*dah* tah-vaw
  gim-*tah*-deah-nis? — *Kada tavo gimtadienis?*

What do you do after school?
  kah tu vay-*ki* paw
  pah-maw-koo? — *Ką tu veiki po pamokų?*

Do you have a pet at home?
  ahr tu-*ri* nah-*mi*-ni
  gee-vu-*lyu*-kah? — *Ar turi naminį gyvuliuką?*

I have a ...	ahsh tu-*ryu* ...	*Aš turiu ...*
bird	powksh-*ta*-li	*paukštelį*
budgerigar	ows-*trah*-lish-kah	*australišką*
	pah-poo-*geh*-la	*papūgėlę*
canary	kah-nah-*reh*-la	*kanarėlę*
cat	kah-*tee*-ta	*katytę*
duck	*ahn*-ti	*antį*
dog	*shu*-ni	*šunį*
fish	zhu-*vee*-ta	*žuvytę*
frog	vahr-*lee*-ta	*varlytę*
guinea pig	*yoo*-raws kyow-*lee*-ta	*jūros kiaulytę*
hamster	zhur-*keh*-nah	*žiurkėną*
horse	*ahrk*-li	*arklį*
tortoise	vehzh-*lyu*-kah	*vėžliuką*

Expressing Feelings

I'm ...	ahsh ...	*Aš ...*
in a hurry	sku-*bu*	*skubu*
right	tay-*si*/tay-*sus*	*teis/teisus* (f/m)
wrong	klees-*tu*	*klystu*

I'm sorry. (condolence)	uzh-*u-aw*-yow-tah	*Užuojauta.*

I'm ...	mahn ...	*Man ...*
afraid	bai-*su*	*baisu*
angry	*pik*-tah	*pikta*
cold	*shahl*-tah	*šalta*
happy	*links*-mah	*linksma*
hot	*kahr-sh*-tah	*karšta*
sad	*lyood*-nah	*liūdna*
sleepy	im-ah *meah*-gahs	*ima miegas*
well	ga-*rai*	*gerai*

I'm ...	ahsh a-*su* ...	*Aš esu ...*
full of energy	*pil*-nahs an-ar-gi-yaws	*pilnas energijos*
hungry	ish-*ahl*-kusi	*išalkusi* (f)
	ish-*ahl*-kas	*išalkęs* (m)
thirsty	ish-*trawsh*-kusi	*ištroškusi* (f)
	ish-*trawsh*-kas	*ištroškęs* (m)
tired	pah-*vahr*-gusi	*pavargusi* (f)
	pah-*vahr*-gas	*pavargęs* (m)
worried	su-si-*roo*-pi-nusi	*susirūpinusi* (f)
	su-si-*roo*-pi-nas	*susirūpinęs* (m)

Expressing Opinions

I like ...	mahn pah-*tin*-kah ...	*Man patinka ...*
I don't like ...	mahn na-pah-*tin*-kah ...	*Man nepa tinka ...*
What a pity!	kaip *gai*-lah	*Kaip gaila!*
I agree.	ahsh su-tin-*ku*	*Aš sutinku.*
I disagree.	ahsh na-su-tin-*ku*	*Aš nesutinku.*
We're very upset.	mas lah-*bai* su-*yow*-din-ti	*Mes labai sujaudinti.*
Good!	ga-*rai*!	*Gerai!*

BODY LANGUAGE

When you go visiting it's proper to take gifts such as flowers for her and perhaps a bottle of drink for him. Don't shake hands across the threshold – it brings bad luck!

If you're due to accept some traditional Lithuanian home hospitality, be prepared to loosen your belt several notches and skip breakfast that morning. There'll be a prolonged period of feasting, punctuated by many *Išgeriam!* (Let's drink!) and *Iki dugno!* (Bottoms up!). Be wary and discreetly ration your intake of food and drink from the start to avoid offending your hosts later, when you find you're too full to accept any more. Starter dishes can be deceptively generous, leading unsuspecting guests to think they're the main meal. To decline further helpings may offend and be taken to mean that you don't like the food or the hospitality.

BREAKING THE LANGUAGE BARRIER

Do you speak English?
  ahr *kahl*-bah-ta *ahn*-glish-kai?   *Ar kalbate angliškai?*

Do you understand me?
  ahr mah-*na* su-*prahn*-tah-ta?   *Ar mane suprantate?*

I understand you.
  ahsh *yus* su-prahn-*tu*   *Aš jus suprantu.*

I don't understand you.
  ahsh *yoo*-soo na-su-prahn-*tu*   *Aš jūsų nesuprantu.*

What does this word mean?
  kah *raysh*-kyah shis *zhaw*-dis?   *Ką reiškia šis žodis?*

Please translate.
  prah-shom ish-*vars*-ti   *Prašom išversti.*

We need an interpreter.
  mums *ray*-kyah var-*teh*-yaw   *Mums reikia vertėjo.*

What do you mean?
  kah yoos tu-ri-ta aw-ma-*nee*-ja?   *Ką jūs turite omenyje?*

What's Lithuanian for ...?
  kaip leah-*tu*-vish-kai ...?   *Kaip lietuviškai ...?*

CLAMBERING FOR AMBER

Amber, found throughout the Baltic region, is one of Lithuania's most distinctive souvenirs. Formed 30-50 million years ago (well after the dinosaurs died out, despite what the makers of *Jurassic Park* would have you believe), amber is fossilised resin of coniferous trees. It ranges in colour from opaque to transparent, from ivory through to black. Yellows and reddish browns are the most common colours, although amber can also be green, blue or cherry.

It has been used as a gemstone for hundreds of thousands of years. Many people believe amber has healing properties. It is said to cure sore throats, asthma and bronchitis.

I speak ...	ahsh kahl-*bu* ...	*Aš kalbu* ...
English	*ahn*-glish-kai	*angliškai*
French	prahn-*tsoo*-zish-kai	*prancūziškai*
German	*vaw*-kish-kai	*vokiškai*
Polish	*lan*-kish-kai	*lenkiškai*
Russian	*rus*-ish-kai	*rusiškai*

Sports & Interests

Do you like ...?	ahr yoos *mehgs*-tah-ta ...?	*Ar jūs mėgs tate* ...?
art	*man*-ah	*meną*
ballet	bah-*lat*-ah	*baletą*
bird watching	*powksh*-chus stab-*eh*-ti	*paukščius stebėti*
the cinema	*ki*-nah	*kiną*
classical music	*klah*-sish-kah *mu*-zi-kah	*klasišką muziką*
exhibitions	*pah*-raw-dahs	*parodas*
fishing	mash-ka-*ryaw*-ti	*meškerioti*
folk dancing	*tow*-ti-nyus *shaw*-kyus	*tautinius šokius*
folk music	*lyow*-deahs *mu*-zi-kah	*liaudies muziką*
gliding	*sklahn*-dee-ti	*sklandyti*
horse riding	yaw-di-*neh*-ti	*jodinėti*
ice fishing	*la*-daw zhuk-la	*ledo žuklę*
opera	*o*-pa-rah	*operą*
reading	skai-*tee*-ti	*skaityti*
rollerblading	rah-*tu*-ki-nehm pah-*choo*-zhawm vah-zhi-*neh*-tis	*ratukinėm pačiūžom važinėtis*
sailboarding	*bur*-lan-ta *plowk*-ti	*burlente plaukti*
the theatre	teh-*aht*-rah	*teatrą*
travelling	kal-*yow*-ti	*keliauti*

I want to go ...	ahsh *naw*-ryu ...	*Aš noriu ...*
bobsleighing	pah-si-vah-zhi-*neh*-ti	*pasivažinėti*
	bob-*sleh*-yu-mi	*bobslėjumi*
canoeing	pah-*plowk*-yaw-ti	*paplaukioti*
	bai-*dah*-ra	*baidare*
cycling	pah-si-vah-zhi-*neh*-ti	*pasivažinėti*
	dvi-rah-chu	*dviračiu*
hiking	ish-kee-*low*-ti	*iškylauti*
jogging	pah-behg-*yaw*-ti	*pabėgioti*
skating	pah-chu-aw-zhi-*neh*-ti	*pačiuožinėti*
skiing	pah-sli-di-*neh*-ti	*paslidinėti*
swimming	pah-si-*mow*-dee-ti	*pasimaudyti*
tobogganing	pah-si-vah-zhi-*neh*-ti	*pasivažinėti*
	raw-*gu*-teh-mis	*rogutėmis*
yachting	pah-bur-*yaw*-ti	*paburiuoti*

I play ...	ahsh ...	*Aš ...*
basketball	zhai-*ju*	*žaidžiu*
	krap-*shi*-ni	*krepšinį*
cards	lawsh-*yu* kor-*taw*-mis	*lošiu kortomis*
chess	lawsh-*yu* shah-*mah*-tais	*lošiu šachmatais*
guitar	*skahm*-bi-nu gi-*tah*-rah	*skambinu gitara*
soccer	zhai-*ju* sok-a-ri	*žaidžiu sokerį*
tennis	lawsh-*yu* tan-i-sah	*lošiu tenisą*
winter sports	zhai-*ju* zheah-*maws* *spor*-tus	*žaidžiu žiemos sportus*

USEFUL PHRASES

Sure.	tik-*rai*	*Tikrai.*
Just a minute.	pah-*low*-ki-ta	*Palaukite*
	mi-*nu*-ta	*minute.*
It's (not) important.	tai (na)-svahr-*bu*	*Tai (ne)svarbu.*
I can't do it.	ahsh *shi*-taw na-gah-*lyu* pah-dah-*ree*-ti	*Aš šito negaliu padaryti.*
Wait!	pah-*low*-ki-ta!	*Palaukite!*
Good luck!	lai-*min*-gai!	*Laimingai!*
That's great!	pwi-*ku*!	*Puiku!*
How awful!	*syow*-bahs	*Siaubas!*

GETTING AROUND

Where's the ...?	kur ee-*rah* ...?	*Kur yra ...?*
airport	aw-raw *u*-aws-tahs	*oro uostas*
booking office	kah-*sah*	*kasa*
bus stop	ow-*taw*-bu-saw staw-*ta*-leh	*autobuso stotelė*
train station	gal-azh-*in*-kal-yaw staw-*tis*	*geležinkelio stotis*
ferry terminal	*kal*-taw staw-*tis*	*kelto stotis*

Is it far from here?
ahr tai taw-*li*?　　　　　*Ar tai toli?*

Can we walk there?
ahr gah-li-mah nu-ay-ti pehs-*chom*?　　　*Ar galima nueiti pėsčiom?*

Can you show me (on the map)?
gah-*leh*-tu-met mahn pah-*raw*-dee-ti (zham-*eh*-lah-pee-ya)?　　　*Galėtumėt man parodyti (žemėlapyje)?*

Please write down the address.
prah-shom pah-rah-*shee*-ti
ahd-ras-ah

Prašom parašyti
adresą.

Are there other means
of getting there?
ahr *gah*-li-mah ki-*taip* tan
nu-*veek*-ti?

Ar galima kitaip ten
nuvykti?

Directions

Turn left at the ...	*su*-ki-ta i *kai*-ra preah ...	Sukite į kairę prie ...
Turn right at the ...	*su*-ki-ta i *dash*-na preah ...	Sukite į dešinę prie ...
traffic lights	shveah-so-*fo*-ro	šviesoforo
next	*sak*-ahn-chaw	sekančio
corner	*kahm*-paw	kampo
back	aht-*gahl*	atgal
behind	uzh	už
far	taw-*li*	toli
in front of	*preah*-shais	priešais
straight ahead	*teah*-say	tiesiai
to the left	i *kai*-ra	į kairę
to the right	i *dash*-na	į dešinę

STREET CRED

GATVĖ	STREET
AIKŠTĖ	SQUARE
PROSPEKTAS/ BULVARAS	AVENUE/ BOULEVARD
KELIAS	ROAD
PLENTAS	HIGHWAY
TILTAS	BRIDGE

LITHUANIAN

Buying Tickets

Where can I buy tickets?
    kur gah-*lyu* nu-si-*pirk*-ti
    bil-eah-tus?
    *Kur galiu nusipirkti
    bilietus?*

I want to travel to ...
    ahsh *naw*-ryu
    nu-vah-*zhu-aw*-ti i ...
    *Aš noriu
    nuvažiuoti į ...*

Do I need to book?
    ahr mahn *ray*-kya
    uzh-si-sah-*kee*-ti?
    *Ar man reikia
    užsisakyti?*

Is it sold out?
    ahr ee-*rah* ish-pahr-*du-aw*-tah?
    Ar yra išparduota?

I'd like to book a seat to ...
    ahsh *naw*-ryu uzh-sah-*kee*-ti
    veah-tah kal-*yaw*-nay i ...
    *Aš noriu užsakyti vietą
    kelionei į ...*

I'd like (a) ...	ahsh naw-*reh*-chow ...	*Aš norėčiau ...*
one-way ticket	*bil*-eah-tah i *veah*-nah gah-*lah*	*bilietą į vieną galą*
return ticket	*bil*-eah-tah i ah-*bu* gah-*lus*	*bilietą į abu galus*
two tickets	du *bil*-eah-tus	*du bilietus*
tickets for all of us	*bil*-eah-tus mums vis-*eahms*	*bilietus mums visiems*
child/pensioner fare	*bil*-eah-tah *vai*-kwi/ *pen*-si-nin-kwi	*bilietą vaikui/ pensininkui*
1st class ticket	pir-*maws klah*-sehs *bil*-eah-tah	*pirmos klasės bilietą*
2nd class ticket	ahn-*traws klah*-sehs *bil*-eah-tah	*antros klasės bilietą*

Air

Is there a flight to ...?
ahr ee-*rah* *ray*-sahs i ...?　　*Ar yra reisas į ...?*

When's the next flight to ...?
kah-*dah* *sak*-ahn-tis *ray*-sahs i ...?　*Kada sekantis reisas į ...?*

What's the flight number?
kawks ee-*rah* *ray*-saw　　*Koks yra reiso*
nu-ma-ris?　　　　　　　*numeris?*

When will the plane arrive at ...?
kah-*dah* lehk-*tu*-vahs　　*Kada lėktuvas*
aht-*skris* i ...?　　　　　*atskris į ...?*

airport	aw-raw *u*-aws-tahs	*oro uostas*
airport tax	aw-raw *u*-aws-taw	*aoro uosto*
	maw-kas-tis	*mokestis*
boarding pass	tah-*lon*-ahs	*talonas*
customs	*mwi*-ti-neh	*muitinė*
customs	*mwi*-ti-nehs	*muitinės*
declaration	dak-lah-*rah*-tsi-yah	*deklaracija*

Bus

Where's the ... stop?	kur ee-*rah* ...	*Kur yra ...*
	staw-*ta*-leh?	*stotelė?*
bus	ow-*to*-bu-saw	*autobuso*
trolleybus	tro-*lay*-bu-saw	*troleibuso*

Which bus goes to ...?
kaw-*kyu* ow-*to*-bu-su *gah*-li-mah　*Kokiu autobusu galima*
nu-vah-zhu-*aw*-ti i-ki ...?　　　　*nuvažiuoti iki ...?*

Does this trolleybus go to ...?
ahr *shi*-tahs tro-*lay*-bu-sahs　*Ar šitas troleibusas*
vah-zhu-*aw*-yah i ...?　　　　*važiuoja į ...?*

Could you let me know
when we get to ...?
ahr gah-*leh*-tu-met *par*-speh-ti　*Ar galėtumėt perspėti,*
kai pri-vah-zhu-*aw*-sim ...?　　*kai privažiuosim ...?*

I want to get off.
 ahsh *naw*-ryu ish-*lip*-ti *Aš noriu išlipti.*
This is your stop.
 dah-*bahr* yums *Dabar jums*
 rayk-yah ish-*lip*-ti *reikia išlipti.*

Train

Is this the right platform for ...?
 ahr ish *shi*-taws plaht-*for*-maws *Ar iš šitos platformos*
 ish-*veeks*-tah trow-ki-*nees* i ...? *išvyksta traukinys į ...?*
The train leaves from platform ...
 trow-ki-*nees* ish-vah-*zhu*-aw-yah *Traukinys išvažiuoja*
 ish ... plaht-*for*-maws *iš ... platformos.*

Passengers must ...	ka-*lay*-vay tu-ri ...	*Keleiviai turi ...*
change trains	*par*-sehs-ti	*persėsti*
go to platform	*ay*-ti i ... pa-*ro*-nah/	*eiti į ... peroną/*
number ...	plaht-*for*-mah	*platformą*

Boat

To cross from the mainland at Klaipėda to the strip of sand dunes called Neringa (the Curonian Spit) you need to take a short ferry ride. In the summer months you can take a ferry along the Nemunas River between Kaunas and Nida, or a boat tour of the Curonian Bay as well as a boat trip from Nida to the mouth of the Nemunas. Overseas ferry services operate between Klaipėda and Germany, Sweden and Denmark.

When does the ...	kah-*dah*	*Kada išplaukia ...*
sail for ...?	ish-plowk-yah ... i ...?	*į ...?*
When does the ...	kah-*dah*	*Kada atplaukia ...?*
arrive?	aht-plowk-yah ...?	
boat	*lai*-vahs	*laivas*
ferry	*kal*-tahs	*keltas*
hydrofoil	rah-*kat*-ah	*raketa*

boat/ferry landing place	*preah*-plow-kah	*prieplauka*
ferry terminal	*kal*-taw *preah*-plow-kah	*kelto prieplauka*
harbour	u-*aws*-tahs	*uostas*

Where does the boat leave from?
  ish kur *lai*-vahs ish-plow-kyah?   *Iš kur laivas išplaukia?*
What time does the boat arrive?
  kah-*dah lai*-vahs aht-plow-kyah?   *Kada laivas atplaukia?*
Which boat goes to ...?
  ku-*ris lai*-vahs plow-kyah i ...?   *Kuris laivas plaukia į ...?*
Which landing is next?
  kahs bus *sak*-ahn-ti *preah*-plow-kah?   *Kas bus sekanti prieplauka?*
Is this the ferry for ...?
  ahr *shis kal*-tahs *plow*-kyah i ...?   *Ar šis keltas plaukia į ...?*

Taxi

Can you take me to ...?
  ahr gah-*leh*-tu-met mah-na nu-*vash*-ti i ...?   *Ar galėtumėt mane nuvežti į ...?*
How much does it cost to go to ...?
  keahk kai-*nu*-aw-yah nu-vah-*zhu*-aw-ti i ...?   *Kiek kainuoja nuvažiuoti į ...?*
Here is fine, thank you.
  deh-kwi ish-*lays*-ki-ta cha   *Dėkui, išleiskite čia.*
The next corner, please.
  prah-*show* ish-*lays*-ki-ta preah *sak*-ahn-chaw *kahm*-paw   *Prašau išleiskite prie sekančio kampo.*
Please slow down.
  prah-*show* su-*leh*-tin-ki-ta *gray*-ti   *Prašau sulėtinkite greitį.*
Please wait here.
  prah-*show* cha pah-*lowk*-ti   *Prašau čia palaukti.*

Car

Where can I hire a car
(for a day/week)?
    kur ahs gah-*leh*-chow
    pah-si-sahm-*dee*-ti
    ow-to-*mob*-i-li
    (*deah*-nai/sah-*vai*-tay)?

Kur aš galėčiau
pasisamdyti
automobilį
(dienai/savaitei)?

Where's the next petrol station?
    kur ee-*rah* sak-ahn-ti
    dag-ah-*li*-neh?

Kur yra sekanti
degalinė?

Please fill the tank.
    prah-*show* pri-*pil*-dee-ki-ta
    ban-*zi*-naw *bah*-kah

Prašau pripildykite
benzino baką.

Please check the oil and water.
    prah-*show* pah-*tik*-rin-ki-ta
    tap-ah-lah ir *vahn*-dan-i

Prašau patikrinkite tepalą
ir vandenį.

Does this road lead to ...?
    ahr shis *kal*-yahs *vad*-ah i ...?

Ar šis kelias veda į ...?

I need a mechanic.
    mahn *rayk*-yah ma-*hah*-ni-kaw

Man reikia mechaniko.

We've had an accident.
    mums ish-*tik*-aw ah-*vah*-ri-yah

Mums ištiko avarija.

I have a flat tyre.
    mahn prah-*doo*-reh
    pah-dahn-gah

Man pradūrė
padangą.

Could you please tow my car?
    ahr na-gah-*leh*-tu-met
    pah-*vilk*-ti mah-naw
    mah-shi-nah?

Ar negalėtumėt
pavilkti mano
mašiną?

The battery is flat.
    ah-ku-mu-*lah*-taw-rus ee-*rah*
    ish-si-ayk-*vaw*-yas

Akumuliatorius yra
išsieikvojes.

The radiator is leaking.
    rah-di-*yah*-taw-rus
    prah-*kew*-ras

Radiatorius
prakiuręs.

LITHUANIAN

It's overheating.
    vah-*rik*-lis *par*-kais-tah   *Variklis perkaista.*
It's not working.
    na-vayk-yah   *Neveikia.*

Useful Words

air (for tyres)	aw-raw *pah*-dahn-goms	*oro padangoms*
battery	ah-ku-mu-*lah*-taw-rus	*akumuliatorius*
brakes	*stahb*-jay	*stabdžiai*
clutch	*sahn*-kah-bah	*sankaba*
driving licence	vai-*ru-aw*-taw-yaw	*vairuotojo*
	pah-zhee-*meh*-yi-mahs	*pažymėjimas*
engine	vah-*rik*-lis	*variklis*
lights	*shveah*-saws	*šviesos*
oil	*tap*-ah-lahs	*tepalas*
puncture	*nu*-lays-tah	*nuleista*
	pah-dahn-gah	*padanga*
radiator	rah-di-*yah*-taw-rus	*radiatorius*
repair shop	*ram*-on-taw *dirb*-tu-vehs	*remonto dirbtuvės*
road map	ow-taw-kal-*yoo*	*autokelių*
	aht-lah-sahs	*atlasas*
spare parts	aht-sahr-*gin*-ehs	*atsarginės*
	dah-lees	*dalys*
spark plug	*zhvah*-keh	*žvakė*
speed limit	*gray*-chaw	*greičio*
	ahp-rib-*aw*-yi-mahs	*apribojimas*
tyre	*pah*-dahn-gah	*padanga*
windscreen	*preah*-ki-nis *stik*-lahs	*priekinis stiklas*

Useful Phrases

The train is delayed/cancelled.
trow-ki-*nees* veh-*lu*-aw-yah/   *Traukinys vėluoja/*
na-ba-vah-*zhu*-aws   *nebevažiuos.*

How long will it be delayed?
keahk il-*gai* veh-*lu*-aw-yah?   *Kiek ilgai vėluoja?*

There's a delay of ... hours.
veh-*lu*-aw-yah ... *vah*-lan-doo   *Vėluoja ... valandų.*

How long does the trip take?
keahk il-*gai* trun-kah   *Kiek ilgai trunka*
kal-*yaw*-neh?   *kelionė?*

Is it a direct route?
ahr kal-*yaw*-neh ba   *Ar kelionė be*
par-seh-di-moo?   *persėdimų?*

I want to hire a bicycle.
ahsh *naw*-ryu   *Aš noriu*
pah-si-sahm-*dee*-ti *dvi*-rah-ti   *pasisamdyti dviratį.*

SIGNS

ATIDARA	OPEN
DĖMESIO!	CAREFUL!
DRAUDŽIAMA STOTI	NO STANDING/ PARKING
DRAUDŽIAMA	ENTRY PROHIBITED
DRAUDŽIAMA	NO ENTRY
IĖJIMAS	ENTRANCE
INFORMACIJA	INFORMATION
IŠĖJIMAS	EXIT
NERŪKOMA	NO SMOKING
PATOGUMAI	PUBLIC TOILET
PERĖJA	PEDESTRIAN CROSSING
REZERVUOTAS	RESERVED
STOK!	STOP!
TAISOMAS KELIAS	ROADWORKS
UŽDARA	CLOSED
VAKANSIJA	VACANT

LITHUANIAN

ACCOMMODATION

Over the last few years a number of new quality hotels have sprung up in the major cities of Lithuania, particularly the capital, Vilnius, offering a welcome alternative to the old Soviet-style accommodation.

Tourist, holiday and health resorts have some exceptional facilities, but you'll have to book well in advance as they're very popular with the locals.

Finding Accommodation

I'm looking for (a) ...	ahsh *yeash*-kow ...	*Aš ieškau ...*
hotel	*veash*-bu-chaw	*viešbučio*
camp site	staw-veek-*lah*-veah-tehs	*stovyklavietės*
somewhere to stay	kur nors ahp-si-*staw*-ti	*kur nors apsistoti*

Could you write down
the address please?

ahr gah-*leh*-tu-met mahn
uzh-rah-*shee*-ti *ah*-dras-ah?

*Ar galėtumėt man
užrašyti adresą?*

At the Hotel

Do you have any rooms available?

ahr *tu*-ri-ta lais-*voo*
kahm-bahr-yew?

*Ar turite laisvų
kambarių?*

I'd like a ...	ahsh *nawr*-yu ...	*Aš noriu ...*
single room	veahn-*veah*-chaw kahm-*bahr*-yaw	*vienviečio kambario*
double room	dvi-*veah*-chaw kahm-*bahr*-yaw	*dviviečio kambario*
room with a bathroom	*kahm*-bahr-yaw su prow-*seek*-lah	*kambario su prausykla*
room with a television	*kahm*-bahr-yaw su te-le-*viz*-aw-ryum	*kambario su televizorium*
room with a window	*kahm*-bahr-yaw su *lahn*-gu	*kambario su langu*

Is there (a) ...?	ahr ee-*rah* ...?	*Ar yra ...?*
hot water	*kahrsh*-tahs vahn-*du*-aw	*karštas vanduo*
bathroom	vawn-*yah*	*vonia*
sauna	pir-*tis*	*pirtis*
shower	*du*-shahs	*dušas*
telephone	te-le-*fo*-nahs	*telefonas*
television	te-le-*viz*-aw-ryus	*televizorius*

How much is it per day (24 hrs)?
    keahk kai-*nu-ah*-yah *pah*-rai?
    Kiek kainuoja parai?

HIP HIP PARAI!

In Lithuania, prices at hotels are often marked *parai*, for a 24-hour day.

How much is it per night, per person?
    keahk kai-*nu*-aw-yah ahp-si-*staw*-ti *nahk*-chay *ahs*-man-wi?
    Kiek kainuoja apsistoti nakčiai asmeniui?

Does it include breakfast?
    ahr kai-*nah* i-*skai*-taw *pus*-ree-chus?
    Ar karina įskaito pusryčius?

Can I see the room?
    ahr gah-*leh*-chow *kahm*-bah-ri pah-mah-*tee*-ti?
    Ar galéčiau kambarį pamatyti?

Are there any cheaper rooms?
 ahr ee-*rah* pi-gas-*new*
 kahm-bahr-yew?
 *Ar yra pigesnių
 kambarių?*

Is there hot water all day?
 ahr ee-*rah* kahrsh-*taw*
 vahn-*dans* vi-sah *deah*-nah?
 Ar yra karšto vandens visą dieną?

It's fine, I'll take it.
 bus *tin*-kah-mah pah-*ims*-yu   *Bus tinkama, paimsiu.*
I'm not sure how long I'm staying.
 ahsh na-su *tik*-rahs   *Aš nesu tikras*
 keahk il-*gai* ahsh boos-yu   *kiek ilgai aš būsiu*
 ahp-si-*staw*-(yu-si/-yas)   *apsistoj (usi/ęs).* (f/m)

I'm going	ahsh ahp-si-*staws*-yu ...	*Aš apsistosiu ...*
to stay for ...		
one day	*veah*-nah *deah*-nah	*vieną dieną*
two days	dvi *deah*-nahs	*dvi dienas*
one week	*veah*-nah sah-*vai*-ta	*vieną savaitę*

I'm leaving ...	ahsh ish-veeks-*tu* ...	*Aš išvykstu ...*
this afternoon	shan-*deahn* paw *peah*-too	*šiandien po pietų*
tonight	*shah*-nahkt	*šiąnakt*
tomorrow morning	ree-*toy* ree-tah	*rytoj rytą*

We're leaving now.
 mas dah-*bahr*   *Mes dabar*
 ish-si-*krows*-taw-ma   *išsikraustome.*
I'd like to pay the bill.
 ahsh *nawr*-yu su-si-maw-*keh*-ti   *Aš noriu susimokėti*
 sah-skai-tah   *sąskaitą.*

Requests & Complaints

Please wake me up at ...
    prah-shom mah-na pah-*zhah*-
    din-ti ...
                       Prašom mane pažadinti ...

The room needs to be cleaned.
    ray-*keh*-tu *kahm*-bah-ri ish-
    vah-*lee*-ti   *Reikėtų kambarį išvalyti.*

Please change the sheets.
    prah-shom pah-*kays*-ti
    pah-*klaw*-das   *Prašom pakeisti paklodes.*

I can't open the window.
    ahsh na-gahl-*yu* ah-ti-dah-*ree*-ti *Aš negaliu atidaryti*
    lahn-gaw   *lango.*

I've locked myself out of my room.
    ahsh a-su ne-*tee*-chah uzh-si- *Aš esu netyčia užsitrenkęs*
    tran-kas du-*ris*   *duris.*

The toilet won't flush.
    ish-veah-tehs vahn-*du*-aw   *Išvietės vanduo*
    na-nu-si-*lay*-jah   *nenusileidžia.*

I don't like this room.
    mahn shi-tahs *kahm*-bah-rees *Man šitas kambarys*
    na-pah-*tin*-kah   *nepatinka.*

It's too ... here.	cha par-na-*leeg* ...	*Čia pernelyg ...*
cold	*shahl*-tah	*šalta*
dark	tahm-*su*	*tamsu*
expensive	brahn-*gu*	*brangu*
hot	*kahrsh*-tah	*karšta*
noisy	truksh-*min*-gah	*triukšminga*

Laundry

Where can I have my things ...?	kur *gah*-li-mah ah-ti-*du-aw*-ti *daik*-tus ...?	*Kur galima atiduoti daiktus ...?*
dry-cleaned	ish-vah-*lee*-ti	*išvalyti*
pressed	ish-*lee*-gin-ti	*išlyginti*
washed	ish-*skahlp*-ti	*išskalbti*

I need my things ...	mah-*naw* daik-*tai* mahn bus ray-kah-*lin*-gi ...	*Mano daiktai man bus reikalingi ...*
today	shan-*deahn*	*šiandien*
tomorrow	ree-*toy*	*rytoj*
the day after tomorrow	paw-*reet*	*poryt*

Please remove this stain.	*prah*-shom ish-*im*-ti shah *deh*-ma	*Prašom išimti šią dėmę.*
This isn't mine.	tai ne *mah*-naw *daik*-tahs	*Tai ne mano daiktas.*

Useful Words

air-conditioning	kon-dits-yo-*neahr*-yus	*kondicionierius*
balcony	bahl-*kon*-ahs	*balkonas*
bathroom	prow-*seek*-lah	*prausykla*
bed	*law*-vah	*lova*
bill	*sah*-skai-tah	*sąskaita*
blanket	vil-*naw*-neh *ahnt*-klaw-deh	*vilnonė antklodė*
chair	keh-*deh*	*kėdė*
dark	tahm-*su*	*tamsu*
dirty	na-shvah-*ru*	*nešvaru*
electricity	al-ak-trah	*elektra*
fan	veh-sin-*tu*-vahs	*vėsintuvas*
heater	*shil*-dee-mahs	*šildymas*

key	*rahk*-tahs	raktas
lift (elevator)	*lif*-tahs	liftas
light bulb	*lam*-pah	lempa
lock (n)	uzh-*rahk*-tahs	užraktas
mattress	maht-*raht*-sahs	matracas
pillow	*pah*-gahl-veh	pagalvė
plug (basin)	*kahmsh*-tis	kamštis
	prows-*tu*-vwi	praustuvui
plug (bath)	*kahmsh*-tis *vawn*-yay	kamštis voniai
quiet	tee-*lah*	tyla
room	*kahm*-bah-rees	kambarys
shower	*du*-shahs	dušas
soap	*mwi*-lahs	muilas
suitcase	lah-gah-*mi*-nahs	lagaminas
toilet	tu-ah-*lat*-ahs	tualetas
toilet paper	tu-ah-*lat*-aw	tualeto popierius
	paw-peahr-yus	
towel	*rahnk*-shlu-aws-tis	rankšluostis
water	vahn-*du*-aw	vanduo
hot/cold water	*kahrsh*-tahs/*shahl*-tahs	karštas/šaltas
	vahn-*du*-aw	vanduo
window	*lahn*-gahs	langas

AROUND TOWN

How do I get	*prah*-shom	Prašom
to the ...?	pah-sah-*kee*-ti	pasakyti,
	kaip pah-*tak*-ti i ...?	kaip patekti į ...?
art gallery	*man*-aw gah-*la*-ri-yah	meno galeriją
cinema	*ki*-nah	kiną
exhibition	*pah*-raw-dah	parodą
museum	mu-*zeah*-yu	muziejų
stadium	stah-di-*yo*-nah	stadijoną
university	u-ni-var-si-*tat*-ah	universitetą
zoo	zaw-*log*-i-yaws *saw*-dah	zoologijos sodą

I'm looking for the ...   ahsh *yeahsh*-kow ...   *Aš ieškau ...*

art gallery	*man*-aw gah-*la*-ri-yaws	*meno galerijos*
barber/	kir-*peek*-laws	*kirpyklos*
hairdresser		
church	bahzh-*nee*-chaws	*bažnyčios*
city centre	*meahs*-taw *tsan*-traw	*miesto centro*
currency	vah-*lyu*-taws	*valiutos*
exchange		
outlet	kay-*teek*-laws	*keityklos*
embassy	ahm-bah-*sah*-daws	*ambasados*
hotel	*veahsh*-buch-aw	*viešbučio*
market	*tur*-gows	*turgaus*
museum	mu-*zeah*-yows	*muziejaus*
old city	san-*ah*-meahs-chaw	*senamiesčio*
police	paw-*lit*-si-yaws	*policijos*
post office	*pahsh*-taw	*pašto*
public toilet	tu-ah-*lat*-aw	*tualeto*
telephone	te-le-*fo*-naw-	*telefono-*
centre	ow-to-*mah*-taw	*automato*
tourist	tu-*ris*-too	*turistų*
information	in-for-*mah*-tsi-yaws	*informacijos*
office	*byoo*-raw	*biuro*

At the Bank

The litas is now the only legal tender in the country. Money can be exchanged at banks and at street kiosks dealing exclusively in money exchange. Cash advances on major credit cards are available from some banks in the major towns.

I want to exchange some money/
travellers cheques.

    ahsh *nawr*-yu ish-*kays*-ti   *Aš noriu iškeisti pinigų/*
    pi-ni-*goo*/kal-ay-*vi*-new chak-ew   *keleivinių čekių.*

What's the exchange rate?

    kawks ee-*rah kur*-sahs?   *Koks yra kursas?*

How many litas per ...?	keahk *li*-too uzh ...?	*Kiek litų už ...?*
Australian dollar	ows-*trah*-li-yaws *do*-la-ri	*Australijos dolerį*
Canadian dollar	kah-*nah*-daws *do*-la-ri	*Kanados dolerį*
English pound	ahn-gloo svah-rah	*Anglų svarą*
German mark	vaw-keah-*chew* *mahr*-ka	*Vokiečių markę*
US dollar	ah-*ma*-ri-kaws *do*-la-ri	*Amerikos dolerį*

bank notes	bahnk-*naw*-tai	*banknotai*
cashier	*kah*-si-nin-kahs	*kasininkas*
coins	maw-*nat*-aws	*monetos*
credit card	kra-*di*-taw kor-*ta*-leh	*kredito kortelė*
exchange	ish-kay-*ti*-mahs	*iškeitimas*

At the Post Office

I'd like to send a ...	ahsh naw-*reh*-chow pah-*syoos*-ti ...	*Aš norėčiau pasiųsti ...*
fax	*fahk*-sah	*faksą*
(registered) letter	(rag-is-*tru*-aw-tah) laish-kah	*(registruotą) laišką*
postcard	aht-vi-*ru*-kah	*atviruką*
parcel	*syun*-ti-ni pah-*kat*-ah	*siuntinį* (large) *paketą* (small)
telegram	te-le-*grah*-mah	*telegramą*

Where's the poste restante counter?
    kur ish-du-aw-dah-*mi* laish-kai   *Kur išduodami laiškai*
    i-ki pah-ray-kah-*lah*-vi-maw?   *iki pareikalavimo?*
Are there any letters for me?
    ahr mahn ee-*rah* laish-koo?   *Ar man yra laiškų?*
Here's my passport.
    shtai mah-naw *pah*-sahs   *Štai mano pasas.*

I'd like some stamps.

    naw-*reh*-chow nu-*pirk*-ti   *Norėčiau nupirkti*
    pahsh-taw zhank-*loo*   *pašto ženklų.*

How much is the postage?

    keahk kai-*nu-aw*-yah   *Kiek kainuoja*
    pahsh-taw zhank-*lai?*   *pašto ženklai?*

aerogram	ah-eh-raw-grah-*mah*	*aerograma*
airmail	*aw*-raw pahsh-*tu*	*oro paštu*
envelope	*vaw*-kahs	*vokas*
express mail	aks-*pras pahsh*-tahs	*ekspres paštas*
mail box	*pahsh*-taw deh-*zheh*	*pašto dėžė*
registered mail	rag-is-*tru-aw*-tahs *pahsh*-tahs	*registruotas paštas*
surface mail	pah-prahs-*tu* pahsh-*tu*	*paprastu paštu*

Telephone & Internet

Would you please put a
call through to ...?

    prah-shom pri-im-ti uzh-*sah*-kee-mah *paw*-kahl-byui su ...   *Prašom priimti užsakymą pokalbiui su ...*

How much do you charge for a
three-minute call?

    keahk kai-*nu-aw*-yah tri-*yoo* mi-*nu*-chew *paw*-kahl-bis?   *Kiek kainuoja trijų minučių pokalbis?*

How much does each
extra minute cost?

    keahk kai-*nu-aw*-yah uzh keahk-*veah*-nah pri-*deh*-ti-na mi-*nu*-ta?   *Kiek kainuoja už kiekvieną pridėtinę minutę?*

It's engaged.

    uzh-im-tah   *Užimta.*

I've been cut off.

    kahzh-*kahs* mus *ish*-yun-geh   *Kažkas mus išjungė.*

telephone	te-le-*fo*-nahs	*telefonas*
telephone number	te-le-*fo*-naw nu-ma-ris	*telefono numeris*
telephone booth	te-le-*fo*-naw boo-*da*-leh	*telefono būdelė*

I need to get access to the Internet.
mahn *rayk*-yah preah
in-ter-*nat*-aw pri-*ay*-ti

Man reikia prie interneto prieiti.

I need to check my email.
mahn *rayk*-yah pah-si-*tik*-rin-ti
al-ak-*tron*-i-ni *pahsh*-tah

Man reikia pasitikrinti elektronini paštą.

Making a Phone Call

Hello.	ahl-*yo*	*Alio.*
I'd like to speak to ...	naw-*reh*-chow pah-kahl-*beh*-ti su ...	*Norėčiau pakalbėti su ...*
Please wait a minute.	*prah*-shom pah-*lowk*-ti mi-nu-*teh*-la	*Prašom palaukti minutėlę*
Speaking!	klow-*sow!*	*Klausau!* (lit: I'm-listening)
This is Tom.	cha *to*-mahs	*Čia Tomas.*

Sightseeing

Do you have a guidebook/local map?
ahr yoos *tu*-ri-ta tu-*ris*-too
vah-*daw*-vah/*veah*-ti-ni
zham-*eh*-lah-pi?

Ar jūs turite turisų vadovą/vietinį žemėlapį?

What are the main attractions?
kawk-yaws ee-rah
pah-grin-*din*-ehs
ah-*trahk*-tsi-yaws?

Kokios yra pagrindinės atrakcijos?

What's that?
kahs tahs?

Kas tas?

How old is it?
    kal-*in*-tah-ma *shimt*-mat-ee-ya   *Kelintame šimtmetyje*
    yis bu-vaw pah-stah-*tee*-tahs?   *jis buvo pastatytas?*
                              (lit: what century
                                  it was built?)

Can I take photographs?
    ahr *lay*-jah-mah fo-to-grah-   *Ar leidžiama fotografuoti?*
    fu-aw-ti?

What time does it open/close?
    kal-*in*-tah *vah*-lahn-dah   *Kelintą valandą*
    aht-si-*dah*-raw/uzh-si-*dah*-raw?   *atsidaro/užsidaro?*

Useful Words

ancient	san-*aw*-vin-is	*senovinis*
archaeological	ar-he-o-*lo*-gin-is	*archeologinis*
building	*pah*-stah-tahs	*pastatas*
castle	pil-*is*	*pilis*
cathedral	*kah*-tad-rah	*katedra*
cemetery	*kah*-pi-nehs	*kapinės*
church	bahzh-*nee*-chah	*bažnyčia*
concert hall	*kon*-tsar-too *sah*-leh	*koncertų salė*
library	bib-*lyo*-tak-ah	*biblioteka*
main square	pah-grin-*di*-neh	*pagrindinė*
	meahs-taw *aiksh*-teh	*miesto aikštė*
monastery	veah-nu-*aw*-*lee*-nahs	*vienuolynas*
monument	pah-*mink*-lahs	*paminklas*
national park	nah-tsyo-*nah*-li-nis	*nacionalinis*
	pahr-kahs	*parkas*
opera house	o-per-aws *roo*-mai	*operos rūmai*
park	*pahr*-kahs	*parkas*
parliament	*say*-maw *roo*-mai	*seimo rūmai*
ruins	groo-*veh*-say	*griuvėsiai*
stadium	stah-di-*yon*-ahs	*stadijonas*
statues	stah-*tu*-laws	*statulos*
synagogue	si-nah-*gog*-ah	*sinagoga*
university	u-ni-var-si-*tat*-ahs	*universitetas*

FOLK SONGS

Lithuanians have many thousands of folk songs in their folkloric treasure chest, most stemming from pre-Christian times. Here is but one of them, heard to be sung by the crowd during a pro-independence demonstration. The song is very old, while the refrain is a popular modern addition:

Augo sode klevelis,	A maple in the garden grew,
Augo sode žaliasai,	A green one in the garden grew,
Po tuo klevu,	Under the maple,
po žaliuoju,	under the green one,
Gul bernelis jaunasai.	Lay a young man sleeping.
(Last 2 lines twice)	

Refrain:
Viens, du, graži Lietuva,	One, two, beautiful Lithuania,
Kaip gėlelė žydi visada.	Like a flower, always in bloom.
- Nepapūski, vėjeli,	"Do not blow, o wind,
Nepapūski, šiaurusai,	Do not blow, o northern one,
Nepajudink klevo šaką,	Do not move the maple branch,
Nepabudink bernelio.	Do not waken the young man."
Ir papūtė vėjelis,	But the wind did blow,
Ir papūtė šiaurusai,	But the northern one did blow,
Pajudino klevo šaką,	And it moved the maple branch,
Pabudino bernelį.	And it woke the young man up.
- Kelkis, kelkis, berneli,	"Get up, get up, o young man,
Gana ilgai miegoti:	You've been sleeping long enough
Laikas stoti tau į kovą,	It's time for you to go to battle,
Ginti laisvę Lietuvos.	To defend the freedom of Lithuania."

Going Out

What's there to do in the evenings?

kur gah-*leh*-tu-ma ish-*ay*-ti
vah-kah-*rais*?

*Kur galėtume išeiti
vakarais?*

Are there any discos?

ahr ee-*rah* dis-ko-*tak*-oo?

Ar yra diskotekų?

Are there places where you can hear
local folk music?

ahr ee-*rah veah*-too kur boo-too
gah-li-mah ish-*girs*-ti lyow-deahs
mu-zi-kaws?

*Ar yra vietų kur būtų
galima išgirsti liaudies
muzikos?*

How much is it to get in?

keahk kai-*nu-aw*-yah
i-eh-*yi*-mahs?

*Kiek kainuoja
įėjimas?*

cinema	*ki*-nahs	*kinas*
concert	*kon*-tser-tahs	*koncertas*
disco	dis-ko-*tak*-ahs	*diskotekas*
jazz	*jyah*-zahs	*džiazas*
nightclub	nahk-*ti*-nis *klub*-ahs	*naktinis klubas*
rock	*rok*-ahs	*rokas*
theatre	teh-*aht*-rahs	*teatras*

PAPERWORK

name	*vahr*-dahs	*vardas*
address	*ahd*-ras-ahs	*adresas*
age	*mat*-ai	*metai*
border	*seah*-nah	*siena*
business trip	ko-mahn-di-*ru*-aw-teh	*komandiruotė*
citizenship	pil-eah-*tee*-beh	*pilietybė*
customs	*mwi*-ti-neh	*muitinė*
customs	*mwi*-ti-nehs	*muitinės*
declaration	dak-lah-*rah*-tsi-yah	*deklaracija*
date of birth	gi-*mi*-maw dah-*tah*	*gimimo data*
driving licence	vai-*ru*-aw-taw-yaw	*vairuotojo*
	pah-zhee-*meh*-yi-mahs	*pažymėjimas*
extension of visa	*viz*-aws	*vizos*
	prah-tas-*i*-mahs	*pratęsimas*
identification	ahs-*mans*	*asmens*
	loo-di-yi-mahs	*liudijimas*
immigration	i-mi-*grah*-tsi-yah	*imigracija*
length of stay	bu-*vim*-aw *lai*-kahs	*buvimo laikas*
marital status	*sahn*-tu-aw-kin-is	*santuokinis*
	stah-tu-sahs	*statusas*
nationality	tow-*tee*-beh	*tautybė*
next of kin	ahr-tim-*yow*-sas	*artimiausias*
	shay-*maws* nah-*rees*	*šeimos narys*
passport number	*pahs*-aw *nu*-ma-ris	*paso numeris*
passport	*pahs*-ahs	*pasas*
place of birth	gi-*mi*-maw veah-*tah*	*gimimo vieta*
profession	pro-*fas*-i-yah	*profesija*
purpose of trip	kal-*yaw*-nehs *tiks*-lahs	*kelionės tikslas*
religion	re-*lig*-i-yah	*religija*
sex	lee-*tis*	*lytis*
tourist trip	tu-*ris*-ti-neh kal-*yaw*-neh	*turistinė kelionė*
visa	*viz*-ah	*viza*

I have only my personal possessions,
nothing dutiable.

    ahsh tik tur-yu ahs-*man*-ish-kus   *Aš tik turiu asmeniškus*
    daik-tus *neah*-kaw ahp-*mwi*-ti-   *daiktus, nieko*
    nah-maw   *apmuitinamo.*

What duty must I pay?

    kaw-ki *mwi*-tah ahsh tur-yu   *Kokį muitą aš turiu*
    maw-*keh*-ti?   *mokėti?*

I have an export
licence for these things.

    ahsh tur-yu lay-*di*-mah   *Aš turiu leidimą*
    ish-*vash*-ti   *išvežti.*

Are these things dutiable?

    ahr sheah daik-*tai*   *Ar šie daiktai*
    ahp-*mwi*-tin-ah-mi?   *apmuitinami?*

I have paid the duty.

    ahsh su-maw-*keh*-yow   *Aš sumokėjau*
    mwi-tah   *muitą.*

SONG TO FREEDOM

On 3 June 1988, a huge rally of Lithuanian demonstrators gathered to support a newly-formed citizens' movement, *Sajūdis*, in its bid to persuade the next Communist Party Conference to grant Lithuania greater national autonomy. That demonstration resulted in the old national flag, banned for 50 years, being reinstated and hoisted on the tower of Gediminas Castle. Further passionate but peaceful demonstrations followed, where people sang the old folk songs which gave them a feeling of unity of purpose. However, the Soviets continued to show a reluctance to grant too many freedoms. After a human chain pro-independence demonstration by nearly two million singing Baltic people on 23 August 1989, President Gorbachev still warned that a split from the Soviet Union would not be tolerated.

Finally on 11 March 1990, in defiance of the Soviets, the Lithuanian Parliament itself declared the restoration of Lithuania's independence.

This was too much for the Soviets and tanks were sent in to intimidate the people. Helicopters scattered leaflets urging them to continue to obey the Soviet Constitution. In a further effort to break the people's will, the Soviets imposed a devastating economic blockade. On the night of Sunday, 13 January 1991, as people held hands and sang while trying to bar the way of Soviet tanks rolling in to capture the TV tower in Vilnius, 14 defenceless Lithuanians were crushed by the tanks. Eventually, by 1993, a complete withdrawal of Soviet troops was achieved as the last Russian soldier left Lithuania.

LITHUANIAN

IN THE COUNTRY

The Lithuanian countryside is spectacular in summer. There's no dangerous wildlife, apart from the possibility of ticks. You may come across the occasional feral pig in some areas. The country is dotted with sights of historic significance and beauty. As always, a knowledgeable guide of the local area adds great value to any outing.

Weather

What's the weather forecast for today/tomorrow?	kaw-*kyah* aw-raw prog-*no*-zeh shan-*deah*-nai/reet-*deah*-nai?	*Kokia oro prognozė šiandienai/rytdienai?*
It's going to (be) ...	bus ...	*Bus ...*
cloudy	dab-as-*u*-aw-tah	*debesuota*
cold	*shahl*-tah	*šalta*
cool	veh-*su*	*vėsu*
drizzly	dulks-*naw*-tah	*dulksnota*
foggy	*tirsh*-taw *roo*-kaw	*tiršto rūko*
hail	*krush*-ah	*kruša*
hot	*kahrsh*-tah	*karšta*
icy	lad-*in*-gahs *aw*-rahs	*ledingas oras*
rain	leah-*tows*	*lietaus*
snow	*sneah*-gaw	*sniego*
sunny	sow-*leh*-tah	*saulėta*
warm	*shil*-tah	*šilta*
windy	veh-*yu*-aw-tah	*vėjuota*

Directions

Is it far?	ahr taw-*li*?	*Ar toli?*
Can I get there on ...?	ahr veah-*taw*-veh pri-*ay*-nah-mah ...?	*Ar vietovė prieinama ...?*
bike	*dvi*-rah-chu	*dviračiu*
foot	pehs-*chaw*-mis	*pėsčiomis*
horseback	ahrk-*lays*	*arkliais*

north	show-*reh*	*šiaurė*
south	*peah*-toos	*pietūs*
east	ree-*tai*	*rytai*
west	vah-kah-*rai*	*vakarai*

Animals, Birds & Insects

bird	*powksh*-tis	*paukštis*
boar	*shar*-nahs	*šernas*
butterfly	dru-*gal*-is	*drugelis*
cat	kah-*teh*	*katė*
chicken (hen)	vish-*tah*	*višta*
cow	*kahr*-veh	*karvė*
deer	*stir*-nah	*stirna*
dog	shu-aw	*šuo*
domestic animal	nah-*mi*-nis gee-vu-*lees*	*naminis gyvulys*
duck	*ahn*-tis	*antis*
elk	*breah*-dis	*briedis*
fish	zhu-*vis*	*žuvis*
fox	*lah*-peh	*lapė*
frog	vahr-*leh*	*varlė*
goat	awzh-*kah*	*ožka*
hare	*kish*-kis	*kiškis*
horse	ahrk-*lees*	*arklys*
insect	vahbz-*dees*	*vabzdys*
lynx	*loo*-shis	*lūšis*
midges	mah-shah-*lai*	*mašalai*
mosquito	u-*aw*-das	*uodas*
otter	ood-*rah*	*ūdra*
pigeon	bah-*lahn*-dis	*balandis*
pig	*kyow*-leh	*kiaulė*
seagull	zhuv-*ehd*-rah	*žuvėdra*
sheep	ah-*vis*	*avis*
snake	gee-*vah*-teh	*gyvatė*
spider	*vaw*-rahs	*voras*
squirrel	*vaw*-va-reh	*voverė*
stork	*gahn*-drahs	*gandras*
swan	*gul*-beh	*gulbė*
tick	*ar*-keh	*erkė*
wild animal	zhveh-*ris*	*žvėris*

Plants

(edible) berry	(*vahl*-gaw-mah)	*(valgoma)*
	u-*aw*-gah	*uoga*
blossom	*zheah*-dahs	*žiedas*
bush (shrub)	*kroo*-mahs	*krūmas*
fir	pu-*shis*	*pušis*
flower	geh-*leh*	*gėlė*
grass	zhaw-*leh*	*žolė*
leaf	*lah*-pahs	*lapas*
mushroom	*gree*-bahs	*grybas*
oak	ah-zhu-*aw*-lahs	*ažuolas*
plant	*ow*-gah-lahs	*augalas*
rue	*roo*-ta	*rūta*
spruce	*ag*-leh	*eglė*
tree	*mad*-is	*medis*
woods/forest	*mish*-kahs	*miškas*

WE LOVE RUE, YES IT'S TRUE

If Lithuania has a national plant, it's the rue, an aromatic shrub with small, yellow flowers. The evergreen leaf of the rue has enough tradition and folk symbolism associated with it to fill this whole book. It plays a major role in many aspects of life, including weddings, celebrations, songs and poetry.

Camping

We'd like to go hiking/camping.

mas naw-*reh*-tu-ma ish-kee-*low*-ti/staw-veek-*low*-ti	*Mes norėtume iškylauti/ stovyklauti.*

Where would you suggest?

kur yoos pah-*tahr*-tu-met?	*Kur jūs patartumėt?*

Are we allowed to camp here?

ahr *gah*-li-mah cha staw-veek-*low*-ti?	*Ar galima čia stovyklauti?*

Am I allowed to light a fire?

    ahr *gah*-li-mah uzh-*kur*-ti *ug*-ni?   *Ar galima užkurti ugnį?*

Can we fish here?

    ahr *gah*-li-mah cha zhu-*vow*-ti?   *Ar galima čia žuvauti?*

Where can I buy a fishing rod?

    kur *gah*-li-mah *pirk*-ti   *Kur galima pirkti*
    mash-ka-ra   *meškerę?*

camping	*kam*-pin-gahs	*kempingas*
axe	*kir*-vis	*kirvis*
backpack	kup-*rin*-eh	*kuprinė*
bottle opener	ah-ti-dah-ree-*tu*-vahs	*atidarytuvas*
	bu-tal-yui	*buteliui*
can opener	kon-*sar*-voo deh-zhu-tehs	*konservų dėžutės*
	ah-ti-dah-ree-*tu*-vahs	*atidarytuvas*
compass	*kom*-pah-sahs	*kompasas*
firewood	*mahl*-kaws *low*-zhwi	*malkos laužui*
gas cylinder	*du*-yoo bon-*kal*-eh	*dujų bonkelė*
insect repellent	vahbz-*jus* aht-*bai*-dahn-ti	*vabzdžius*
	preah-maw-neh	*atbaidanti*
		priemonė
matches	dak-*tu*-kai	*degtukai*
penknife	pay-*lyu*-kahs	*peiliukas*
rope	*vir*-veh	*virvė*
sleeping bag	*meahg*-mai-shis	*miegmaišis*
stove	kraws-*nal*-eh	*krosnelė*
tent	pah-lah-*pin*-eh	*palapinė*
tent pegs	kawl-*yu*-kai	*kuoliukai*
	pah-lah-*pin*-ay	*palapinei*
water bottle	vahn-*dans bu*-tal-is	*vandens butelis*

Useful Words

beach	*plazh*-ahs	pliažas
bridge	*til*-tahs	tiltas
castle mound	pil-*yah*-kahl-nis	piliakalnis
cemetery	*kah*-pin-ehs	kapinės
farm	*oo*-kis	ūkis
forest	*mish*-kahs	miškas
harbour	u-*aws*-tahs	uostas
hill	*kahl*-nahs	kalnas
lake	*azh*-a-rahs	ežeras
map	zham-*eh*-lah-pis	žemėlapis
national park	nah-tsyon-*ah*-li-nis	nacionalinis
	pahr-kahs	parkas
river	u-*peh*	upė
road	*kal*-yahs	kelias
sand dune	*kaw*-pah	kopa
scenery	*vaiz*-dahs	vaizdas
sea	*yoo*-rah	jūra
town	*meahs*-tahs	miestas
track	*tah*-kahs	takas
valley	sleh-*nees*	slėnys
village	*kai*-mahs	kaimas
waterfall	krawk-*lees*	krioklys

CREEPY CRAWLIES

There's not much in the way of insect repellents to be found in Vilnius pharmacies or shops dealing in hygiene products. Travellers are advised to carry their own roll-on repellent, as midges are prevalent and these annoying little creatures can spoil your summer holiday.

LITHUANIAN

FOOD

Traditional Lithuanian food consists of simple dishes based on potato, milk, pork or poultry and fresh fish, often served with black rye bread. Meat was often smoked as a common means of preservation. Modern Lithuanian cuisine has developed out of these traditions. Much of the especially tasty and exotic fare is reserved for festive occasions and events. These delectable dishes are not generally available in the cities where the more familiar, inexpensive, easier to prepare food of Western cafes greets the tourist. This picture is changing slowly, however, with some restaurants offering style, service and fine traditional food.

The staple food is dark brown rye bread, which is eaten practically at every meal. For breakfast Lithuanians traditionally prefer pickled herring (*silkė*) with black rye bread. Breakfast cereals are still something of a novelty to many. After bread, salted or smoked pork dishes are second in importance. An essential dairy food is a hard cottage cheese with caraway. There are lots of traditional potato dishes, of which *cepelinai* ('zeppelins') take top place and *kugelis* ('cannon ball') takes second. Pancakes, fresh fish, pickled herrings, smoked eels, mushrooms, beetroot and cabbage are the other traditional staples.

Where's the nearest ...?	kur ahr-tim-yow-sa/as ...?	*Kur artim-iausia/as ...?* (f/m)
cafe	kah-*vi*-neh	*kavinė* (f)
dining room	vahl-*geek*-lah	*valgykla* (f)
fast-food outlet	uzh-kahn-*din*-eh	*užkandinė* (f)
restaurant	ras-to-*rah*-nahs	*restoranas* (m)
Let's have lunch!	*ay*-kim pah-peah-*tow*-ti!	*Eikim papietauti!*

At the Restaurant

A table for ..., please.
stah-lah ... prah-*show* — Stalą ..., prašau.

May I see the menu, please?
ahr gah-*leh*-chow gow-ti — Ar galėčiau gauti
man-*yew* prah-*show*? — meniu prašau?

I'd like the set lunch.
ahsh naw-*reh*-chow — Aš norėčiau
nu-stah-*tee*-tah *lan*-chah — nustatytą lenčą.

Do you have the menu in English?
ahr yoos *tu*-ri-ta man-*yew* — Ar jūs turite meniu
ahn-glish-kai? — angliškai?

I'd like to try that.
ahsh naw-*reh*-chow — Aš norėčiau
ish-bahn-*dee*-ti taw — išbandyti to.

This isn't my order.
ahsh taw na-uzh-sah-*kyow* — Aš to neužsakiau.

Is service included in the bill?
ahr pah-tahr-*nah*-vi-mahs — Ar patarnavimas
i-*skai*-taw-mahs sah-skai-taw-ya? — įskaitomas sąskaitoje?

Useful Words

bill	sah-skai-*tah*	sąskaita
bottle	*bu*-tal-is	butelis
butter	*sveahs*-tahs	sviestas
coffeepot	kah-vi-*nu*-kahs	kavinukas
cup	pu-aw-*du*-kahs	puodukas
drinks/beverages	*geh*-ri-mai	gėrimai
fork	shah-*kut*-eh	šakutė
glass	stik-*lin*-eh	stiklinė
knife	*pay*-lis	peilis
meal/dish	*vahl*-gis	valgis
menu	man-*yew*	meniu
napkin	sar-*vat*-eh	servetė
pepper	pip-*i*-rai	pipirai
plate	lehksh-*teh*	lėkštė

salt	*drus*-kah	*druska*
serviette	sar-vat-*eh*-leh	*servetėlė*
spoon	*showksh*-tahs	*šaukštas*
Waiter!	pah-dah-*veh*-yah!	*Padavėja!* (f)
	pah-dah-*veh*-yow!	*Padavėjau!* (m)

Vegetarian Meals

I don't eat ...	ahsh na-*vahl*-gow ...	*Aš nevalgau ...*
meat	*meh*-sish-kaw	*mėsiško*
dairy products	*peah*-nish-kaw	*pieniško*

Breakfast & Lunch

bacon	bak-*on*-ahs	*bekonas*
boiled eggs	*vir*-tahs kyow-*shin*-is	*virtas kiaušinis*
bread	*du*-aw-nah	*duona*
butter	*sveahs*-tahs	*sviestas*
cheese	*soo*-ris	*sūris*
coffee	kah-*vah*	*kava*
cottage cheese	*vahrsh*-keh	*varškė*
eggs	kyow-*shin*-ay	*kiaušiniai*
fried eggs	*kap*-ti kyow-*shin*-ay	*kepti kiaušiniai*
kefir (a kind of low-fat natural yoghurt)	ka-*fee*-rahs	*kefyras*
milk	*peah*-nahs	*pienas*
oatmeal porridge	ah-vi-zhoo *kaw*-sheh	*avižų košė*
omelette	om-*lat*-ahs	*omletas*
pancakes	blee-*nal*-ay/sklin-jay	*blyneliai/ sklindžiai*
sandwiches	su-mush-*tin*-ay	*sumuštiniai*
sausages	dash-*ral*-ehs	*dešrelės*
scrambled eggs	kyow-shin-*eah*-neh	*kiaušinienė*
semolina porridge	*mah*-noo *kaw*-sheh	*manų košė*
tea	ahr-bah-*tah*	*arbata*

LITHUANIAN

MENU DECODER

Soup

kopūstų sriuba	kaw-*poos*-too sru-*bah*	cabbage soup
lietuviški barščiai su grybais	leah-*tu*-vish-ki *bahrsh*-chay su *gree*-bais	Lithuanian borscht with mushrooms
šaltibarščiai	shahl-*ti*-barsh-chay	beetroot and sour cream soup (cold)
žirnelių sriuba	zhir-*na*-lew sru-*bah*	green pea soup

Meat

jautiena su svogūnais	yow-*teah*-nah su svaw-*goo*-nais	beef with onions
mėsos asorti	meh-*saws*-ah-sor-*tee*	meat assortment
bifšteksas	bif-*shtak*-ahs	beefsteak
liežuvis drebučiuose	leah-*zhu*-vis drab-*uch*-aw-sa	jellied ox tongue
kotlietai	*kot*-leah-tai	rissoles
kiaulienos muštinis su lietuvišku įdaru	kyow-*leah*-naws mush-*ti*-nis su leah-*tu*-vish-ku *i*-dah-ru	stuffed pork
karbonadas veršiena su morkomis arba su grybais	kahr-bon-*ah*-dahs var-*sheah*-nah su *mor*-kaw-mis ahr-bah su *gree*-bais	breaded pork chop veal with carrots or mushrooms
cepelinai	tsap-al-*in*-ai	boiled potato dumplings stuffed with meat and covered with bacon, cream and butter sauce
kaldūnai	kahl-*doo*-nai	Lithuanian dim sims
skilandis	ski-*lahn*-dis	pork sausage

MENU DECODER

Seafood

juodi/raudoni ikrai	yu-aw-*di*/ row-daw-*ni ik*-rai	black/ red caviar
žuvies asorti	zhu-*veahs* ah-sor-*tee*	fish assortment
silkė lietuviškai/ rusiškai	*sil*-keh leah-*tu*-vish-kai/ *rus*-ish-kai	herring Lithuanian/ Russian style
rūkytas ungurys	roo-*kee*-tahs un-gu-*rees*	smoked eel
rūkytas eršketas	roo-*kee*-tahs arsh-*kat*-ahs	smoked white sturgeon
kalmarai tešloje	kahl-*mah*-rai *tash*-law-ya	calamari (in dough)
midijos su ryžiais	*mi*-di-yaws su *ree*-zhays	mussels with rice

Poultry & Game

vištos kojelė	*vish*-taws kaw-*yal*-eh	chicken leg
vištienos kotletas su razinomis	vish-*teah*-naws *kot*-lat-ahssu rah-*zi*-naw-mis	chicken cutlet with raisins
įdarytas vištienos kotletas	i-dah-*ree*-tahs vish-*teah*-naws *kot*-lat-ahs	stuffed chicken cutlet
vištienos sultinys	vish-*teah*-naws sul-ti-*nees*	chicken bouillon

LITHUANIAN

MENU DECODER

Salads

burokėlių salotos	bu-raw-*keh*-lew sah-*law*-taws	baby beetroot salad
pupelių salotos	pu-*pal*-yew sah-*law*-taws	bean salad
morkų salotos su slyvomis	*mor*-koo sah-*law*-taws su *slee*-vaw-mis	carrot and plum salad
lietuviškos salotos su kumpiu	leah-*tu*-vish-kaws sah-*law*-taws su *kum*-pyu	ham salad
apelsinų salotos su alyvuogemis	ah-pal-*si*-noo sah-*law*-taws su ah-*leev*-u-aw-geh-mis	orange and olive salad
krevečių salotos	krav-*ach*-ew sah-*law*-taws	shrimp salad
pomidorų salotos	po-mi-*daw*-roo sah-*law*-taws	tomato salad

Meat

beef	yow-*teah*-nah	*jautiena*
ham	*kum*-pis	*kumpis*
lamb	a-*reah*-nah	*ėriena*
mutton	ah-*veah*-nah	*aviena*
pork	kyow-*leah*-nah	*kiauliena*
veal	var-*sheah*-nah	*veršiena*

Seafood

cod	*man*-keh	*menkė*
crab	*krah*-bahs	*krabas*
crawfish/crayfish	*yoo*-raws veh-*zhay*	*jūros vėžiai*
eel	un-gu-*rees*	*ungurys*
herring	*sil*-keh	*silkė*
lobster	*aw*-mah-rahs	*omaras*
shellfish	maw-*lyus*-kai	*moliuskai*
mussels	dvi-*gal*-dehs *kryowk*-lehs	*dvigeldės kriauklės*
oysters	*ows*-trehs	*austrės*
perch	*star*-kahs	*sterkas*
pike	lee-dak-*ah*	*lydeka*
plaice	*plaksh*-neh	*plekšnė*
salmon	lah-shi-*shah*	*lašiša*
shrimp	vehzh-*lyu*-kahs	*vėžiukas*
sturgeon	arsh-*kat*-ahs	*eršketas*
trout	u-*peh*-tah-kis	*upėtakis*

Poultry & Game

chicken	vish-*teah*-nah	*vištiena*
duck	ahn-*teah*-nah	*antiena*
goose	zha-*seah*-nah	*žąsiena*
hare	*kish*-kis	*kiškis*
rabbit	*zwi*-kis	*zuikis*
turkey	kah-lah-*ku*-tahs	*kalakutas*
wild pig	*shar*-nahs	*šernas*

LITHUANIAN

Vegetables

beans	*pu*-paws	*pupos*
beetroot	bu-raw-*keh*-lay	*burokėliai*
cabbage	ko-*poos*-tai	*kopūstai*
carrots	*mor*-kaws	*morkos*
cauliflower	kah-lahf-*yaw*-rai	*kalafiorai*
celery	sah-*leah*-rahs	*salieras*
cucumbers	ah-*gur*-kai	*agurkai*
green beans	*pu*-paws	*pupos*
lentils	*la*-shay	*lęšiai*
lettuce	sah-*law*-taws	*salotos*
mushrooms	*gree*-bai	*grybai*
onions	svo-*goo*-nai	*svogūnai*
peas	zhir-*nal*-ay	*žirneliai*
pepper	pi-*pi*-rai	*pipirai*
potatoes	*bul*-vehs	*bulvės*
radishes	ri-di-*keh*-lay/ri-*di*-kai	*ridikėliai/ridikai*
spinach	shpi-*nah*-tai	*špinatai*
tomatoes	po-mi-*daw*-rai	*pomidorai*
vegetables	dahr-*zhaw*-vehs	*daržovės*

EGGSTRAVAGANZA!

Šakotis (shah-*kaw*-tis) is a special celebration cake that looks like a yellow tree trunk with lopped branches (similar to German *Baumkuchen*). It's made with 60 eggs and is very popular for special occasions, such as weddings.

Fruit

apple	aw-baw-*lees*	*obuolys*
apricot	ahb-ri-*ko*-sahs	*abrikosas*
banana	bah-*nah*-nahs	*bananas*
bilberries	meh-*lee*-nehs	*mėlynės*
blackberries	*garv*-u-aw-gehs	*gervuogės*
cherries	*veesh*-nyaws	*vyšnios*
cranberries	*spahn*-gu-ah-lehs	*spanguolės*
fruit	*vai*-say	*vaisiai*
gooseberries	*ahg*-rahs-tai	*agrastai*
grapes	*veen*-u-aw-gehs	*vynuogės*
lemon	tsit-*ri*-nah	*citrina*
mulberries	*shilk*-maj-aw u-aw-gaws	*šilkmedžio uogos*
orange	ah-pal-*si*-nahs	*apelsinas*
peach	*par*-si-kahs	*persikas*
pear	*krow*-sheh	*kriaušė*
pineapple	ah-nah-*nah*-sahs	*ananasas*
plum	*slee*-vah	*slyva*
prune	jaw-*vin*-tah *slee*-vah	*džiovinta slyva*
raisins/sultanas	rah-*zi*-naws	*razinos*
raspberries	ah-*veah*-tehs	*avietės*
strawberries	*brahsh*-kehs	*braškės*

Desserts

fruit compote	*kom*-pot-ahs	*kompotas*
honey cake	mad-*ow*-nin-kahs	*medauninkas*
hot fudge	*karsh*-tahs	*karštas*
	sho-ko-*lah*-dahs	*šokoladas*
ice cream	lad-*ai*	*ledai*
chocolate	sho-ko-*lah*-dahs	*šokoladas*
fruit	*vai*-say	*vaisiai*
mousse	pu-*teh*-say	*putėsiai*
pastries	pee-rah-*gai*-chay	*pyragaičiai*
pastry with jelly	pee-rah-*gai*-tis	*pyragaitis*
	su zhal-*eh*	*su želė*
... with nuts	... reah-shu-*tais*	*... riešutais*

AT THE MARKET

Basics

bread	*du*-aw-nah	duona
butter	*sveahs*-tahs	sviestas
cereal	yah-*vai*-nyay	javainiai
cheese	*soo*-ris	sūris
chocolate	sho-ko-*lah*-dahs	šokoladas
eggs	kyow-*shin*-ay	kiaušiniai
flour	*mil*-tai	miltai
margarine	mahr-gah-*ri*-nahs	margarinas
marmalade	u-ah-*geah*-nah	uogienė
milk	*peah*-nahs	pienas
olive oil	praw-*vahn*-si-nis	provansinis
	ah-*leah*-yus	aliejus
pasta	*pahs*-tah	pasta
rice	*ree*-zhay	ryžiai
sugar	*tsuk*-rus	cukrus
water	van-*du-aw*	vanduo
yogurt	*yaw*-gur-tahs	jogurtas

Meat & Poultry

beef	yow-*teah*-nah	jautiena
chicken	vish-*teah*-nah	vištiena
ham	*kum*-pis	kumpis
lamb	a-*reah*-nah	ėriena
mutton	a-*veah*-nah	aviena
pork	kyow-*leah*-nah	kiauliena
turkey	kah-lah-*ku*-tahs	kalakutas
veal	var-*sheah*-nah	veršiena

Vegetables

(green) beans	*pu*-paws	pupos
beetroot	bu-raw-*keh*-lay	burokėliai
cabbage	ko-*poos*-tai	kopūstai
carrots	*mor*-kaws	morkos
cauliflower	kah-lahf-*yaw*-rai	kalafiorai
celery	sah-*leah*-rahs	salieras
cucumbers	ah-*gur*-kai	agurkai
lettuce	sah-*law*-taws	salotos
mushrooms	*gree*-bai	grybai

AT THE MARKET

onions	svo-*goo*-nai	*svogūnai*
peas	zhir-*nal*-ay	*žirneliai*
potatoes	*bul*-vehs	*bulvės*
radishes	ri-di-*keh*-lay/ri-*di*-kai	*ridikėliai/ridikai*
spinach	shpi-*nah*-tai	*špinatai*
tomatoes	po-mi-*daw*-rai	*pomidorai*
vegetables	dahr-*zhaw*-vehs	*daržovės*

Seafood

cod	*man*-keh	*menkė*
crayfish	*yoo*-raws veh-*zhay*	*jūros vėžiai*
crab	*krah*-bas	*krabas*
fish	*kah*-lah	*kala*
herring	*sil*-keh	*silkė*
lobster	*aw*-mah-rahs	*omaras*
mussels	dvi-*gal*-dehs	*dvigeldės*
	kryowk-lehs	*kriauklės*
plaice	*plaksh*-neh	*plekšnė*
salmon	lah-shi-*shah*	*lašiša*
trout	u-*peh*-tah-kis	*upėtakis*

Fruit

apple	aw-baw-*lees*	*obuolys*
apricot	ahb-ri-*ko*-sahs	*abrikosas*
banana	bah-*nah*-nahs	*bananas*
blackberries	*garv*-u-aw-gehs	*gervuogės*
cherries	*veesh*-nyaws	*vyšnios*
fruit	*vai*-say	*vaisiai*
grapes	*veen*-u-aw-gehs	*vynuogės*
lemon	tsit-*ri*-nah	*citrina*
mulberries	*shilk*-maj-aw	*šilkmedžio*
	u-aw-gaws	*uogos*
orange	ah-pal-*si*-nahs	*apelsinas*
peach	*par*-si-kahs	*persikas*
pear	*krow*-sheh	*kriaušė*
plum	*slee*-veh	*slyva*
raspberries	ah-*veah*-tehs	*avietės*
strawberries	*brahsh*-kehs	*braškės*

Condiments, Herbs & Spices

caraway	*kmee*-nai	*kmynai*
chives	tsi-bul-*yu*-kai	*cibuliukai*
cinnamon	tsi-nah-*maw*-nahs	*cinamonas*
cloves	gvahz-*dik*-ai	*gvazdikai*
garlic	chas-*nah*-kahs	*česnakas*
gherkin	roogsh-*tus* ah-*gur*-kahs	*rūgštus agurkas*
ginger	*im*-bi-rahs	*imbieras*
gravy	meh-*saws sul*-tees	*mėsos sultys*
horseradish	*kreah*-nai	*krienai*
nutmeg	mush-*kah*-tahs	*muškatas*
olive oil	praw-*vahn*-si-nis	*provansinis*
	ah-*leah*-yus	*aliejus*
parsley	pat-*rush*-kaws	*petruškos*
salt	*drus*-kah	*druska*
sugar	*tsuk*-rus	*cukrus*
vinegar	*ahts*-tahs	*actas*

Cooking Methods

baked/fried	*kap*-tahs	*keptas*
boiled	*vir*-tahs	*virtas*
rare	na vi-*sai* ish-kap-tah	*ne visai iškepta*
smoked	roo-*kee*-tah	*rūkyta*
steamed	*gah*-rin-tah	*garinta*
stewed	trawsh-*kin*-tah	*troškinta*
well done	lah-*bai* ga-*rai*	*labai gerai*
	ish-kap-tah	*iškepta*

Non-Alcoholic Drinks

Very strong black coffee seems to be the preferred daily drink these days, although various herb or fruit teas are also popular. Country people use all kinds of home grown products to make beverages: camomile, beetroot and honey, sour milk, berry or fruit marmalades, mint, birch or maple sap, acorns, rhubarb, cucumbers and honey, vegetable juices and more.

Alcoholic drinks are also often home made from items such as honey, fruits, vegetables, grains, bread, milk, and even horseradish.

cocoa	kah-*kah*-vah	*kakava*
coffee	kah-*vah*	*kava*
black coffee	yu-aw-*dah* kah-*vah*	*juoda kava*
coffee with cream	kah-*vah* su greah-tin-*eh*-la	*kava su grietinéle*
coffee with ice cream topping	kah-*vah* su lad-*ais*	*kava su ledais*
fruit juice	*vais*-yew *sul*-tees	*vaisių sultys*
orange juice	ah-pal-*si*-noo *sul*-tees	*apelsinų sultys*
tomato juice	po-mi-*daw*-roo *sul*-tees	*pomidorų sultys*
soft drinks	gai-*vi*-nah-meah-yi geh-ri-mai	*gaivinamieji gėrimai*
tea	ahr-bah-*tah*	*arbata*
black tea	yu-aw-*daw*-yi ahr-bah-*tah*	*juodoji arbata*
tea with lemon	ahr-bah-*tah* su tsit-*ri*-nah	*arbata su citrina*
tea with milk	ahr-bah-*tah* su peah-nu	*arbata su pienu*
water	vahn-*du*-aw	*vanduo*
mineral water	mi-ner-*ah*-li-nis vahn-*du*-aw	*mineralinis vanduo*
soda water	gah-zu-*aw*-tahs vahn-*du*-aw	*gazuotas vanduo*

LITHUANIAN

Alcoholic Drinks

beer	ah-*lus*	*alus*
local beer	*veah*-ti-nehs	*vietinės*
	gah-*mee*-baws ah-*lus*	*gamybos alus*
brandy/cognac	*kon*-yah-kahs	*konjakas*
champagne	shahm-*pah*-nahs	*šampanas*
cider	*sid*-rahs	*sidras*
cocktails	kok-*tay*-lay	*kokteiliai*
honey liqueur	*krup*-ni-kahs	*krupnikas*
mead	mi-*dus*	*midus*
whisky	*vis*-kis	*viskis*
vodka	dag-*tin*-eh	*degtinė*
red/white wine	row-*daw*-nahs/	*raudonas/*
	bahl-tahs vee-nahs	*baltas vynas*

From the Bar

chewing gum	*krahm*-taw-maw-yi gu-mah	*kramtomoji guma*
chocolate	sho-ko-*lah*-dahs	*šokoladas*
cigarettes	tsi-gah-*rat*-ehs	*cigaretės*
cigars	tsi-*gah*-rahs	*cigaras*
crisps	trahsh-*ku*-chay	*traškučiai*
salted nuts	*soo*-roos reahshu-*tai*	*sūrūs reišutai*

SHOPPING

You'll find many craft shops in Vilnius where you can buy good
quality handicrafts such as pottery, leather, cast iron, jewellery
and amber as well as souvenirs. A number of shops stock Western
goods but these are generally more expensive.

bakery	*du-aw*-naws	*duonos*
	pahr-daw-*tu*-veh/	*parduotuvė/*
	kap-*eek*-lah	*kepykla*
bookshop	knee-*gee*-nahs	*knygynas*
butcher	*meh*-sin-eh	*mėsinė*
camera shop	fo-to-ah-pah-*rah*-too	*fotoaparatų*
	pahr-daw-*tu*-veh	*parduotuvė*
clothing store	drah-*bu*-zyew	*drabužių*
	pahr-daw-*tu*-veh	*parduotuvė*
delicatessen	da-li-kah-*tas*-oo	*delikatesų*
	pahr-daw-*tu*-veh	*parduotuvė*
general store	*krow*-tu-veh	*krautuvė*
greengrocer	*vais*-yew ir	*vaisių ir*
	dahr-*zhaw*-view	*daržovių*
	pahr-daw-*tu*-veh	*parduotuvė*
kiosk	*kyos*-kahs	*kioskas*
market	*tur*-gus	*turgus*
newsagency	*laik*-rahsh-chew	*laikraščių*
	krow-tu-veh	*krautuvė*
pharmacy	*vais*-tin-eh	*vaistinė*
shoe shop	*bah*-too	*batų*
	pahr-daw-*tu*-veh	*parduotuvė*
souvenir shop	su-van-*ee*-roo	*suvenyrų*
	krow-tu-veh	*krautuvė*
supermarket	sah-*vi*-tahr-naws	*savitarnos*
	pahr-daw-*tu*-veh	*parduotuvė*

LITHUANIAN

Making a Purchase

I want to buy ...	ahsh *naw*-ryu	*Aš noriu*
	nu-si-*pirk*-ti ...	*nusipirkti ...*
How much is it?	keahk kai-*nu-aw*-yah?	*Kiek kainuoja?*
Can I see it?	ahr gah-*leh*-chow ish	*Ar galėčiau iš*
	ahr-*chow*	*arčiau*
	pah-mah-*tee*-ti?	*pamatyti?*
It doesn't fit.	na-*tin*-kah	*Netinka.*
It's too ...	par-*dowg* ...	*Perdaug ...*
big	*did*-al-is	*didelis*
small	*mah*-zhahs	*mažas*
short	*trum*-pahs	*trumpas*
long	*il*-gahs	*ilgas*
loose	*lyu-aw*-sahs	*liuosas*
tight	*ahnksh*-tahs	*ankštas*

Essential Groceries

batteries	bah-*ta*-ri-yos	*baterijos*
bread	*du-aw*-nah	*duona*
butter	*sveahs*-tahs	*sviestas*
candles	*zhvah*-kehs	*žvakės*
cereal	yah-*vai*-nyay	*javainiai*
cheese	*soo*-ris	*sūris*
chocolate	sho-ko-*lah*-dahs	*šokoladas*
eggs	kyow-*shin*-ay	*kiaušiniai*
flour	*mil*-tai	*miltai*
gas cylinder	*du*-yoo bon-*kal*-eh	*dujų bonkelė*
ham	*kum*-pis	*kumpis*
honey	ma-*dus*	*medus*
insect repellent	vahbz-*jus*	*vabzdžius*
	aht-*bai*-dahn-ti	*atbaidanti*
	preah-maw-neh	*priemonė*
marmalade	u-ah-*geah*-neh	*uogienė*
margarine	mahr-gah-*ri*-nahs	*margarinas*
matches	dak-*tu*-kai	*degtukai*
milk	*peah*-nahs	*pienas*
pepper	pi-*pi*-rai	*pipirai*
rice	*ree*-zhay	*ryžiai*

salt	drus-kah	druska
shampoo	shahm-poo-nahs	šampūnas
soap	mwi-lahs	muilas
sugar	tsuk-rus	cukrus
toilet paper	tu-ah-lat-aw	tualeto
	paw-peah-ryus	popierius
toothpaste	dahn-too pahs-tah	dantų pasta
washing powder	skahl-bi-maw mil-ta-lay	skalbimo milteliai
yogurt	yaw-gur-tahs	jogurtas

LUCKY IN LOVE

There are many different fortune-telling games played in Lithuania at different times of the year. At Midsummer they usually involve a wreath of flowers. A girl stands with her back to a tree and throws her wreath over her head to try to hook it on a branch. The number of times she succeeds indicates the number of years before she marries. Pairs of wreaths labelled with boys' and girls' names are thrown into a stream and those which come together indicate who will become couples. A wreath which sinks foretells a person's imminent death. One which floats easily represents a happy life. Boys and girls link arms and jump over the dying bonfire embers. If they land still linked and unscathed, love and marriage will ensue.

At Christmas, the games involve straw from the Christmas table. The young people draw straws from under the table cloth and the length and shape of the straw drawn is said to give a clue as to the height and shape of their future spouse. Bunches of twigs are counted to see who will be married in the coming year – an even number indicates a wedding. Another clue to a person's future is gained when they turn their back to the door and throw a shoe over their shoulder in the direction of the door – if it lands with the toe end pointing towards the door, they'll leave the family home next year and marry someone who lives far away.

LITHUANIAN

Souvenirs

amber ...	gin-tah-*ri*-n(eh/ehs) ...	*gintarin(ė/ės)* ... (f, sg/pl)
	gin-tah-*ri*-n(is/ay) ...	*gintarin(is/iai)* ... (m, sg/pl)
carving	draw-zhi-*neh*-lis	*drožinėlis*
cast iron	*kat*-ai	*ketai*
clogs	*klum*-pehs	*klumpeės*
folk art	lyow-deahs *man*-ahs	*liaudies menas*
handicrafts	*rahnk*-dahr-bay	*rankdarbiai*
jewellery	brahn-gan-*ee*-behs	*brangenybės*
necklace	kah-*rawl*-ay	*karoliai*
picture/ painting	pah-*vayks*-lahs	*paveikslas*
statuette	stah-tu-*leh*-leh	*statulėlė*
trinket	dir-bi-*neh*-lis	*dirbinėlis*

Clothing

blouse	pah-lai-di-*nu*-keh	*palaidinukė*
clothing	drah-*bu*-zhay	*drabužiai*
coat/overcoat	*pahl*-tahs	*paltas*
dress	suk-*nal*-eh	*suknelė*
jacket	*shvahr*-kahs	*švarkas*
jeans	*jin*-sai	*džinsai*
jumper/sweater	mags-*tin*-is	*megztinis*
shirt	mahrsh-kin-*ay*	*marškiniai*
shoes	*bah*-tai	*batai*
skirt	si-*yaw*-nahs	*sijonas*
trousers/pants	*kal*-nehs	*kelnės*
windcheater	*stroo*-keh	*striukė*

Materials

amber	gin-tah-*ri*-neh	*gintarinė* (f)
	gin-tah-*ri*-nis	*gintarinis* (m)
brass	zhal-vah-*ri*-neh	*žalvarinė* (f)
	zhahl-vah-*ri*-nis	*žalvarinis* (m)
cotton	*mad*-vil-neh	*medvilnė*
gold	owk-*si*-neh	*auksinė* (f)
	owk-*si*-nis	*auksinis* (m)
handmade	*rahn*-koo *dahr*-baw	*rankų darbo*
leather	*aw*-dah	*oda*
silk	*shil*-kahs	*šilkas*
silver	si-dah-*bri*-neh	*sidabrinė* (f)
	si-dah-*bri*-nis	*sidabrinis* (m)
wool	*vil*-nah	*vilna*

Toiletries

condoms	pre-zer-vah-*tee*-vai	*prezervatyvai*
deodorant	de-o-*daw*-rahs	*deodoras*
hairbrush	plow-koo shap-at-*ees*	*plaukų šepetys*
moisturiser	*aw*-dai	*odai*
	su-*shval*-ni-ni-maw	*sušvelninimo*
	kram-ahs	*kremas*
razor	sku-*ti*-maw-si	*skutimosi*
	pay-*lyu*-kahs	*peiliukas*
electric razor	al-ak-*tri*-nis	*elektrinis*
	skus-*tu*-vahs	*skustuvas*
sanitary napkins	*bin*-tai	*bintai*
shampoo	shahm-*poo*-nahs	*šampūnas*
shaving cream	sku-*ti*-maw-si *mwi*-lahs	*skutimosi muilas*
soap	*mwi*-lahs	*muilas*
sunblock cream	*sow*-lehs *kram*-ahs	*saulės kremas*
tampons	tahm-*pon*-ai	*tamponai*
toilet paper	tu-ah-*lat*-aw	*tualeto*
	paw-peah-ryus	*popierius*
toothbrush	dahn-too shap-at-*ees*	*dantų šepetys*
toothpaste	dahn-too *pahs*-tah	*dantų pasta*

Stationery & Publications

I want to buy	ahsh *naw*-ryu	*Aš noriu*
(a/an) ...	nu-si-*pirk*-ti ...	*nusipirkti ...*
English-	*ahn*-gloo-	*anglų-*
Lithuanian	leah-*tu*-view	*lietuvių*
dictionary	kahl-*baws*	*kalbos žodyną*
	zhaw-*dee*-nah	
guidebook in	tu-*ris*-taw vah-*daw*-vah	*turisto vadovą*
English	*ahn*-gloo kahl-baw-ya	*anglų kalboje*
newspaper in	*laik*-rahsh-ti	*laikraštį anglų*
English	*ahn*-gloo kahl-baw-ya	*kalboje*
novels in	raw-*mah*-noo	*romanų anglų*
English	*ahn*-gloo kahl-baw-ya	*kalboje*
map	zham-*eh*-lah-pis	*žemėlapis*
newspaper	*laik*-rahsh-tis	*laikraštis*
paper	*paw*-peah-ryus	*popierius*
pen	tu-shi-*nu*-kahs	*tušinukas*

Photography

How much is it to
process this film?

keahk kai-*nu*-*aw*-yah	*Kiek kainuoja*
ish-*aish*-kin-ti shi *fil*-mah?	*išaiškinti šį filmą?*

When will it be ready?

kah-*dah* bus *gah*-tah-vah?	*Kada bus gatava?*

I'd like a ... film	ahsh naw-*reh*-chow ...	*Aš norėčiau ... filmo*
for this camera.	*fil*-maw sham	*šiam fotoaparatui.*
	fo-to-ah-pah-*rah*-twi	
B&W	yu-*aw*-daw	*juodo*
	bahl-taw	*balto*
colour	spahl-*vaw*-taw	*spalvoto*

Smoking

May I smoke?
   ahr *gah*-li-mah roo-*kee*-ti?   *Ar galima rūkyti?*
A packet of cigarettes, please.
   pah-*kal*-i tsi-gah-   *Pakelį*
   rach-ew prah-*show*   *cigarečių, prašau.*

Colours

black	*yu-aw*-dah	*juoda*
blue	*meh*-lee-nah	*mėlyna*
brown	*ru*-dah	*ruda*
green	*zhahl*-yah	*žalia*
pink	*roo*-zhah-vah	*rūžava*
red	row-*daw*-nah	*raudona*
white	*bahl*-tah	*balta*
yellow	gal-*taw*-nah	*geltona*

Sizes & Comparisons

small	*mah*-zhahs	*mažas*
big	*did*-al-is	*didelis*
heavy	sun-*kus*	*sunkus*
light	*lang*-vahs	*lengvas*
more	dowg-*yow*	*daugiau*
less	mahzh-*yow*	*mažiau*
too much/many	par-*dowg*	*perdaug*
many	dowg	*daug*
enough	uzh-*tan*-kah	*užtenka*
a little bit	tru-*put*-i	*truputi*

HEALTH

Where's the ...?	kur ee-*rah* ...?	*Kur yra ...?*
chemist	*vais*-ti-neh	*vaistinė*
dentist	*dahn*-too	*dantų*
	gee-dee-taw-yahs	*gydytojas*
doctor	gee-dee-taw-yahs	*gydytojas*
hospital	li-*gaw*-ni-neh	*ligoninė*

Ailments

I have (a/an) ...	mahn ...	*Man ...*
She/He has (a/an) ...	yay/yahm ...	*Jai/Jam ...*
ache	*skows*-mahs	*skausmas*
appendicitis	ah-pan-di-*tsi*-tahs	*apendicitas*
burn	nu-dag-*i*-mahs	*nudegimas*
cold	*slaw*-gah	*sloga*
fever	*kahrsh*-tis	*karštis*
flu	*grip*-ahs	*gripas*
food poisoning	ahp-si-*nu-aw*-di-yi-mahs	*apsinuodijimas*
	mais-*tu*	*maistu*
fracture	*loo*-zhis	*lūžis*
headache	gahl-*vaws*	*galvos*
	skows-mahs	*skausmas*
heart attack	shir-*deahs*	*širdies*
	preah-pu-aw-lis	*priepuolis*
infection	in-*fak*-tsi-yah	*infekcija*
nausea	veh-*mim*-ahs	*vėmimas*
sprain	ish-nah-*rin*-i-mahs/	*išnarinimas/*
	pah-tam-*pim*-ahs	*patempimas*
stroke	in-*sul*-tahs	*insultas*
swelling	ish-ti-*nim*-ahs	*ištinimas*
temperature	tam-pa-rah-*too*-rah	*temperatūra*
trauma	*trow*-mah	*trauma*
venereal disease	van-a-ri-neh li-*gah*	*venerinė liga*

LITHUANIAN

At the Doctor

I'm sick.	ahsh sar-*gu*	*Aš sergu.*
Where does it hurt?	kur *skow*-dah?	*Kur skauda?*
It hurts here.	cha *skow*-dah	*Čia skauda.*
Could I see a female doctor?	ahr gah-*leh*-chow kon-sul-*tu-aw*-ti *maw*-ta-ri gee-dee-taw-yah?	*Ar galėčiau konsultuoti moterį gydytoją?*

Parts of the Body

My ... hurt(s).	mahn ... *skow*-dah	*Man ... skauda.*
back	*nu*-gah-rah	*nugara*
buttocks	seh-*dee*-neh	*sėdynė*
chest	kroo-*ti*-neh	*krūtinė*
ear	*ow*-sis	*ausis*
elbow	ahl-*koo*-neh	*alkūnė*
eye	ah-*kis*	*akis*
finger	*pirsh*-tahs	*pirštas*
foot	peh-*dah*	*pėda*
gums	*dahn*-tan-aws	*dantenos*
head	gahl-*vah*	*galva*
knee	*ka*-lis	*kelis*
leg	*kaw*-yah	*koja*
mouth	*bur*-nah	*burna*
shoulder	pat-*ees*	*petys*
skin	*aw*-dah	*oda*
stomach	*skrahn*-dis	*skrandis*
teeth	*dahn*-tees	*dantys*
throat	*gark*-leh	*gerklė*

TICKED OFF

Ticks occur in Lithuania, so it's wise to be on the lookout for them when you're out and about in a forrested area.

LITHUANIAN

At the Chemist

I need medication for ...
    mahn *rayk*-yah vais-*too* ...   *Man reikia vaistų ...*
I have a prescription.
    ahsh tur-*yu* rat-sap-tah   *Aš turiu receptą.*

At the Dentist

I have a toothache.
    'mahn *dahn*-tis *skow*-dah   *Man dantis skauda.*
I've lost a filling.
    ahsh a-su pah-*mat*-us/as   *Aš esu pametus/ęs*
    plom-bah   *plombą.*
I have broken a tooth.
    mahn *dahn*-tis *loo*-zhaw   *Man dantis lūžo.*
My gums hurt.
    mahn *dahn*-tan-aws *skow*-dah   *Man dantenos skauda.*
I don't want it extracted.
    ahsh ne-*naw*-ryu kahd yis   *Aš nenoriu, kad jis būtų*
    boo-*too* *ish*-trowk-tahs   *ištrauktas.*
Please give me an anaesthetic.
    prah-*show* uzh-mah-*rin*-ki-ta   *Prašau užmarinkite.*

Useful Words & Phrases

I'm ...	ahsh a-su ...	*Aš esu ...*
diabetic	di-yah-*bat*-i-keh	*diabetikė* (f)
	di-yah-*bat*-i-kahs	*diabetikas* (m)
epileptic	api-*lap*-ti-keh	*epileptikė* (f)
	api-*lap*-ti-kahs	*epileptikas* (m)
asthmatic	ahs-*mah*-ti-keh	*asmatikė* (f)
	ahs-*mah*-ti-kahs	*asmatikas* (m)
I'm allergic to ...	ahsh ah-*lar*-gish-k	*Aš alergišk*
	(ah/ahs)	*(a/as) ...* (f/m)
antibiotics	ahn-ti-bi-*yaw*-ti-kahms	*antibiotikams*
penicillin	pan-it-si-*lin*-wi	*penicilinui*

LITHUANIAN

I feel ...	yow-*chu* kahd mahn ...	*Jaučiu, kad man ...*
weak	*silp*-nah	*silpna*
dizzy	*svaigs*-tah *gahl*-vah	*svaigsta galva*

I'm pregnant.
    ahsh nehsh-*cha*   *Aš nėščia.*
I haven't had my
period for ... months.
    ahsh yow na-tur-*yu*   *Aš jau neturiu*
    meh-nas-*in*-yaw ...   *mėnesinio ...*
    meh-nas-yus   *mėnesius.*
I have my own syringe.
    ahsh tur-*yu* sah-vaw   *Aš turiu savo*
    shvirksh-tah   *švirkštą.*
I have a tick bite.
    mahn i-*kahn*-daw ar-keh   *Man įkando erkė.*

accident	na-lai-*min*-gahs	*nelaimingas*
	aht-si-ti-*kim*-ahs	*atsitikimas*
road accident	ah-*vah*-ri-yah	*avarija*
addiction	zhah-*lin*-gahs i-*praw*-tis	*žalingas įprotis*
antiseptic	daz-in-fak-*wah*-yah-	*dezinfekuojamoji*
	maw-yi maj-ah-*gah*	*medžiaga*
bandage	*tvahrs*-tis	*tvarstis*
blood pressure	*krow*-yaw	*kraujo*
	spow-*di*-mahs	*spaudimas*
blood test	*krow*-yaw	*kraujo*
	pah-*tik*-ri-ni-mahs	*patikrinimas*
injection	i-shvirksh-*tim*-ahs	*įšvirkštimas*
pharmacy on duty	*bu*-din-ti *vais*-ti-neh	*budinti vaistinė*

SPECIFIC NEEDS
Disabled Travellers

I'm disabled/handicapped.
| ahsh in-vah-*li*-d(eh/ahs) | *Aš invalid(ė/as).* (f/m) |

I need assistance.
| mahn *ray*-kyah pah-*gahl*-baws | *Man reikia pagalbos.* |

What services do you have
for disabled people?
| kaw-*kew pah*-slow-goo joos | *Kokių paslaugų jūs teikiate* |
| *tay*-kyah-ta in-vah-*li*-dahms? | *invalidams?* |

Is there wheelchair access?
| ahr ee-*rah* pri-vah-*zhah*-vi-mahs | *Ar yra privažiavimas* |
| in-vah-*li*-doo va-zhi-*meh*-lams? | *invalidų vežimėliams?* |

I'm deaf. Speak more
loudly, please.
| ahsh *kur*-chas prah-*show* | *Aš kurčias. Prašau* |
| kahl-*beh*-ki-ta gahr-*syow* | *kalbėkite garsiau.* |

I have a hearing aid.
| ahsh na-*shaw*-yu klow-saws | *Aš nešioju klausos* |
| ah-pah-rah-*teh*-li | *aparatėlį* |

I'm blind.
| ahsh *ahk*-lahs | *Aš aklas.* |

Are guide dogs permitted?
| ahr *lay*-jah-mah *vas*-tis | *Ar leidžiama vestis* |
| ahk-*loo*-yoo shu-ni? | *aklųjų šunį?* |

I'm mute.
| ahsh na-bi-*lees* | *Aš nebylys.* |

Braille library
| *brai*-lyaw *shrif*-taw *knee*-goo | *Brailio šrifto knygų* |
| bib-*lyaw*-ta-kah | *biblioteka* |

disabled person
| in-vah-*li*-d(eh/ahs) | *invalid(ė/as)* (f/m) |

guide dog
| ahk-*loo*-yoo shu-ah | *aklųjų šuo* |

wheelchair
| in-vah-*li*-daw va-zhi-*meh*-lis | *invalido vežimėlis* |

TIME & DATES

What time is it?	keahk dah-bahr *lai*-kaw?	*Kiek dabar laiko?*
It's ... (o'clock).	dah-*bahr* ...	*Dabar* ...
	(vah-lahn-*dah*)	*(valanda).*
2.00	ahn-*trah*	*antra*
5.30	pu-seh shash-*yew*	*pusė šešių*
11.45	ba pank-*yaw*-li-kaws	*be penkiolikos*
	dvee-lik-tah	*dvylikta*

in the morning	*ree*-taw	*ryto*
in the afternoon	paw *peah*-too	*po pietų*
in the evening	*vah*-kah-raw	*vakaro*

Days of the Week

Monday	pir-*mah*-deah-nis	*pirmadienis*
Tuesday	ahn-*trah*-deah-nis	*antradienis*
Wednesday	trach-*ah*-deah-nis	*trečiadienis*
Thursday	kat-vir-*tah*-deah-nis	*ketvirtadienis*
Friday	pank-*tah*-deah-nis	*penktadienis*
Saturday	shash-*tah*-deah-nis	*šeštadienis*
Sunday	sak-*mah*-deah-nis	*sekmadienis*

Months

January	*sow*-sis	*sausis*
February	vah-*sah*-ris	*vasaris*
March	*kaw*-vahs	*kovas*
April	bah-*lahn*-dis	*balandis*
May	gag-*uzh*-is	*gegužis*
June	bir-*zhal*-is	*birželis*
July	*leah*-pah	*liepa*
August	rug-*pew*-tis	*rugpiūtis*
September	rug-*seh*-yis	*rugsėjis*
October	*spah*-lis	*spalis*
November	*lahp*-krit-is	*lapkritis*
December	gru-*aw*-dis	*gruodis*

Seasons

summer	*vah*-sah-rah	*vasara*
autumn	ru-*du*-aw	*ruduo*
winter	zheah-*mah*	*žiema*
spring	pah-*vah*-sah-ris	*pavasaris*

Present

today	shan-*deahn*	*šiandien*
this morning	shi *ree*-tah	*šį rytą*
tonight	shi *vah*-kah-rah	*šį vakarą*
this week	shah sah-*vai*-ta	*sią savaitę*
this year	shays *mat*-ais	*šiais metais*
now	dah-*bahr*	*dabar*

Past

yesterday	*vah*-kahr	*vakar*
day before yesterday	uzh-vah-kahr	*užvakar*
yesterday morning	*vah*-kahr *ree*-tah	*vakar rytą*
last night	*vah*-kahr vah-kah-ra	*vakar vakare*
last week	par-ay-tah sah-*vai*-ta	*pereitą savaitę*
last year	par-ay-tais *mat*-ais	*pereitais metais*

Future

tomorrow	ree-*toy*	*rytoj*
day after tomorrow	paw-*reet*	*poryt*
tomorrow ...	ree-*toy* ...	*rytoj ...*
morning	*ree*-tah	*rytą*
afternoon	paw-*peah*-too	*popietų*
evening	vah-kah-*ra*	*vakare*
next week	ah-*tay*-nahn-cha sah-*vai*-ta	*ateinančią savaitę*
next year	ah-*tay*-nahn-chays *mat*-ais	*ateinančiais metais*

Dates

What date is it today?	kawk-*yah* shan-*deahn* dah-*tah*?	*Kokia šiandien data?*
It's 1 April.	shan-*deahn* pir-*mah* bah-*lahn*-jaw	*Šiandien pirma balandžio.*

During the Day

afternoon	*paw*-peah-teh	*popietė*
dawn	owsh-*rah*	*aušra*
day	deah-*nah*	*diena*
early	ahnks-*ti*	*anksti*
midnight	vi-*dur*-nahk-tis	*vidurnaktis*
morning	*ree*-tahs	*rytas*
night	nahk-*tis*	*naktis*
noon	vi-*dur*-deah-nis	*vidurdienis*
sunset	sow-*leh*-lee-dis	*saulėlydis*

Useful Words

a year ago	preahsh mat-*us*	*prieš metus*
always	vi-sah-*dah*	*visada*
at the moment	shyaw mo-*man*-tu	*šiuo momentu*
early	ahnks-*ti*	*anksti*
every day	kahs-*deahn*	*kasdien*
forever	ahm-zhin-*ai*	*amžinai*
late	veh-*lai*	*vėlai*
later on	vehl-*yow*	*vėliau*
never	neah-kah-*dah*	*niekada*
not yet	dahr na	*dar ne*
now	dah-*bahr*	*dabar*
since	nu-aw	*nuo*
sometimes	*kahr*-tais	*kartais*
soon	grayt	*greit*
still	dahr	*dar*
straight away	toy-*ows*	*tuojaus*

LITHUANIAN

FESTIVALS & HOLIDAYS
National Holidays

Naujų Metų Diena
now-*yoo* mat-oo deah-*nah*
New Years Day (1 January)

Nepriklausomybės Šventė
nap-rik-low-saw-*mee*-behs *shvan*-teh
Independence Day (16 February)

Velykos
veh-*lee*-kaws
Easter (March/April)

Valstybės Diena
vahl-*stee*-behs deah-*nah*
Statehood Day (6 July)

Visų Šventujų Šventė
vi-*soo* shvan-*too*-yoo *shvan*-teh
All Saints Day (1 November)

Kalėdos
kah-*leh*-daws
Christmas (25 & 26 December)

For greetings used on various holidays, see the Special Occasions section on page 199.

Festivals

National Song Festival   *Dainų šventė*
Every five years hundreds of choirs and folk dance groups from all over Lithuania and Lithuanian communities overseas converge on Vilnius to perform. You'll see many different regional folk costume styles worn by participants in this massive outdoor spectacular.

Folk music has always formed a vital part of the Lithuanian soul. During the Soviet regime a certain amount of the content of the Song Festival had to reflect a devotion to communism, but today the event has become an outpouring of the true spirit of the people.

Midsummer Night   *Joninės*

Midsummer Night was originally a pagan festival. For Christians the night of 23 June became the feast of St John the Baptist, '*Joninės*', and also the name day of all men named John ('*Jonas*').

Since pagan times, when people believed that fires would scare off witches and evil spirits which were lurking about seeking to damage their crops and livestock, bonfires were lit on hilltops on midsummer night. Sometimes burning cartwheels are hoisted on poles decorated with wreaths of herbs and flowers. The wheels symbolise the sun and the wreaths symbolise growth. Girls wear floral wreaths, which are also used in fortune-telling games.

There's a myth that the fern will produce a magic blossom on this night, and that whoever finds it will gain amazing magical powers, including the ability to understand all human and animal languages and read people's thoughts, know where treasures lie buried and foresee who will live and who will die. So at midnight everyone goes on a fern blossom hunt. Finally, those who stay around to see the sunrise will enjoy health and happiness throughout the year.

St Casimir's Fair   *Kaziuko mugė*

Lithuania has the distinction of being the last European country to accept Christianity, which was not fully established there until the 16th century. There's only one Lithuanian saint, the popular St Casimir (*Šventas Kazimieras*). He was Lithuanian by birth, a royal prince who rejected the trappings of royalty to don sack cloth and live a life of prayer and good works. He died of tuberculosis on 4 March 1483, aged 25. His best known miracle was his apparition to a small force of Lithuanian soldiers, whom he led to victory in a battle against a large Russian army in 1518. Because pilgrims used to flock to his burial place in Vilnius on St Casimir's Day, outdoor stalls were set up to cater for them. Hence the '*Kaziuko mugė*' ('Casi's' Fair) which survives to this day and is held on the Sunday closest to 4 March.

LITHUANIAN

Summer Music Festival

This happens in the historic setting of the Old Town sector of Vilnius in July, with music, dance, street theatre, masked parades and craft stalls for your enjoyment.

Vilnius City Days

A three-day festival in mid-September, Vilnius City Days is filled with an amazing diversity of entertainment including folk and international music such as country, gipsy, French, African and jazz. There's also modern ballet and dance, circus acts, bands, a carnival parade, children's theatre, pantomime, puppets, comedy, satire, art exhibitions, films, disco, cabaret, ethnic food tastings, air balloons and more!

All Souls Day   *Vėlinės*

Lithuanian cemeteries are always lovingly tended and on All Souls Day, 2 November, they're at their most beautiful.

HORSING AROUND

Lithuania's biggest horse races take place on the first Saturday in February at Lake Sartai in Dusetos, near Utena.

LITHUANIAN

Christmas Eve   *Kūčios*

For Lithuanians the main family event of the year is Christmas Eve. The celebration centres mostly on the table which is laid with a fresh white cloth and a handful of hay, representing the hay in the manger where Jesus lay, is spread over it. The places of deceased or absent family members are marked by a fir twig and a burning candle. There are at least twelve different dishes on the table to symbolise both the twelve apostles at the Last Supper and the twelve months of the year, but no meat or alcohol. *Šližikai* (dice-sized plain biscuit cubes) with poppy-seed milk are a must.

The meal begins when the first star appears in the sky. After the head of the family says grace, a Christmas Eve holy wafer is passed around the table to be broken and shared together with everybody's good wishes to each other. It's not proper to talk or joke too loudly during this meal, which is a sacred occasion. Ancient lore says that you should try some of every dish on the table or you won't survive until next Christmas Eve.

The table is left uncleared that night, so that the souls of ancestors can come down and partake of the remaining food.

After the meal, young people play traditional fortune-telling games aimed at determining their future marriage prospects. Then it's time to gather around the decorated Christmas tree for each person to recite or sing before receiving their Christmas present.

At midnight it's customary for families to attend a midnight mass.

CROSS MY HEART

In the village of Jurgaičiai stands *Kryžių kalnas*, the Hill of Crosses. Crosses were first planted here in the middle of the 14th century. During the Soviet era, the crosses came to symbolise not only Christianity, but nationalism. The hill was bulldozed at least three times and the Red Army destroyed all the crosses, sealed off all access to the hill and dug ditches around its base, but still crosses appeared. Today the hill is covered with over 20,000 crosses of all descriptions.

LITHUANIAN

NUMBERS & AMOUNTS
Cardinal Numbers

0	*nul*-is	nulis
1	*veah*-nahs	vienas
2	du	du
3	trees	trys
4	kat-u-*ri*	keturi
5	pan-*ki*	penki
6	shash-*i*	šeši
7	sap-tee-*ni*	septyni
8	ahsh-tu-aw-*ni*	aštuoni
9	dav-ee-*ni*	devyni
10	*dash*-imt	dešimt
11	veah-*naw*-lik-ah	vienuolika
12	*dvee*-lik-ah	dvylika
13	*tree*-lik-ah	trylika
14	kat-u-*raw*-lik-ah	keturiolika
15	pank-*yaw*-lik-ah	penkiolika
16	shash-*yaw*-lik-ah	šešiolika
17	sap-teen-*yaw*-lik-ah	septyniolika
18	ahsh-tawn-*yaw*-lik-ah	aštuoniolika
19	dav-een-*yaw*-lik-ah	devyniolika
20	*dvi*-dash-imt	dvidešimt
21	*dvi*-dash-imt *veah*-nahs	dvidešimt vienas
30	*tris*-dash-imt	trisdešimt
40	*kat*-ur-as-dash-imt	keturiasdešimt
50	*pank*-as-dash-imt	penkiasdešimt
60	*shash*-as-dash-imt	šešiasdešimt
70	sap-*teen*-as-dash-imt	septyniasdešimt
80	ahsh-*tu-aw*-nas-dash-imt	aštuoniasdešimt
90	dav-*een*-as-dash-imt	devyniasdešimt
100	*shim*-tahs	šimtas
101	*shim*-tahs *veah*-nahs	šimtas vienas
500	pan-*ki* shim-*tai*	penki šimtai
1000	*tooks*-tahn-tis	tūkstantis
100,000	*shim*-tahs *tooks*-tahn-chew	šimtas tūkstančių
one million	mi-li-*yaw*-nahs	milijonas

Ordinal Numbers

1st	pir-*mah*/*pir*-mahs	*pirm(a/as)* (f/m)
2nd	ahn-*trah*/*ahn*-trahs	*antr(a/as)* (f/m)
3rd	trach-*ah*/*trach*-ahs	*treči(a/as)* (f/m)
4th	kat-vir-*tah*/*kat*-vir-tahs	*ketvirt(a/as)* (f/m)
5th	pank-*tah*/*pank*-tahs	*penkt(a/as)* (f/m)
6th	shash-*tah*/*shash*-tahs	*šešt(a/as)* (f/m)
7th	sap-tin-*tah*/*sap-tin*-tahs	*septint(a/as)* (f/m)
8th	ahsh-tun-*tah*/ *ahsh-tun*-tahs	*aštunt(a/as)* (f/m)
9th	dav-in-*tah*/*dav-in*-tahs	*devint(a/as)* (f/m)
10th	dash-im-*tah*/*dash-im*-tahs	*dešimt(a/as)* (f/m)
11th	veah-nu-aw-lik-*tah*/ veah-*nu-aw*-lik-tahs	*vienuolikt(a/as)* (f/m)
12th	dvee-lik-*tah*/*dvee*-lik-tahs	*dvylikt(a/as)* (f/m)

ORDINAL STRESS

Note that for ordinal numbers the stress in the masculine form falls on the first syllable, but in the feminine form it falls on the last syllable.

Fractions

1/4	kat-vir-*tah*-dah-lis	*ketvirtadalis*
1/3	*trach*-dah-lis	*trečdalis*
1/2	*pu*-seh	*pusė*
3/4	trees *kat*-vir-chay	*trys ketvirčiai*

Useful Words

calculate	ahp-skai-*chu*-aw-ti	*apskaičiuoti*
a little (amount)	*tru*-pu-ti	*truputi*
double	dvi-gu-*bah*/dvi-gu-bahs	*dvigub(a/as)* (f/m)
a dozen	*tu*-zin-ahs	*tuzinas*
few	na-*dowg*	*nedaug*
less	mahzh-*yow*	*mažiau*
many	dowg	*daug*
more	dowg-*yow*	*daugiau*
once	*veah*-nah *see*-ki	*vieną syki*
pair	*paw*-rah	*pora*
percent	nu-*aw*-shim-tis	*nuošimtis*
some	*kal*-at-ahs	*keletas*
too much	par-*dowg*	*perdaug*
twice	du *seek*-yus	*du sykius*

ABBREVIATIONS

ež.	*ežeras*	lake
g.	*gatvė*	street
ir t.t.	*ir taip toliau*	and so on/etc
kl.	*kalnas*	mountain/hill
LAL	*Lietuvos Avialinijos*	Lithuanian Airlines
mst./m.	*miestas*	town/city
pvz.	*pavyzdžiui*	for example

EMERGENCIES

Help!	*gal*-beh-ki-te!	*Gelbékite!*

It's an emergency.
  krit-ish-kah pah-deh-*tis*   *Kritiška padétis.*
There's been an accident.
  i-*vee*-kaw na-*lai*-meh   *Įvyko nelaimé.*

Call ...!	ish-*show*-ki-ta ...!	*Iššaukite ...!*
a doctor	gee-dee-taw-yah	*gydytoją*
an ambulance	gray-tah-yah	*greitają*
	pah-*gahl*-bah	*pagalbą*
the police	paw-*lit*-si-yah	*policiją*

Stop it!	nu-*stawk*!	*Nustok!*
Go away!	ayk shah-*lin*!	*Eik šalin!*
Watch out!	*sow*-gaw-kis!	*Saugokis!*
Thief!	vah-*gis*!	*Vagis!*
Fire!	*gais*-rahs!	*Gaisras!*

I've been raped.
  mah-*na* ish-preah-vahr-   *Mane išprievartavo.*
  tah-vaw
I've been robbed.
  mah-*na* *ahp*-vaw-geh   *Mane apvogé.*
I'm ill.
  ahsh sar-*gu*   *Aš sergu.*
I'm lost.
  ahsh pah-*klee*-d(usi/as)   *Aš paklyd(usi/ęs).*
I'll get the police.
  ahsh pah-*showk*-syu   *Aš pašauksiu*
  paw-*lit*-si-yah   *policiją.*
Where's the police station?
  kur paw-*lit*-si-yaws   *Kur policijos*
  nu-*aw*-vah-dah?   *nuovada?*
Where are the toilets?
  kur tu-ah-*lat*-ai?   *Kur tualetai?*
Could you help me please?
  ahr gah-*leh*-tu-met mahn   *Ar galétumét man*
  pah-*deh*-ti?   *padéti?*

Could I please use the telephone?
ahr gah-*leh*-chow pah-now-*daw*-ti
te-le-*fo*-nah?
Ar galėčiau panaudoti telefoną?

I want to contact my embassy/consulate.
ahsh *naw*-ryu su-si-*seahk*-ti su
sah-vaw ahm-bah-*sah*-dah/
kon-su-*lah*-tu
Aš noriu susisiekti su savo ambasada/konsulatu.

I speak English.
ahsh kahl-*bu* ahn-glish-kai
Aš kalbu angliškai.

I didn't realise I was doing anything wrong.
ahsh na-*su*-vawk-yow kahd ahsh
kah-nors *blaw*-gaw dahr-*yow*
Aš nesuvokiau, kad aš kąnors blogo dariau.

I didn't do it.
ahsh taw na-pah-dahr-*yow*
Aš to nepadariau.

I'm sorry.
ahsh aht-si-prah-*show*
Aš atsiprašau.

My blood group is (A, B, O, AB) positive/negative.
mah-naw *krow*-yaw
gru-*pu-aw*-teh
ee-*rah* (ah beh aw ah-beh)
po-zi-tee-*vus*/*nay*-gyah-mahs
Mano kraujo grupuotė yra (A, B, O, AB) pozityvus/neigiamas.

I've lost my ...	ahsh *pah*-mach-ow sah-vaw ...	*Aš pamačiau savo ...*
bags	lah-gah-*min*-us	*lagaminus*
money	*pi*-ni-gus	*pinigus*
passport	*pah*-sah	*pasą*

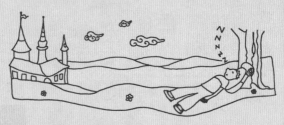

INDEX

Read it, hear it, speak it!